VENEZUELA ALIVE

ARNOLD GREENBERG

**PUBLISHED BY ALIVE PUBLICATIONS
NEW YORK CITY**

Published By
Alive Publications Ltd.
32 East 57th St.
New York, N.Y. 10022

Distributed by
Hunter Publishing, Inc.
300 Raritan Center Parkway, CN 94,
Edison, N.J. 08818

ISBN 1-55650-193-5

Interior Design Bob Silverman and Morrie Brown
Cover Design Bob Silverman, Inc.
Maps and MacTypography by DeskTop Graphix - Morrie Brown

Printed In Hong Kong by Colorcraft Ltd.

ABOUT VENEZUELA ALIVE

For the imaginative traveler who wants to plan a trip that suits his (or her) own pace, interests, style and pocketbook, we offer this sixth edition of Venezuela Alive, the best selling guidebook to an exotic country. Old friends of the Alive Series will notice the expanded size (although still small enough to tuck into a pocket) and our new format. As always the Alive guide is designed to increase your knowledge of Venezuela before you depart and to be carried with you each day as you explore the nation in depth. To help you do so, we have added new hotels and restaurants and deleted others. A new feature, the Alive Price Scale will help you plan a trip budget.

In the wide margins you'll find our personal tips and notes which offer tidbits of information that will add to your understanding and enjoyment. Facts you'll want at your fingertips are located there too.

We hope you'll find the "notes" pages scattered throughout the book helpful. Use them to jot down a shop you'd like to return to or a restaurant you loved or even hated. Selfishly, we hope when you return home you'll share some of your "notes" with us and with other Alive travelers in the next edition of Venezuela Alive.

CONTENTS

* Indicates map of Venezuela with specific city location highlighted

To my niece, Bari
With Love
Uncle Arnold

An Acknowledgement

To my friend Bram Gunther

My sincerest thanks for your help in researching and writing this book – and my heartfelt gratitude for traipsing around Venezuela and for the many sleepless nights you spent. I couldn't have done it without you. Muchas Gracias

PREFACE

We visited Caracas in 1966 to research the city for inclusion in an upcoming edition of our best selling guidebook "South America On $30 A Day" ($10 then). Although we spent sometime visiting other parts of the country, space considerations did not allow us to include them in that guide. But we were so impressed with the variety of the experiences we had, that a few years later we penned "Caracas Alive" followed by "Venezuela Alive". Most travellers picked up a copy of Caracas Alive, visited that cosmopolitan city and its nearby beaches and headed home, failing to appreciate that the "interior" (as the Caraqueños call the rest of the country) can be a fascinating travel experience. Albeit , at that time an expensive one – since prices in Venezuela were very high – among the highest in the world.

It has become obvious from the phone calls we receive that many travellers, those having visited Caracas several times and those looking for an exciting travel experience, want to explore this multi-dimensional country in depth. Arthur Frommer in his new book names Venezuela as the next travel "must" and happily at this writing the experience will be far less costly since Venezuela at this writing has rock bottom prices.

Because Caracas is such a magnet, the U.S. press rarely mentions other parts of Venezuela, which can be a provocative and different tourist destination – ranging from the 16,000 foot Espejo Peak (reached via the world's highest cable car in Merida) to the jungle camps of Canaima; from the sparkling little known beaches of Margarita to the boom town of Maracaibo. Add to this the romantic beaches of Puerto La Cruz. We will guide you to all of these exotic destinations and more. Some of you may know us as the authors of Rio Alive, Guatemala Alive, Virgin Islands Alive, Miami Alive and Panama Alive. In the Alive Series, we emphasize the best there is in the way of hotels, restaurants, clubs and shops. By "best" we do not mean the most expensive, we mean the best value. The newest additions to the Alive Travel Series will include Buenos Aires and Mexican beaches. To get the maximum benefits from our guides, carefully set a budget in advance. No matter what your budget you can plan around our listings, for they include the widest possible range of accommodations and dining choices, as well as night clubbing, sight seeing and shopping options. Now all you have to do is come Alive in Venezuela.

Buen Viaje! Arnold & Harriet Greenberg

NOTES:

Venezuela

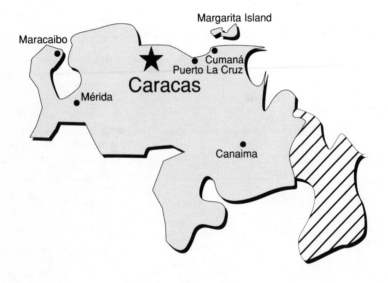

INTRODUCTION TO VENEZUELA

A quick two hours from Miami and a scant 4 1/2 hours from New York, this marvelously diverse country offers travelers a range of vacations that can include sophisticated Caracas a contemporary city that offers the added plus of a resort atmosphere with its deluxe hotels and at the beaches 45 minutes to the North. Then there is the Caribbean island of Margarita, the oil-boom city of Maracaibo, the fisherman's nirvana of mountainous Mérida, the beach-rich historic city of Cumaná, the jungle village of Canaima with nearby wilderness camps and the beautiful beaches of Puerto La Cruz.

For years Venezuela's reputation for sky-high prices was a deterrent to visitors. Happily we can report that as of this writing due to the devaluation of the Venezuelan currency, prices in Venezuela are among the lowest in the world.

That kind of trip should entice anyone seeking a change of pace from the typical expensive large-city tour that snares most travelers whether in Europe or South America. And for that reason we have concentrated in Venezuela Alive on just this contrasting series of areas to create something different in travel guides. In each area – there will be additional cities in later editions – you will find a traveler's orientation, a summary of the best hotels, restaurants and night clubs, sightseeing recommendations, and the best in shopping. In short, a succinct yet complete guide for North Americans.

GETTING TO VENEZUELA

Chances are you will enter Venezuela by air (via **Avensa**, **Viasa**, **Pan Am**, **Eastern** or **American**) which means you will come in at Maiquetía Airport outside of Caracas. From there you can pick up your **Avensa** flight to your interior destination. U.S.-Caracas air fares are quite low for excursion from New York and Miami. Package tours can cut your costs considerably so check these out through your airline. An **Airpass** special ticket will enable you to explore the interior inexpensively. (See below)

Keep in mind that the **Airpass** must be purchased before you enter Venezuela. You cannot buy it there. **Check with Avensa before you leave.**

THE VENEZUELAN AIRPASS

TIP

For infants carried along by an airpass card holder, a domestic ticket will be issued locally at a special domestic fare.

The **Avensa/Airpass** offers wide and attractive possibilities for journeys within Venezuela. You can fly an unlimited number of flights and miles during 7, 14 or 21 days.

The **Airpass** is an essential complement that allows you to make the most of your journey, and travel as much as you wish throughout the country.

The **Airpass** may be obtained from travel agents, Airlines offices or **Avensa's** offices by means of an **MCO** (Miscellaneous Charges Order) which will be exchanged for an airpass travel card, upon arrival in Venezuela, and only to passengers outside the country.

You don't have to arrange the complete itinerary of your trip within Venezuela at the time of purchase, you may decide step by step all the flights you wish during the validity of your **Airpass** travel card.

When holding an **Avensa/Airpass** travel card you will only pay the airport embarkation tax where applicable.

The **Airpass**, **MCO's** and tickets are not endorsable. The period of validity may not be extended and refunds will be made only if the **MCO** is completely unused.

At the time of this writing the **Airpass** fares are as follows:

Adult Fare	7 Days	$110.00
Adult Fare	14 Days	$125.00
Adult Fare	21 Days	$139.00
Children Under 12	7 Days	$55.00
Children Under 12	14 Days	$62.50
Children Under 12	21 Days	$69.50

AQUI SE HABLA INGLES

The result of North American oil investment in Venezuela is reflected in a relatively high standard of living – Caracas has a higher living standard than any other Latin American city. A happy fact is that English is the number two language. Therefore, hotel clerks, shop managers and restaurant maitre d's often speak English. Too, there are English-language TV and radio shows as well as theater (though non-professional, the performers are highly regarded). Finally, the English-language daily, The Daily Journal, is Latin America's best.

In short, you will feel comfortably at home in Venezuela.

READY TO GO

Happily the Venezuelan government makes life

NOTE

Avensa/Airpass passengers are granted the same baggage allowance and conditions as those of any international journey. Travel is only permitted on Domestic routes operated by *Avensa* and to Aruba.

easy for tourists. All you need to enter Venezuela is a tourist card. To obtain one, when purchasing your airline or steamship ticket, bring with you proof of citizenship – such as passport, birth certificate or voter registration card. The carrier will issue the tourist card and that's all you need to bring to Venezuela.

A MONETARY NOTE

Venezuela's currency, which for many years held fast at 4.3 bolívares to the U.S. dollar, was devalued in February 1983 to 14 bolívares to the dollar.

Since then it has skid to more than 37 to the dollar and still sinking. How long will this last, who knows? You should check the rate before you leave to have an up to date idea of the exchange. There is no black market or parallel market.

As long as this devaluation of the bolivar to the dollar remains, Venezuela will be inexpensive for anyone arriving with dollars.

For quick reference, here's a breakdown of Venezuelan currency:

Coins

5 céntimos

12 1/2 céntimos (a locha)

25 céntimos (a medio) (pronounced "medeeo")

50 céntimos (a real) (pronounced "rayal")

1 bolívar (1 B)

2 bolívares (2 Bs)

5 bolívares (5 Bs)

TIP

North Americans generally abbreviate bolivar to "B". Thus a typical cab ride will run you 20 Bs. Avoid saying "bolivares".

TIP

Bring about $10 with you into Venezuela to cover incidental arrival expenses.

NOTE

Try to avoid exchanging dollars at your hotel, which will invariably offer less for your money.

Bills

Denominations are in 5, 10, 20, 50, 100 and 500 bolívares.

You can purchase Bs at Perera's (this international money dealer has offices in most major cities) or in the international department of any large U.S. bank. Once in Venezuela, Cambios (places where you can change money) are readily available and all banks will offer the official exchange rate for your dollars. Shops too will gladly exchange your dollars for Bs with no discount.

THE CASHLESS SOCIETY

Credit cards – Master Charge, BankAmericard, American Express, Diner's Card, and others – are widely used in Venezuela. Some bills can take up to two months to reach you – a happy thought. You should carry Travelers Checks – any will do.

WHAT TO PACK

Stick to our suggestion and you will ease your life considerably. Don't –as most travelers do – over-pack. Only in Caracas will you need somewhat dressy clothing. and even there you can do well on a minimum. In the other cities in this guide you will require only casual comfortable lightweight outfits. Only in Mérida will warm clothing be necessary. In summary these are our tips.

Women

Emphasize summer clothing. White dresses are popular from December to February. Nylon, and polyesters are great because they don't crease. Pants outfits are OK everywhere. Leave home fur pieces. No one wears them here. Two bathing suits and resort wear are a must for Margarita, Cumaná, Puerto La Cruz and Maracaibo. For

Canaima you'll need slacks and comfortable shoes if you stay over. In Mérida you'll need a warm sweater or poncho for the trip up Pico Espejo. From December to February bring a lined raincoat, other times a raincoat is important as well. In general, the sporty informal look predominates.

Men

Lightweight suits or jackets and slacks for evening wear. Better restaurants require jackets and ties. Bathing suits and beach wear are a must. Sport shirts and light cottons are ideal for the daytime. Travel light.

Sundries

Bring sunglasses and suntan lotions. These are expensive here but they are widely available. Pharmacies, plentiful in all cities, are well stocked with North American non-prescription items. So don't become a walking drugstore. U.S. cigarettes and pipe tobacco are expensive here. Bring your own poison or stick to local brands.

Luggage

You are allowed 2 suitcases and there's no reason why you should exceed that. One 26-inch bag per adult plus a small tote bag for cameras and such should do nicely.

Laundry

In most better hotels, laundry and valet service is fine. Nevertheless, for a short trip, you will find wash-and-wear articles most convenient.

HOTELS IN VENEZUELA

Venezuela has many fine hotels, ranging from deluxe five star hotels down to basic hostelries.

There are only a few five star hotels in the country now, but several more are in the planning, with one of them almost constructed. The abundance of hotels are in the four-star and three-star range, all of them clean, comfortable and private. The majority of these hotels are more than just functional; they are quite nice, a place that is attractive and exciting.

Hotels are rated by the government and a 1 star to 5 star basis. These hotels have price limits that are in tandem with their rating. Only five star hotels are free from this system and can charge any rate they want although for international prices the rates are incomparably low.

Hotel Prices

Our price scale is designed to give you a ball-park figure to plan with. It is based solely on the price for a double room. Single rooms are only 20% less.

THE ALIVE SCALE	
Deluxe	$80
Expensive	$40
Moderate	$30
Inexpensive	below $15

VENEZUELAN FOODS

Most traditional dishes of Venezuela have been adopted from Spanish foods. They lean to sharp tangy sauces not as hot as in Mexico but sample before you plunge. Shrimp, lobster, beef and chicken are extremely popular but most menus are extensive and you can find virtually any kind of food you get an urge for.

Ever have an avocado stuffed with shrimp or lobster? Or a shellfish casserole in a piquant creole sauce? You are in for an unusual gustatory experience in your travels. While certain foods are popular throughout Venezuela, each section adds a nuance.

Venezuela has its own style and flavor of food. With its many regions and styles and mini cultures, the cuisine is diverse. But there is one dish that stands out as unified: it is called **hallaca**, and it is made up of small pieces of pork, chicken, beef and seasoned with olives, raisins, onions, garlic and rolled into a layer of corn dough and wrapped plantain leaves. The corn bread **arepa** is also common to the country.

There are many regional specialities (they will be covered in each chapter as it corresponds), but here is a brief survey to get an idea of how Venezuelan's eat.

The State of Zulia, centered around Maracaibo, specializes in meats in coconut, chiefly rabbit, and, having a great lake as its nucleus, fish abounds. **Tostones** are round slices of green plantain, which are common to the area.

In Caracas, international food dominates, but local cuisine is still somewhat popular. **Pabellon**, a melange of shredded meat, black beans, boiled rice and fried slices of ripe plantain, is the most common.

The Andean region, Mérida in particular, is abundant in trout dishes, the trout of the region being considered some of the best in the world. Also, a dish called **mojos**, scrambled eggs with milk, tomato and Tabasco is served.

The northeast area of Cumaná and Puerto La Cruz, being on the Caribbean, is obviously replete with fish dishes, but there are also dishes like **cuajao**, a dish made with mullet or loach roe, and **cuajao de chucho**, a similar dish, that are popular. And **cachapas**, a thin tortilla made with young corn,

TIP

Venezuelans usually dine late in the evening. Often well after 8 p.m. Lunch, served between noon and 3 p.m. is usually a heavy meal. Tea at 5 p.m. is a good local custom that holds you nicely until your late dinner.

TIP

Most restaurants charge a "cubierto", or cover, for bread, rolls, butter and other extras.

salt and sugar, is sold all along the road between Puerto La Cruz and Cumaná.

So, there are many option for native food, as well as a variety of good international cuisine. Before going further, we would like to review dining customs, mores and the most popular Venezuelan foods. Regional specialities will be described in each chapter. Tip 10% will be added to your bill for service. If service has been satisfactory, add another 5%. Venezuelans tend to give the waiter the benefit of the doubt. Some representative dishes.

Appetizers

A true local delicacy is **aguacate relleno con camarones** which is avocado stuffed with shrimp served with a Russian dressing type sauce. You can have your avocado stuffed with crab meat or lobster as well. Tangier is **ceviche de mero** a marvelous bass dish marinated in a vinaigrette sauce. Often shrimp **(camarones)** is substituted. If you're partial to smoked salmon order **salmon ahumado**, it comes without cream cheese.

Soups

Your trip here would be seriously deficient if you do not sample the Turtle Soup, either as broth with wine **(consomé de tortuga)** or in a cream turtle soup **(crema de tortuga)**.

The **gazpacho** soup, which should need no description, is much as it is in good New York restaurants, except that here the tomatos, onions, peppers, and other vegetables are fresh indeed. A refreshing cold luncheon dish on a warm day.

Venezuelans go delirious over a thick vegetable soup called **sancocho** which actually can serve as a full meal, especially when fish or beef chunks are added.

Main Courses

An extremely tender steak called **punta trasera** is a constant in most local restaurants. Definitely sample it. Argentine-style steaks served with a hot red pepper relish and a cool green pepper relish are popular too. Common designations include **Lomito**, **Churrasco** and **Baby Bife**.

Particularly filling is the **pabellón**, a casserole-type melange of shredded beef, black beans, white rice, and large plantains (banana-like fruit, called platanos in Spanish).

Turning from beef to seafood, there is a remarkable casserole called **cazuela de mariscos** which is a perfectly baked blend of clams, mussels, lobster, shrimp and squid served in a hot creole sauce. Then too is the ubiquitous **Paella Valenciana** comprised of chicken, lobster, shrimp, clams, mussels, olives and saffron rice. Moreover, you can order **arroz con mariscos** (a mixed seafood platter with Spanish rice).

Since seafood is extremely popular here, we are providing you with a capsule vocabulary:

Langosta - lobster served in many different ways

Langostinos - large shrimps (cray fish)

Cangrejo - crab meat

Pargo - red snapper

Mero - bass

Trucha - trout

Lenguado - sole

Mejillones - mussels

Desserts

Venezuelans adore strawberries and most restaurant menus include one strawberry dish, typically

fresas con crema, which is the red fruit with whipped cream. Guava fruit is in demand too and one popular dessert is **cascos de gauyaba con queso crema** (red guava fruit in syrup with cream cheese). Ice cream is very good indeed and the **flan**, or caramel custard, is worth sampling.

Special Dishes

Hallacas, recommended, is a leaf stuffed with a corn dough and tiny bits of chicken, pork, beef, olives, raisins, and onions. Quite good. A corn bread called **arepa**, served hot at many restaurants, is recommended too.

Cocktails

Rum is the king of hard liquor here, and little wonder since Venezuela produces some of the world's best rum. Try **ponche crema**, an egg nog rum drink, a tall **rum punch** or the **cuba libre**, or the daiquiris. Scotch, bourbons, and blends are available at relatively high prices. Local beers are quite good, particularly **Cardenal** and **Solera** premium brands which are exported. Most popular are the **Polar**, **Caracas**, and **Zulia** brands. And finally, the water is quite drinkable at all the restaurants in this book.

HOW ALIVE LISTINGS WORK

We've scoured Venezuela for the restaurants that offer the best values in all price ranges. Categories are arranged by nationality or type of restaurant (such as French, Chinese, fast food or cafes).

Our price scale is based on the cost of a 4-course dinner (per person) – appetizer or soup, main dish, dessert and cafe – and includes the cover and a 10% service charge. Cocktails and wine are extra, of course.

PRICE SCALE	
Expensive	*$30 + (per person)*
Moderate	*$20-30*
Inexpensive	*Under$20*

Credit cards are accepted at all the restaurants we have listed.

SHOPPING TIPS

In general your best buys are native handicrafts which range from colorful wool ruanas in Mérida to rugs woven by the Guajiro Indians of Maracaibo. Margarita is the place for pearl lovers and ceramics. Other items of interest include modern art, wood carvings, colorful devil masks, multihued hand woven hammocks and many other unusual gift ideas.

Bargaining is generally out except in Indian markets.

At this writing leather goods are a fraction of what they would cost in North America. As one example, a good pair of ladies dress leather shoes can be purchased at Charles Jourdan for $40. Many people from Miami fly here for shopping sprees.

Most good shops accept credit cards including Master charge, American Express, Diners and Carte Blanche.

Store hours are generally 9 a.m. to 7 p.m., including Saturdays, but most take a noon to three midday break.

Sizes (Tamaños)

Just a reminder, sizes here differ from North America. Rely on the comparison chart below, but try everything on first to be safe.

First the U.S. size, followed by its corresponding size in Venezuela.

Women

Shoes (Zapatos)			Dresses (Vestidos)		
4	-	34	8	-	34
4 1/2	-	35	10	-	38
5	-	36	12	-	42
5 1/2	-	37	14	-	44
6 1/2	-	38	16	-	46
7 1/2	-	39	18	-	48
8 1/2	-	40	20	-	50

Men

Shoes (Zapatos)			Suits (Trajes)		
6 1/2	-	39	40	-	32
7 1/2	-	40	42	-	34
8	-	41	44	-	36
8 1/2	-	42	46	-	38
9 1/2	-	43	48	-	40
10 1/2	-	44	50	-	42
11	-	45	52	-	44
12	-	46	54	-	46
12 1/2	-	47			

CLIMATE

Located just north of the equator, Venezuela is warm all year round. Temperatures range from quite warm at sea level to moderate in more elevated sites. It matters little what time of year you visit. Venezuela's climate generally is perfect for vacationing.

SPORTS

Baseball is the national sport. There is a Venezuelan professional league that lasts for four months and culminates with the Caribbean Series. There are several Venezuelans either in, or having been in, the majors in the U.S.: Dave Concepcion, Luis Aparicio, Andres Galaragga, Tony Armas, Manny Trillo and Luis Salazar. In popularity, soccer, basketball, boxing and horse-racing follow.

HISTORY OF VENEZUELA

Venezuela is one of Columbus's many children. Of course he was an absent, even indifferent father, but, nonetheless, Venezuela's modern history begins with Columbus discovering the islands of Margarita and Cubagua in 1498. (This does not negate Venezuela's pre-Columbus history, made by its original members the Indians.) It was a year later, in 1499, that Venezuela received its name. Alonso de Ojeda and Amerigo Vespucci, sailing along Venezuela's coast, encountered the Indians of Guajira, who lived around Lake Maracaibo in the northwest region of the country. Their houses are built upon piles over the water, and this inspired the two explorers to name the area Venezuela, Little Venice.

It is a year later that Venezuela's, and South America's, first settlement of Europeans is created on the island of Cubagua. The island was settled by Cristobal de la Guerra and Pedro Alonso Nino because of its abundance of pearls. The year before, 1499, the two men went back to Spain with 80 pounds of pearls, sweaty with anticipation, and on their return wasted no time in settling Cubagua and beginning a frenzy of mining.

In 1501 Venezuela's shores are mapped, and the cartographer, Rodrigo de Bastidas, used the name Venezuela on his map, cementing the name's permanence.

In 1520 Fray Bartolome de las Casas began a community on the northern coast of Venezuela, near present day Cumaná. His vision was to create a small society of artisans, including Indians. It fails, but the area stays populated and structured.

The province of Margarita is established in 1525, and in 1527 Coro, in the present State of Falcon, is founded and soon after leased to a family of German bankers named Welser. The contract allows the Welsers control of the area, but they must use their own money to make the region productive. For 17 years the bankers search the northwest region of Venezuela for gold, diamonds and valuable raw materials, plugging the earth and trooping all over to find wealth. In 1546 the lease is not renewed, and although the Welsers have not come up with the envisioned natural factory of riches, the region has been settled, explored and routed.

Cubagua, Venezuela's, and South America's, first community comes to an eternal end because of a massive earthquake and tidal wave. The waters had been pillaged of pearls, and the Indians drowned, en masse, as they dove, day after day, for the opaque pink treasure.

Diego de Losada founds Caracas in 1566. Eleven years later the capital is moved from El Tocuyo, set-up by the Germans, to Caracas.

The next 100 years see Venezuela forming, shifting, settling and expanding. This is still its childhood, the outline of the country being inexorably drawn and muddled. Maracaibo is established in 1574; Venezuela's main port La Guaira is begun in 1589; the Andean province of Merida is unveiled in 1622; the Archbishop of Coro is moved to Caracas in 1637, beginning the trend to centralize in that city; the Viceroyalty of Nueva Granda is formed in 1739, furthering the movements towards a centralized government of the area; and finally in 1777 the Captaincy-General of Venezuela is created, linking the country's six older provinces – Margarita, Merida, Maracaibo, Nueva Andalucia, Guayana, Trinidad (which cedes in 1802) and Venezuela – into one territory.

It is actually in 1776 when the first rumblings of independence are felt. Francisco de Miranda travelled to Europe to muster-up support for the idea of Venezuelan independence. But it is not until 1806 that he tests his might with the Spanish. With the assistance of American volunteers, Miranda's excited swing of the sword is begun; it is quickly dulled by the Spanish off the coast of Ocumare de la Costa. Vengeful, the Spanish hang 10 American officers (unimaginable today) and imprison 50 others. Slippery Miranda, though, makes it to the State of Falcon, where he briefly flies a Venezuelan flag of his design, and revs the engine for future events.

On April 19, 1810 a renegade commission declares Venezuela independent. This event catapulted the country into civil war. On July 5, 1811 Venezuela's independence is reiterated, and this ignites rebellions throughout the territory. Almost a year later, Caracas and its periphery is leveled by an earthquake, and the Spanish try to advertise this as an act of God. The fighting, though, begins to boil, with Miranda battling on the western front and several generals sweeping the Spanish away from the eastern coast. Miranda eventually loses out and is imprisoned, but, simultaneously, Simon Bolivar, Venezuela's most famous and revered citizen, is steamrolling towards Caracas.

Bolivar initially enters Venezuela from Colombia (then Nueva Granada) in 1813. On June 15 he issues the "War to the Death" promise from Trujillo, and on Aug. 7 enters and takes Caracas for the first time. The tides eventually turn, and on

June 15, 1814 Bolivar and General Marino's forces are almost eliminated, and he is forced to flee.

The Spanish try to fortify in the next year – 15,000 troops from Spain arrive. On Sept. 6, 1815 Bolivar reared his head again, with the publication of his "Letter From Jamaica," which reiterates his, and the independence force's, temerity. Twice he tries to climb onto the mainland, but was repelled. Margarita is made the transitory capital on May 8, 1817. In the same year Bolivar sets-up a provisional government in the jungle city of Angostura (now Ciudad Bolivar).

With the shroud of peace at Angostura, work is begun on a constitution, and the final push for independence is begun. Yet independence does not come until the independence of Colombia is secured on Aug. 7, 1819. June 24, 1821 is recognized as Venezuela's independence day, with the battle of Carabobo; but it is not technically secured until June 24, 1823 when the last of the Spanish loyalist forces are defeáted on Lake Maracaibo. In between those dates Bolivar has proposed the Gran Colombian Union, which included present day Venezuela, Colombia, Panama and Ecuador. This, of course, is short-lived, and Venezuela splits from this pact on May 6, 1830, and names revolutionary star Jose Antonio Paez its first president.

Bolivar is the secular icon of Venezuela. His name is glorified in every city and town of Venezuela, and he is the namesake for far more things in Venezuela than Roosevelt, Kennedy or Washington is in America. Even the currency bears his name.

He was born in Caracas on July 24, 1783. His short life was a chain on liberations, starting with Colombia's and continuing to Venezuela's, Ecuador's, Peru's and Bolivia's. Although Miranda was the initial spark for Venezuela's independence, Bolivar was the dynamite. But his role was not only militaristic. He is famous for several publications – the "Letter From Jamaica" and "Manifest" being the most well-known – his speeches and political ideas. It was his dream to see a combined Colombia, Venezuela, Ecuador and Panama, all functioning under one central government; and it was also his dream to be its president. He died at the age of 47 in San Pedro Alejandino, an estate on the outskirts of Santa Marta, Colombia.

On March 24, 1854 slavery is outlawed, and 1864 the United States of Venezuela is constituted.

From 1830 to 1958 Venezuela flip-flops between democracy and dictatorship. Venezuela's most indelible period is constructed at the hands of Antonio Leocadio Guzman, who ruled intermittently in the second half of the 19th century. His initial rise to power comes on the ruinous tail of a civil war, called the Federal War. When in power he began reshaping and rebuilding the country in his secular vision. He makes education free and obligatory, and fosters an atmosphere of cultural excitement. He was no democrat, Venezuela's Peron, and he let little interfere with his goals; civil liberties were irrelevant. His reign, though, filled Venezuela out in many ways – architecturally, educationally and culturally.

The next three successors to Guzman were pale, and in 1908 the country is taken over by Cipriano Castro, who plowed his way to Caracas from the Andes. Yet his military might did not transfer to government, and the country began to crack under his incompetency. Arrogance, and the military, kept him politically alive, but he was immediately dethroned when on a trip to Europe.

His successor, Juan Vicente Gomez, rejuvenated the ailing governmental structure, paid-off Venezuela's debt to Europe and kept them neutral in WWI. Gomez's term was undeniably autocratic, and the government became corpulent, while the infrastructure, civil services and regional communities became emaciated.

Gomez ruled until his death and was replaced by General Lopez Contreras in 1936. He brought back a touch of democracy, which was even furthered by General Isaias Medina Angarita, the next president. But again the flapping winds brought in a dictator, ironically in the year 1945. Romulo Betancourt was the head of this regime, that quickly flattened Angarita's advances. Betancourt was followed by a brief scent of democracy in the famous writer Romulo Gallegos. General Marcos Perez Jimenez, next in line, ignoring civil liberties, built up the country's infrastructure with airports, roads, hospitals, etc. – a legacy felt today. He was punted out in 1958, and since that date Venezuela has had an uninterrupted string of freely elected presidents, with the present one elected in Dec. 1988.

NOTE

President Carlos Andres Perez was re-elected in December 1988.

THE COUNTRY TODAY

Venezuela is a large country with a population of 18,000,000. It is divided into 20 states, the Federal District around Caracas, two territories and 72 islands. Its borders are the Atlantic and Guyana on the east, Brazil to the south, Colombia on the west and the Caribbean to the north.

Its government is broken up similarly to the U.S.'s, with an executive branch, a legislative branch and a judicial branch. Nineteen ministries, with its ministers, make-up the executive branch. The legislative branch is the combination of 50 senators, 47 elected and three ex-presidents who become permanent, and a Chamber of Deputies that has 199 elected officials. The judicial branch has a reigning supreme court and 768 lower courts.

Demographically, the country is divided into 58% of mixed race, 29% white, meaning European, 11% black, of African descent, and finally 2% native Indians. 75,000 Americans actually live in Venezuela.

There are 17 universities and 47 colleges, and there is one English language newspaper, available in Caracas, titled the Daily Journal.

Although Venezuela is considered a developing country by the U.N., its texture and life are basically not. The country's infrastructure is close to perfect; there are less pot holes in Caracas than on Broadway in New York. The standard of living is noticeably middle class, with the poorer neighborhoods of Caracas not the inhospitable wrecks that do exist in other parts of South America. In Mérida, for example, the city is steadily growing with white clean towers, making it look more and more like a mountainous Swiss town.

The country does not have the look of a destitute place, and that is predominantly because of the barrels-full of money received from once sacred oil. Oil has allowed a greater standard of living for everyone, and has given the country a neater, cleaner look.

But oil is glutted, and once terribly expensive Caracas, ten years ago one of the world's most expensive cities, is now very inexpensive. When the city sat in that poodle of affluence tourism was nonexistent. With oil as rare as daisies now, the country has tried to redirect its money into tourism, highlighting the bargain but modernity of the country. It is now a fantastic middle class tourist magnet, with prices astoundingly low – four star chic hotels go for $25 a night. The country has also tried to diversify into aluminum, metals, iron and ore, and agriculture.

Venezuela's cultural pedigree is mainly European, with its art very heavily influenced by Christianity. Much native Indian arts and crafts are available, but the country is dominated by European-styled art, which is seen in many of its churches, both architecturally and artistically.

Music bloomed in early colonial Venezuela. A school created by Father Pedro Sojor (1739-1799) became a breeding ground for young composers. With the rising hoots of independence, the school, and its composers, began to transfuse the atmosphere into music. Many of its students would see their music as rebellious and necessary. The most notable musicians of the time were Jose Angel Lamas, Cayetano Carreno, Mateo Villa Lobos and Juan Manuel Olivares.

Venezuela's most famous writer is Romulo Gallegos, author of "Doña Barbara" (1929), "Cantaclaro" (1934) and "Canaima" (1935).

GEOGRAPHY

The country is chopped-up geographically into the coastal region, which runs for a total of 300 miles, the Andean region of snow-capped peaks and temperate, deciduous forests, the tropical Maracaibo region and finally the southern region called the Guyana Shield. The Shield is made-up of the State of Bolivar and the Amazonas Federal Territory. It is savannah and rain forest. The savannahs are great plains dotted with hulking mesas. The rain forests shelter Venezuela's most wild animals, and some untouched tribes.

The climate, nation-wide, varies little, with the average temperature being about 80 degrees. The two exceptions are Mérida, with temperatures swaying minimally between 60 - 65 degrees, and Caracas, with a slightly higher range of 65 - 70. The rainy season is from June to November, and the dry season from December to May.

NOTES:

INTRODUCTION TO CARACAS

Only 2 1/2 hours from Miami, this cosmopolitan city of sophisticated women, chic boutiques and super highways rivals New York and Paris in its restaurants, shops and standard of elegance. And all this within 45 minutes of superb beaches that are open the year round. Since this city of almost four million is just slightly north of the equator, the seasons hardly change – it seems like early summer much of the year – and with 3,000 feet of elevation the breezes dissipate the warmth of the afternoons.

The skyline is rapidly changing with new communities being added constantly. Real estate is booming. An adjunct of the city's rapid growth are urban problems (pollution – air and traffic variety), unknown a decade ago. But birds still chirp in the center of town and the air has a crispness that reminds us of San Francisco.

AQUÍ SE HABLA INGLES

The result of North American oil investment in Venezuela is reflected not only in a relatively high standard of living – Caracas has a higher living standard than any other Latin American city, including Mexico City – but in the happy fact that English is the number two language. Therefore, hotel clerks, shop managers and restaurant maitre d's often speak English. Sometimes with an accent that requires patience to decipher but at least you will find yourself on familiar ground. Too, there are English-language TV and radio shows as well as theater (though non-professional, the performers are highly regarded). Finally, the English-language daily, The Daily Journal, is Latin America's best.

In short, you will feel comfortably at home in much of what you do and see in Caracas. It is a contemporary city for the contemporary traveler that offers the added plus of a resort atmosphere with its deluxe hotels and at the beaches 45 minutes to the North. We think it offers the best of two worlds: city and beach.

ARRIVAL

Your first glimpse of Venezuela in all likelihood will be through the window of your jet as it approaches modern **Simon Bolivar International Airport** on the Caribbean in the coastal town of **Maiquetía** ($2^{1/2}$ air hours from Miami and 30 cab minutes from Caracas).

On the flight you will be given a tourist card that must be filled in. After your baggage is claimed, which is easy and hassle-free, head toward customs which is per-functory – but you must save the part of the tourist card that they hand back to you! It would be wise to leave the card in your passport, and it can serve as identification if necessary.

Those arriving by ship will land at the adjacent town of **La Guaira**, Venezuela's major port. Another nearby airport in Maiquetía services national traffic.

The airport is in mint condition, air conditioned, and streamlined. Unlike JFK which can make you dizzy with its complications, Simon Bolivar airport is layed-out well. Baggage claim is never more than five minutes from the gate, all on the same level, and once out of customs, the services for tourists are immediately visible. **Corpoturismo**, Venezuela's tourist corporation, is marked by an orange and black sign. They will provide information on hotels, restaurants, trips, prices, crime, etc. and will have literature available. To the right of Corpoturismo is a booth for hotel reservations, and next to that are several car rental outlets – Hertz, Avis, etc. There is also an exchange bank, and it is wise to cash some money here because the rates will be better than at your hotel; and you of course you will have to pay for your ride into Caracas.

If you are not staying in Caracas, are immediately leaving for another destination, there are buses to the domestic terminal, which is only a three minute walk if your load is light.

GETTING TO YOUR HOTEL FROM THE AIRPORT

Two options exists for getting into the city. A por puesto, a public transportation van or bus, will take you to **Parque Central**, near the Hilton Hotel, for about $1. For taxis, which will cost about $7, you should go to the sign, in black and orange letters, **Venta de Boletos**. At this station you will receive a receipt for a taxi into the city, which you will then give to your driver. This is the safest way. There are a lot of taxi drivers hawking rides, and although they will get you to your destination with no problem, they will be more expensive. If you choose to find a taxi yourself, make sure not to pay more than an equivalent of about $10.

Once outside the airport the first charge of warm air reminds you that you are now on the Caribbean and were you in a bathing suit, you would be rejoicing. The sun is strong and haughty, and sweat accumulates quickly. The airport is located in the town of Maiquetía, which is adjacent to the port city of La Guaira. The taxi ride to Caracas is about 30 minutes, and it is a climb.

NOTE

They have been carved out of the mountains that encircle Caracas.

There are three tunnels that must be driven through before Caracas unfolds, and after the first one, the heat begins to dissipate. Climbing higher, small shacks and houses (ranchitos) dot the mountainsides; but they don't have the muddy and destitute look that one associates with South American poverty. Low income high-rises have been built on the mountainside, next to the ranchitos. Small brown poles that are billboards for advertisements line the shoulder of the highway. The heat has really evaporated at this point, and suddenly you come through the third tunnel and the city is there. It is quite startling and spectacular to have just a split second separating darkness from a 12 mile high-rise city; there is no slow approach.

Caracas sits in a valley surrounded on the north and south by towering peaks, the highest being Mt. Avila on the north side. A cable car will put you on top in 15 minutes.

It is like a city in a bathtub, and you have to climb out of it. The buildings are tall and predominantly white, with a glass twin towers, government buildings, being the most outstanding.

You will enter Caracas through the Western section, **El Silencio**, the oldest and most heavily commercial part of the city. To the east, the city becomes more residential.

TO THE BEACHES

Most beach hotels are within 20 minutes of the airport. The landing field is on the Caribbean as are these hostelries. Look to your left as the cab speeds along the main beach road, **Avenida Playa**, and catch the sea waves gently beating against the shore.

Notice the casual dress and relaxed pace of the residents. You will quickly be transmitted to a leisurely attitude toward life. The beaches are discussed in detail in a later Chapter.

ORIENTATION

Coming from the airport via the Autopista La Guaira-Caracas, your first sight is the El Silencio District, one of Caracas' oldest areas with narrow streets and many government buildings. From here you will proceed along one of the three main east-west thoroughfares that cut through the city.

NOTE

*The **Cota Mil**, the newest of the three, runs along the northernmost sections and due to its elevation offers a stunning view. **Libertador** runs through the center, while **Autopista del Este** serves the southernmost districts.*

Caracas is unusual in that neighborhood districts (urbanizaciones) change rapidly and even radically within a few blocks as you proceed through the city. Within minutes you leave Silencio behind and enter the El Conde District, followed by San Bernardino District and then Mariperez, each one distinctive. To get to know Caracas quickly, keep in mind two facts:

First: Caraqueños rarely uses street numbers. Rather, the location of a restaurant or a hotel is noted in terms of the district and the street, sometimes the nearest intersecting avenue and occasionally the building, but seldom is the exact street number noted. Therefore, the Hotel Avila address is Avenida Jorge Washington, San Bernardino District. Period. Cabbies have no trouble at all with this system and you won't either.

Second: Each neighborhood district has one main street invariably called "Avenida Principal" which is followed by the name of the district. Thus La Estancia, a recommended restaurant, is located on the Avenida Principal de La Castellana, while the Hotel Tamanaco is on Avenida Principal de Las Mercedes. By the way, when you see a street designated "la Calle", that means "First (primera) Street" and usually is the initial street crossing the Avenida Principal. Below, we have noted some important urbanizaciones for quick reference (West to East):

EL SILENCIO

Important historically, this district is the first you see normally as you enter the city on your trip from Simon

TIP

We recommend a walking tour through this area in chapter Caracas Sunup To Sundown page 81.

Bolivar International Airport. The area's landmark is **Centro Simon Bolivar,** a large government office complex marked by twin 32-story towers that dominate the skyline nearby. The main plaza, **The Plaza Bolivar**, is flanked by the gold-domed Congress Building and the Cathedral of Caracas.

El CONDE

East of El Silencio, this district too is a part of the city's older heritage. Heavily commercial, El Conde houses the **Caracas Hilton Hotel**, the **Museums of Art** and **Natural Sciences**, a large amusement park and the **Nuevo Circo Bull Ring**.

PARQUE CENTRAL

A modern urban renewal area that features some of the city's finest apartment houses (mostly condominiums), shopping centers, and the Museum of Contemporary Art. Located near the Hilton Hotel, "Central Park" is home to the **Teatro Teresa Carreño**, one of the most incredible cultural centers in the world, and the main office of the government tourist office.

SAN BERNARDINO

North of El Conde, this largely residential area is home to the **Hotel Avila** and the **Colonial Art Museum**. The higher area is scenically lovely and is home to many of the Jewish families living here.

MARIPEREZ

Just east and north of San Bernardino is this blue collar residential area. The cable car (Teleferico) terminal is here.

PLAZA VENEZUELA

While not technically a district, still it is important enough for separate mention. The plaza, which is the beginning point for the Sabana Grande shopping district (below), houses many night clubs, restaurants, movie theatres, and two of the city's tallest office towers, the **Edificio Phelps** and **Centro Capriles**.

SABANA GRANDE

NOTE

There is a METRO stop at each end for the subway that runs below.

Heading East from the Plaza Venezuela, you come upon the city's true center, the large and bustling Sabana Grande shopping district. Shop after shop lines the main thoroughfare, **Avenida Abraham Lincoln**, known as **Calle Real de Sabana Grande**. Many of our recommended restaurants and night clubs are here. The hotels **Tampa**, **Kings Inn** and **Savoy** are located in this section.

BELLO MONTE

This tiny district on the southern edge of the Sabana Grande area is noteworthy as the home of the first class **Hotel Las Americas**, and the main branch of Sears, considered a fine shop in Latin America.

CHACAÍTO

Bordering Sabana Grande on its East side, Chacaíto houses the **Centro Comercial Chacaíto**, one of the city's poshest shopping centers, with fashionable boutiques, art galleries, outdoor cafes and night clubs.

EL ROSAL

Just southeast of Chacaíto is El Rosal, home to splendid restaurants, popular night spots, as well as shops and banks.

LAS MERCEDES

Across the river just south of El Rosal is the North American residential area of Las Mercedes. Lined with lovely homes and fine shops and restaurants, the area's landmark is the magnificent **Hotel Tamanaco** on the

Avenida Principal de las Mercedes as well as the **Hotel Paseo Las Mercedes** and a shopping center. There is even an English-language theater group in nearby San Roman.

COUNTRY CLUB DISTRICT

This section, east of Chacaíto, is where wealthy Caraqueños reside in eye-popping mansions. The hub is an exclusive club called, appropriately, **The Country Club**.

LA CASTELLANA

NOTE

As previouly stated, birds chirp in this scenic plaza.

Heading East from the Country Club is this upper middle class residential area which also houses a number of recommended restaurants and discotheques. Stop at the fountain in the plaza for a relaxing moment if you're in the neighborhood.

ALTAMIRA

Within walking distance of La Castellana is this section of modern high-rise apartment houses, fashionable night clubs, Cleopatra's Obelisk, and a lovely park and fountain. The **Hotel Continental Altamira** is a few blocks North.

LOS PALOS GRANDES

NOTE

Av. Francisco de Miranda is the continuation of Libertador.

A short stroll East from Altamira is the site of the U.S. Embassy on Avenida Francisco de Miranda. The modern shopping center here housed a large *Sears* unit.

CIUDAD UNIVERSITARIA

South of the Plaza Venezuela is the huge 500 acre University City campus which embraces mammoth futbol (soccer) and beisbol stadiums, as well as the botanical gardens.

Two other areas of Caracas worth knowing are **La Florida** north of Sabana Grande and **Chacao** just before Altamira where there is a twice weekly flea market.

WEATHER BEACON

Caracas temperatures are near perfect with sunny afternoons (highs in the 70's and 80's) and pleasant evenings (lows in the 60's) most of the year. At the beaches the mercury appropriately hovers in the 90's. There is year-round swimming here.

GETTING AROUND TOWN

Cabs

NOTE

Waiting time is inexpensive compared to U.S. prices.

Cabs are cheap, plentiful and most have meters. Cabs with meters should never cost more than $2-3 dollars for any point within the city, and a bit more for the suburbs, beaches and airport. In fact, most rides within city limits will rarely be more than a dollar. A trip from El Conde to Altamira, not short in kilometers will be just about a dollar. Cabs without meters should not be more, but they might try to charge you more. Be alert. Cabs are not identified by color, but only by the exterior top light reading "taxi" or "libre."

Por Puestos

Por Puestos (literally translated "by the place") are small buses that travel along fixed routes. A por puesto is identified by a sign in the front window indicating its last stop. Routes include all major thoroughfares, and the fare is usually under 25 cents.

Buses

Buses are also about 25 cents and routes are marked on the side of the bus. The routes are extensive.

The Subway

Finally, there is Caracas' subway system, the **Metro** Built in 1976 by the French (it is obvious immediately, if you have ever been to Paris), the subway system is eventually supposed to cover 51 stations and 32 miles. Now, though, it is much more clipped but still efficient and useful. As clean as a hospital maternity ward, the subway is so efficient and regular that, if coming from New York, you'll probably faint. Covering the main tourist line of Caracas, from Bellas Artes, which is the stop for the Hilton, to Altamira and Parque del Este, and even further east.

The entrances are marked by a big orange M, and the ticket system is the exact same as the Parisian one. You can either buy a ticket from a manned booth, or from a ticket machine, that takes only exact change. No ride is more than 6 Bs. The yellow ticket that you receive is necessary to get in and exit. You put it is the slot on the turnstile, and at entrance it flips out back to you, and on exit does not.

Wide and large subway maps line the walls of each station, and it is as clear to read as a billboard.

An arrow will mark the station you are at then, and all you must do is find the direction of your destination.

There are two lines, but line one is probably all you will use. It travels east to west and is marked in orange. It covers the area from Propatria to Parque del Este.

The metro runs from 5 am to 11 pm, and should be avoided late at night. The cars are clean, brand-new and air conditioned. Even if you don't need to use the metro, try it, it is worth it.

A CAPSULE HISTORY

Caracas was officially founded on July 25, 1567 by Diego de Losada. Its original name was Santiago de Leon de Caracas.

The baby city was just a 25-block compound between the Catuche, Caroata and Guaire Rivers; there were only 60 families at the time.

Caracas was declared the capital of Venezuela in 1731,

yet it was still a small city. In 1807 there were only 47,000 people, and the city was quiet and tiny. It wasn't until the end of the 19th century that Caracas began to grow. That growth was spurred by President Guzman. He expanded its districts, adding schools, churches and theaters.

Around 1930, with oil's first remote discovery, Caracas took another leap forward - it began to modernize. Since World War II (30 years ago there were 400,000 people) the city has grown exponentially. There are now close to 4,000,000 people in the city, pushing its capacity to its limit, if not more.

Caracas is part of the **Distrito Federal** (Federal District) which also includes the coastal region. Yet, the city has spread so much that it has spilled over into the Sucre District of the neighboring State of Miranda.

CARACAS' HOTELS

s befits a cosmopolitan city, Caracas has an abundance of good first class hotels. But for purposes of this guide we have selected what we consider the 20 best hotels in Caracas. In addition, in our chapter on the beach areas, we have chosen additional recommended hotels. Many of you are coming to Caracas as part of a package tour which includes your hotel. For those of you planning to select your own hotels, read this and the beach chapter carefully to help you decide whether you wish to bed down in Caracas and make day trips to the beaches or whether you should split your visit between the city and the beach.

There are only four five star hotels in the city now, with at least one more in the planning. One of them, Eurobuilding, has just opened. The abundance of hotels are in the four-star and three-star range, all of them clean, comfortable and private. The majority of these hotels are more than just functional; they are quite nice, a place that is attractive and exciting. The hotels recommended are spread all throughout the city.

Hotels are rated by the government on a 1 star to 5 star basis. These hotels have price limits that are in tandem with their rating. Only five star hotels are free from this system and can charge any rate they want;

although, for international prices the rates are incomparably low.

HOTEL PRICES

Our price scale is designed to give you a ball-park figure to plan with. It is based solely on price for a double room. Single rooms are only 20% less.

THE ALIVE SCALE

Deluxe	$80
Expensive	$40
Moderate	$30
Inexpensive	below $15

CARACAS HILTON 5 *
(El Conde Section)
905 Rooms, 20 Suites
Pool and Tennis Courts
Phone: 574-11-22
Telex: 21171
Deluxe

The elegant Caracas Hilton has become a mecca for prominent international personalities in business, entertainment the arts and Venezuelan society. Its convenient location only a ten minute drive from the shopping and business district and across the street from the city's major museums and cultural center,is especially attractive for the business and vacation traveler. The Caracas Hilton is a unique combination of cosmopolitan city hotel with attractive resort facilities, two adjacent swimming pools and terrace cafe, tennis court, and health club. La Rotisserie, its elegant restaurant recreating the dining room of a Spanish hacienda, has won the highest award for the best hotel restaurant in Venezuela since the hotel opened.

Be sure to try the danish pastries and croissants in the hotel's Los Caobos coffee shop. On the premises, other facilities include a beauty salon and barber shop, gym, car rental, florist, photo shop, an **H. Stern** jewelry

TIP

For dining and dancing, the panoramic view from La Cota 880 nightclub is a must for any visitor to Caracas.

Deluxe	$80+
Expensive	$40
Moderate	$30
Inexpensive	below $15

shop, boutique, newsstand, bank and airline office.
Handy for the business traveler is a secretarial service.

The Caracas Hilton was built about 20 years ago, and is
the nexus for activity in the El Conde, Parque Central
area of Caracas. Identified all over the city by its tall white
tower, the Hilton is deluxe occupancy. Its lobby has the
glaze of marble and it is opulent. It is also busy, with a
stream of people pacing the central hallway enroute to
either several shops, the hotel's seven restaurants, the
pool, the bookstore, or merely criss-crossing between
the two towers.

The rooms are plush and large. There is a mini-bar in
each, in-room movies, direct dialing telephones, 24-
hour service and central air conditioning. The majority
of the rooms have spectacular views of the city because,
if you are up high, there are no tall buildings near the
Hilton.

Suites are large, roomy and homey, with kitchens,
refrigerators and two bathrooms in each. The Presidential Suite is majestic, being a duplex.

On the 22nd floor complimentary breakfast is served
between 6:30 and 11 (coffee, tea, refreshments and
sweets are always served), and a selection of international and local newspapers, magazines and television
is available. There is a large conference room on the
executive floors, and the hotel provides telex and fax
and secretarial services.

■■■■■ **THE HOTEL TAMANACO 5***

THE HOTEL TAMANACO 5 *
Av Principal de Las Mercedes
(Las Mercedes District)
600 Rooms
Tennis Courts, Large Pool
Air Conditioning
Phone: 208-7000
Telex: 23260
Deluxe

NOTE

*A fabulous urban
mall adjacent to the
Caracas Hilton called
Parque Central with
shops, restaurants, a
Museum of contem-
porary Art and one of
the most modern
Concert Halls in
South America, the
Teatro Teresa
Carreño.*

TIP

*The higher priced
executive floors are
on the 22-29th floors
of the new tower.*

This magnificent 600-room Inter-Continental Hotel, a true luxury resort hotel that still retains the flavor of Venezuela, is located in one of the city's plushest areas. In some ways typical of the elegant hostelries in plush Caribbean islands, the Tamanaco is considered by some to be the premier hotel, not only of Caracas, but of all South America. The Tamanaco houses Le Gourmet, a first class restaurant overlooking the city, La Brasserie, a large American-style coffee shop, several bars with phenomenal views of the city and a renowned night club called La Boite as well as banquet-convention rooms for 10 to 2,000 persons, where such names as Sammy Davis, Jr. and Engelbert Humperdinck appear. Virtually a small city unto itself, the Tamanaco also is home to a bank, beauty shop, boutique gift shops, an H. Stern branch, airline offices, a Hertz Rent-A-Car branch, a cable office, a sauna and health club, and a book shop that carries English-language periodicals, including the New York Times, Newsweek and Time. TV in all rooms.

Activities are available around the large pool, which also contains a children's area. A good value is the combination sauna, massage, and health club. A lovely moment is having a cocktail at sundown on the terrace of the El Punto (off the lobby) or the Cacique Bar while overlooking the city. Located in the hilly Las Mercedes section, where many North Americans live, the Tamanaco's views are spectacular. Even if not a guest, hop a cab and stop in for a drink. Reservations can be made here for Inter-Continental hotels in Maracaibo, Guayana, Valencia, and elsewhere.

NOTE

The hotel is genuinely spectacular, for both its geography and its lavishness.

Deluxe	$80+
Expensive	$40
Moderate	$30
Inexpensive below	$15

■ RESIDENCIAS ANAUCO HILTON 4*
317 Units 44 Floors
(El Conde Section)
Phone: 573-4111, 573, 5702
Expensive

A unique sister to the Caracas Hilton, the Anauco Hilton is a hotel for long-term residential stays, and is

TIP

An ideal choice for families or long stays

aimed for large families or large groups. Doubling as a residence for Venezuelans, the hotel's style is much more in tune with apartment buildings than with hotels. Even more than the Caracas Hilton, the Anauco Hilton is identifiable from most points in the city with its long broad shoulder look.

The range of rooms are from studios to four bedrooms, all with private baths and refrigerators (most have kitchens also).

The hotel is part of Parque Central, a sprawling urban complex, that includes shops, restaurants, museums and a concert hall. The mall is under the hotel, and Hilton International runs several of the restaurants in the mall: **La Canoa**, **La Pergola** and a snack bar.

Connected by a plaza to the Caracas Hilton, all the facilities there are available for Anauco residents.

A nice, more family oriented indigenous stay is what the Anauco provides, with all the trimmings of hotel excitement and opulence.

■■■■■■■■ **HOTEL CCT 5 ***
Centro Ciudad Comercial Tamanaco
80 rooms, 122 suites
Phone: 926122
Telex: 29815
Deluxe

NOTE

A spanking new hotel right in a bustling shopping center

Located in Caracas' best shopping center, the hotel is a hub of activity. A triangle gray structure, the hotel features suites because it is geared towards businessmen. The hotel has an exceptional conference center, with a private entrance, private access to its restaurants, soundproof walls, recording equipment, orchestra, telex and photo copy machines, and secretarial services.

The hotel is fairly new, and is an addition to Caracas' five star network. The hotel has a pool and tennis courts.

■■■■ **EUROBUILDING
CARACAS HOTEL 5 ***
**Calle Amazonas
(Chuao District)
473 Rooms - Main Building
180 Suites - Suite Building
2 Pools, Tennis, Spa
Phone: 923-470 921-193
Deluxe**

*The newest 5 star
hotel in Caracas*

From conception to completion and operation, the Eurobuilding Hotel was created to offer the ultimate in service, comfort and excellence.

Overlooking Mt. Avila on one side and the skyline of Caracas on the other, the hotel is a welcome addition to Caracas.

Ideally located, this magnificent hotel offers everything for a complete vacation or business stay: It has two pools, tennis courts, a spa, a gym, panoramic elevators, Carrara marble covering wall and floor space, **Casandra** - a gourmet restaurant offering Spanish nouvelle cuisine, and **Verde Lecho** - a vegetarian restaurant.

Rooms are tastefully decorated and feature built-in hair dryers, mini bars and individual safety deposit boxes which permit the guests to set their own combinations. Double thick windows keep out street noises and provide quiet repose. Thoughtful extra touches include a small bar and barbecue near the pool, afternoon tea and pastries, a cocktail lounge and an executive bar.

For those guests interested in shopping – welcome to heaven. You are nearby the finest shopping center complex in Caracas, the Centro Comercial Ciudad Tamanaco (C.C.C.T.) featuring hundreds of fine shops and boutiques. On the premises is a good English language book shop, an H. Stern outlet and hosts of other fine shops.

The service staff has been specially selected. Add to this

Deluxe	*$80+*
Expensive	*$40*
Moderate	*$30*
Inexpensive below $15	

an internationally trained team of management experts and you have all the ingredients for a perfect vacation or business trip.

■ HOTEL PASEO LAS MERCEDES 4*
Av Principal de Las Mercedes
(Las Mercedes District)
200 Rooms
Phone: 910444
Telex: 23127
Expensive

Formerly the Holiday Inn, Paseo Las Mercedes is the highest class of the four star hotels. Connected to the Paseo Las Mercedes shopping mall, the hotel is smaller but no less comfortable or elegant than some of the five stars. The rooms are spacious, and are air conditioned. There are several restaurants, a piano bar with occasional live music and a swimming pool. Soda machines are located on each floor.

■ THE HOTEL AVILA 4*
Av Jorge Washington
(San Bernardino District)
120 Rooms, Four Floors
Pool
Phone: 515128 & 515228
Expensive

The most relaxing hotel in town on 14 acres of land

The relatively small Avila founded by Nelson Rockefeller offers one hard-to-match advantage-its natural setting. Situated high above the city on 14 acres of trees and subtropical flowers and plants, this exquisite hotel, in our opinion, is the most thoroughly relaxing hotel in Caracas. Early in the morning or at dusk you can stroll through the grounds marveling at the birds, the mango trees, and ever-changing flowers. The modest pool is surrounded by beach chairs and a lawn perfect for sunning. You can enjoy breakfast and lunch at poolside. The lack of air conditioning is no problem since evenings are always breezy and the nights are delightful for sleeping. Most rooms are terraced and face the pool. Furnishings are in charming Spanish colonial style with rich dark woods and wrought iron dominating. The ubiquitous TV set is standard, of course. A bookstore is off the lobby (English-language periodicals are sold). You will need a taxi to get around.

◼◼◼◼ AVENTURA CARACAS 4 *
Av Francisco Fajardo
(San Bernardino District)
93 Rooms
Phone: 514011
Telex: 27359
Deluxe

TIP

Try this if the nearby Avila is full.

A hotel almost strictly for business people, the Aventura Caracas has four conference rooms, executive center, bar and restaurant, spa, swimming pool, English television stations, air conditioning and two presidential suites.

A good value hotel located near the Avila hotel and cable car terminal.

◼◼◼◼ HOTEL CONTINENTAL ALTAMIRA 3 *
Av San Juan Bosco
(Altamira District)
Pool
Air Conditioned
Phone: 262-0243
Expensive

NOTE

Among the newer hotels in Caracas, the Continental resembles a luxury terraced apartment house more than a hotel. Most rooms are small suites.

Super modern in furnishings and decor, this hotel, is located near the night life district of Altamira, a desirable feature for night people. Appropriately, a prime draw is My Piano Bar, a delightful cocktail nook that pulls many Caraqueños as well as Continental guests. And for overcoming that morning-after heavy-headedness, the pool and deck to the rear are ideal. We are partial to terraces and the Altamira has one for every room. That is comfort indeed.

Deluxe	$80+
Expensive	$40
Moderate	$30
Inexpensive below $15	

HOTEL CRILLON 3 *
Av Liberatador & Av Las Acacias
(Sabana Grande District)
80 Rooms 13 Floors
Air Conditioned
Phone: 71-4411
Expensive

For travelers who prefer roominess or who like to entertain in their hotel rooms, the plush Crillon is perfect since most accommodations are two-room suites, complete with carpeting, refrigerator, couch, TV and terrace. Interestingly, each suite is different in decor and colors. Some are furnished in neo-Danish, others are in more traditional style. In all rooms, the accent is on comfort. A couple of blocks away is the Sabana Grande shopping district. Since the hotel is near a main thoroughfare try to avoid lower front floors, opting instead for the quieter upper rear suites.

HOTEL TAMPA 3 *
Av Francisco Solano Lopez No. 9
(Sabana Grande District)
135 Rooms 8 Floors
Phone: 723771, 723831
Telex: 24403 Tampa VC
Moderate

A clean comfortable and pretty hotel, that has more of a motel look. Once again, in the Sabana Grande area, the hotel is in the center ring of activity in Caracas. It is also a great segue point for the many discos and bars that line the area. The hotel has a restaurant and bar.

HOTEL SAVOY 3 *
2a Av Las Delicias de Sabana Grande
(Sabana Grande District)
100 Rooms
Phone: 721971
Telex: 21031 Savoy VC
Moderate

Bolivar for bolivar, the best value in Caracas probably is the Savoy which is ideally located a short stroll from the Centro Comercial Chacaíto, whose rates are certainly moderate. While the rooms are small, they are neat, and clean, and some come with terrace, private bath (as do all our selections), wall-to-wall carpeting and pipe-in music as a bonus. The restaurant and bar are more than adequate. You can have a perfectly comfortable stay here.

HOTEL EL CONDOR 3*
3a Av Las Delicias
(Sabana Grande District)
73 Rooms
Phone: 729911, 12, 13, 14, 15
Inexpensive

A stocky brick building in the shopping area, again, the Condor, for its money, is a deal. With a glassy neon look, the rooms are reasonably large, and fitted tight with leather furniture. A restaurant and bar compliment conference space for 30.

HOTEL LAS AMERICAS 3*
Calle Los Cerritos
(Bello Monte District)
72 Rooms 7 Floors
Small Pool
Air Conditioned
Phone: 951-7387
Moderate

TIP

Great location for walkers. Las Americas caters to businessmen who find the location convenient and the rate right.

Deluxe	$80+
Expensive	$40
Moderate	$30
Inexpensive below $15	

If you are a walker, Las Americas is for you. Ideally located in virtually the geographical center of Caracas, Las Americas provides a focal point for sightseeing by foot or por puesto or even bus. Rooms are small but adequate with acceptable furnishings. The roof-top pool offers a pleasant interlude and a good view of Caracas. Try the pool-side bar and restaurant. Although centrally situated, nights are quiet since the hotel is not located on a major traffic street.

PLAZA CATEDRAL HOTEL 3*
Boulevard Plaza Bolivar
75 Rooms
Phone: 5637022
Inexpensive

NOTE

*A hotel next to
historic Plaza Bolivar.*

Smack in the center of the financial and historical area of Caracas, the hotel adopts its style from its colonial past. Its colonial set-up is very genuine, and it gives an aged feeling to the place. Its restaurant looks over Plaza Bolivar, and serves international food.

KING'S INN HOTEL 3*
Calle Olimpio
(Sabana Grande District)
60 Rooms 6 Floors
Air Conditioned
Phone: 782-7033 & 782-7534
Moderate

Small, informal and reasonably-priced, the King's Inn offers modest carpeted rooms which represent good value. All rooms are air conditioned, have TV, piped-in music and there is free parking for guests. Location is convenient to the busy Sabana Grande district where in all likelihood you will do most of your shopping.

A Couple of Residential Hotels

Resembling a residence more than a hotel, these choices are fine for families or for longer stays.

HOTEL RESIDENCIA MONTSERRAT
Av Avila Sur Altamira
(Altamira)
Phone: 2843111
Moderate

More a residency than a hotel, Montserrat is nonetheless a good comfortable place to stay in the high and nice Altamira district. If you're staying for a week or more you should inquire.

■■■■ **HOTEL LA FLORESTA**
Av Avilla Sur Plaza Altamira
(Altamira)
Phone: 2844111
Moderate

Like the Montserrat, this hotel is geared more for long term residency than overnights. The location is fabulous.

A Couple of Final Choices

■■■■ **Hotel Santa Fe Suites Gardens 4 ***
Av Jose Maria Vargas
(Santa Fe Norte District)
100 Suites
Phone: 979-8355 or 979-8033
Expensive

Excellent for family or groups, the hotel features a pool and restaurant – but the draw is the 4 room suites complete with kitchen and 3 baths. Located in a quiet residential district between the Tamanaco Hotel and Prados del Este section, you can not go wrong here.

■■■■ **Hotel President 4 ***
Av Valparaiso
(Los Caobos District)
165 Rooms
Phone: 782-6390 or 782-6791
Expensive

Located near the Plaza Venezuela Metro station, the President offers large rooms with great views of Mt. Avila or the valley in which Caracas sits. The swimming pool is in constant uses and the restaurant is excellent.

Deluxe	$80+
Expensive	$40
Moderate	$30
Inexpensive below	$15

NOTES:

CARACAS' BEST RESTAURANTS

Whether your taste in food leans to French, Italian, Spanish, Chinese, German, Argentinian or U.S. style cuisine, you are only a cab ride away from a first class restaurant.

Beyond all this is Venezuelan food which is a must. After all, what would life be like without succulent avocados stuffed with shrimp? Or without shellfish casserole in a blistering hot creole sauce? Or a delicate shredded beef dish served with black beans, white rice, and large fried plantains?

After that Continental, Italian and Steak Houses are the most dominant, and provide for the best meals in the city. Slightly less popular, but sitting on the top level of dining, is French food. Then there is bound to be at least one restaurant of every cuisine you can think of, probably.

Colonel Sanders has invaded Venezuela with his Kentucky Fried Chicken. There is Pizza Hut and Burger King too.

If you can delay your headlong rush to a table, we would like first to review local dining customs, mores, and the most popular Venezuelan foods.

First, Venezuelans usually dine late in the evening, often well after 9 pm. Thus, many restaurants are open to midnight and later. Lunch, served between noon and 3 pm, is usually a heavy meal. Tea at 5 pm is a good local custom that holds you nicely until your late dinner.

Second, most restaurants charge a "cubierto", or cover for bread, rolls, butter and other extras.

Third, 10% will be added to your bill for service. If service has been satisfactory, add another 5%. Caraqueños tend to give the waiter the benefit of the doubt.

VENEZUELAN FOODS

Like the Parisians, Caraqueños like their sauces, but unlike the French, the locals lean to a sharp tanginess that can tingle North American taste buds. These piquant sauces – while certainly not volcanically hot as in Mexico – are hardly delicate either, so sample before you plunge. Shrimps, clams, beef, and chicken dominate many menus but combinations seem endless. Here are some representative dishes.

APPETIZERS

TIP

You can have your avocado stuffed with crabmeat or lobster as well.

A true local delicacy is **aguacate relleno con camarones** which is avocado stuffed with shrimp served with a Russian dressing type sauce. Tangier is **ceviche de mero** a marvelous bass dish marinated in a vinagrette sauce. Often shrimp **(camarones)** is substituted. If you're partial to smoked salmon order **salmon ahumado**. It comes without cream cheese.

SOUPS

Per Person:
Expensive $30+
Moderate $20-30
Inexpensive below $20

Your trip here would be seriously deficient if you do not sample the turtle soup, either as broth with wine **(consome de tortuga)** or in a cream turtle soup **(crema de tortuga)**.

The **gazpacho** soup, which should need no description, is much as it is in good New York restaurants, except that here the tomatos, onions, peppers, and other vegetables are fresh indeed. A refreshing cold luncheon dish on a warm day.

MAIN COURSES

NOTE

Venezuelans go delirious over a thick vegetable soup called sancocho which actually can serve as a full meal, especially when fish or beef chunks are added.

An extremely tender steak called **punta trasera** is a constant in most local restaurants. Definitely sample it. Argentine-style steaks served with a hot red pepper relish and a cool green pepper relish are popular too. Common designations include **Lomito**, **Churrasco** and **Baby Bife**.

Turning from beef to seafood, there is a remarkable casserole called **cazuela de mariscos** which is a perfectly baked blend of clams, mussels, lobster, shrimp and squid served in a hot creole sauce. Then too there is the ubiquitous **Paella Valenciana** comprised of chicken, lobster, shrimp, clams, mussels, olives and saffron rice. Moreover, you can order **arroz con mariscos** (a mixed seafood platter with Spanish rice).

TIP

*Particularly filling is the **pabellon**, a casserole-type melange of shredded beef, black beans, white rice, and large plantains (banana-like fruit, called platanos in Spanish).*

Since seafood is extremely popular here, we are providing you with a capsule vocabulary:

Langosta - lobster served in many different ways
Langostinos - large shrimps (cray fish)
Camarones - shrimp
Cangrejo - crab meat
Pargo - red snapper
Mero - bass
Trucha - trout
Lenguado - sole
Mejillones - mussels

DESSERTS

Venezuelans adore strawberries and most restaurant menus include one strawberry dish, typically

TIP

*Ice cream is very good indeed, and the **flan**, or caramel custard, is worth sampling.*

fresas con crema, which is the red fruit with whipped cream. Guava fruit is in demand too and one popular dessert is **cascos de guayaba con queso crema** (red guava fruit in syrup with cream cheese).

SPECIAL DISHES

Hallacas is a leaf stuffed with a corn dough and tiny bits of chicken, pork, beef, olives, raisins, and onions. Quite good. A corn bread called **arepa**, served hot at many restaurants, is recommended also.

COCKTAILS

TIP

Scotch, bourbons, and blends are available at relatively high prices.

Rum is the king of hard liquor here, and little wonder since Venezuela produces some of the world's best rum. Try **ponche crema**, an eggnog rum drink, a tall **rum punch**, the **cuba libre**, or the **daiquiris**. Local beers are quite good, particularly **Cardenal** and **Solera**, premium brands which are exported. More popular are the **Polar**, **Caracas**, and **Zulia** brands. And finally, the water is quite drinkable at all the Caracas restaurants in this book.

HOW ALIVE LISTINGS WORK

We've scoured Caracas for the restaurants that offer the best values in all prices ranges. Categories are arranged by nationality or type of restaurant (such as French, Chinese, fast food or cafes).

Our price scale is based on the cost of a 4-course dinner (per person) – appetizer or soup, main dish, dessert and cafe –and includes the cover and a 10% service charge. Cocktails and wine are extra of course. Locally produced liquors are much cheaper than imported brands. Make your choice known, if price is a consideration.

Per person:
Expensive $30+
Moderate $20-30
Inexpensive $20 Under

ALIVE SCALE

Expensive	*(per person) $30+*
Moderate	*$20-30*
Inexpensive	*Under $20*

Credit cards are accepted at all the restaurants we have listed.

THE BEST FRENCH AND CONTINENTAL RESTAURANTS

A Caraqueño anxious to impress a dinner guest invariably will escort him to one of the first class French restaurants in Caracas. And thus we begin our tour of the city's best restaurants in the so-called French quarter. Without exception, our selections are elegant (therefore coats and ties are de rigueur) and reservations are a must. It's fashionable to dine after nine. And understandably prices are high. Remember, prices are estimated for a four-course dinner with cover and service, but cocktails and wines are additional.

GAZEBO
Av Rio de Janeiro
(Las Mercedes District)
12 - 3, 8 - 11:30, Sat dinner only
(Closed Sunday)
Phone: 925568
Expensive

Considered by some the best restaurant in Caracas. The food can be roughly categorized as nouvelle cuisine, but what makes it a bit more distinct is that the French foundation has been given a tropical twist. So nothing is that predictable, and, of course, that is good.

The fish dishes stand out, and the mousses are excellent. There is also a more than adequate wine reserve.

Silver plates are dimmed by candle light. Seats are white cushioned couches, a bit bad for the back. The central room is divided by pink columns, and the walls are soft pink and near invisible gray. The walls are covered with a balloon like material that muffles the sounds, and gives a private feel to your space.

There is no menu, but the captain, Jacques, is highbrow, triple languaged and precise. He is as sparkling clean as the restaurant itself. Reservations are a must.

NOTE

The interior design is super modern and super opulent, so pushed-up with luxury that it is startling at first.

■ AVENTINO
Av San Felipe
(La Castellana District)
Noon - 3 pm
7 pm-midnight (Closed Sunday)
Phone: 32-2640
Expensive

NOTE

Presidents Leoni and Caldera both have signed the Aventino's Gold Book (Livre dór) which is reserved for those patrons ordering the pressed duck who also are awarded a gastronomical diploma for their adventurousness.

In a magnificent private estate in the residential La Castellana District is the elegant Aventino through whose massive doors you might expect Louis XIV to make a regal entrance. Set amid flourishing trees and shrubbery, this restaurant is rather formal with high ceilings, dark wood paneling, and silver and china crystal chandeliers that befit a luxury villa. The ambience is muted – you will find yourself speaking softly – and the food is appropriately splendid. The restaurant specialty is **caneton a' la presse** (pressed duck) for which Latin Americans travel great distances to sample. It is a dish for presidents. Other recommendations include the **fonds d´Artichauts** (artichokes) as an appetizer; **bisque de langosta** (lobster bisque); **Chateaubriand bairnaise** (steak in sauce); **beef filet Wellington**; and for dessert a crepe suzette or the **Georgette Romanoff** (a crepe with cognac, grand marnier and almonds).

Per Person:
Expensive	$30+
Moderate	$20-30
Inexpensive	below $20

NOTE

Aventino is a member of the prestigious Confrerie des Chevalieres du Tastevin.

TIP

Hard to find since it is located in an apartment house.

This award winning restaurant features 10,000 bottles of wine – hundreds of brands – ranging from such popular favorites as a beaujolais to a vintage 1966 Chateau Lafite Rothchild.

Ask the owner, Dino Riocci, or his son, Giovanni, for a tour of their truly spectacular wine cellar. It is a grand experience.

GIRAFE
Av Venezuela
Edifico Venezuela
(El Rosal District)
12 - 12
Phone: 261-8218
Expensive

In an elegant large apartment house, the restaurant is, like Gazebo, washed in a light pink. The space is not large or grand, but restful and quaint.

My favorite dishes were the **Corazon de Lomito** (basically steak) and the **Minuta de Pechuga de Pato** (duck).

A fine French restaurant. Live music adds to your dining enjoyment.

PATRICK
Calle Trinidad
(Las Mercedes District)
Noon - 11, Sat dinner only
(Closed Sunday)
Phone: 916641
Expensive

In a hard to find corner, Patrick is placed in a garden setting, which gives off a country, suburban feel. The restaurant itself is dark and intimate, and layed-out elegantly.

The beef and the veal are its specialties, and there is a poached dish of the day.

CAFE NAIF
Calle Madrid
(Las Mercedes District)
12 - 12
Phone: 752-9298
Expensive

TIP

Come for the Indonesian specialities on Wednesdays.

With a hot house motif, Cafe Naif is illuminated with sky lights, and is packed tight with flowers and plants, giving a formal picnic atmosphere. Surrounded by green gardens, the restaurant features a fine **Atun fra diavolo** (tuna) and **Solomo Bourgingnon** (steak), both excellent. On Wednesday nights there is Indonesian food.

BARRIO FRANCES
Av Principal La Castellana
at J. Felix Rios
(La Castellana District)
12 - 1 am, Sat dinner only
(Closed Sunday)
Phone: 333570
Expensive

NOTE

French food plus Dixie Jazz in the tropics

Erected in homage to New Orleans and their style of French cuisine, Barrio Frances has live Dixie Jazz, New Orlean's street signs, brass rails and mementos to the great New Orlean's jazz greats, particularly Louis Armstrong.

The restaurant specializes in **steak Lomito Barnaise**, **Lomito Strogonoff**, **Escalopine de Pavo** (turkey) and **Strogonoff de Mero** (bass).

RESTAURANT LASSERRE
3rd Avenida, Los Palos Grandes
12 - 3, 6 - 2 am (Closed Sunday)
Phone: 283-4558
Expensive

Per Person:
Expensive $30+
Moderate $20-30
Inexpensive below $20

Lasserre is a smaller version of the super-elegant Aventino. And that's no coincidence since two brothers independently operate both restaurants. Jimmy runs his own kitchen which is fortunate for his patrons because the food is remarkable in a city where good restaurants are the only restaurants. A shade less formal than brother Dino's Aventino, this eatery features wine, cheese, and fruit carts that move up and down the aisles in the dining room. Organ music begins at 8 nightly. Jimmy wisely uses a tri-lingual (French-Spanish-English) menu. He is justly proud of his **Ostras Rockefeller** (Oysters Rockefeller served with spinach and a cheese dressing); his **steak flambee poivre** (steak with pepper sauce); and his **brochette**. Jacket and tie.

██████████ **PETITE BISTRO DE JACQUES**
Av Principal de Las Mercedes
(Las Mercedes District)
12 - 2:30 am
Sat dinner only
(Closed Sunday)
Phone: 918108, 910975
Moderate

A small French bistro, this restaurant has specials each night. The service is personal and the menu is on the mirror.

If this bistro doesn't make you believe you're back in Paris, no one will.

██████████ **ALFI'S**
Centro Comercial Chacaíto
Noon - 3, 7 - 12
Phone: 723509
Moderate

Well-kept and elegant, Alfi's has international food that ranges from **Pato Naranja** (duck in orange sauce), to **Steak Pimienta** (pepper steak) and **quiche lorraine**. There is a piano bar.

ANATOLE
Av La Estrella (corner Av Avila)
(San Bernardino District)
Noon - 3:30, 6 - 11(Closed Sunday)
Phone: 52-4353
Moderate

Considered one of Caracas' best restaurants, Anatole's offers no less than eight private salons (one table per salon) as well as a large dining space furnished in imperial French style. Looking like a private club, the plushness is excessive but tasteful.

The menu is bi-lingual and features **pato a la naranja** (duck with orange sauce), **frog legs provencal**, **coq au vin**, and pork chops.

LA ROTISSERIE
Hilton Hotel
Dinner Only
Expensive

NOTE

Award winning restaurant in Hilton's main level.

Award winning and fine dining are provided by the Hilton's premier restaurant. Definitely nouvelle cuisine, the restaurant menu will range from typical French dishes to stranger arcane ones. Very formal.

THE BEST VENEZUELAN RESTAURANTS

It will be your loss if you fail to savor at least one truly Venezuelan meal. You will be depriving yourself of a gastronomical experience that cannot be duplicated in North America or Europe. Review our discussion of Venezuelan foods at the beginning of this chapter.

EL PORTON
Av Pichincha No. 18
(El Rosal District)
11 am - 1 am (Daily)
Phone: 71-6071 & 71-0401
Inexpensive

Per Person:
Expensive   *$30+*
Moderate   *$20-30*
Inexpensive below $20

Spanish-colonial in decor, the Porton is delightfully comfortable, especially the outdoor dining in the rear. Masks, hammocks and handwoven tapestries enliven the walls. High on our recommended list is **aguacate relleno con camarones** (avocadoes stuffed with shrimp). We lean to the **sancocho** (thick vegetable soup) served only on Sundays, the **pabellon** (beef, beans, rice and plantains); and the **parrillada** (a mixed meat grill). Definitely try the **arepas** (corn rolls), **hallacas** (leaf stuffed with chicken, pork, beef, olives and onions), the **yuca** (potato-like mantioc vegetable) and **crema de nata** (a sour-cream-like spread). For dessert, sample the **flan** or the **cascos guayaba** (guava fruit). No music on Sundays. Weekend reservations a must. Informal dress.

> ███████ **EL CARRIZO**
> *Av Blandin*
> *(La Castellana District)*
> *Noon - 2:30 pm*
> *7 pm - 11 pm*
> *Sundays: Noon - 11 pm*
> *Phone: 32-9370*
> *Inexpensive*

El Carrizo's rustic log cabin simplicity and superb kitchen make it the favorite of several Venezuelan friends of ours. Co-owner David Gomez, a delightful Portuguese-born epicure whose English is perfect, will be pleased to order for you and certainly have him do so. He formerly worked at the Lee Hamilton Steak House and now is working hard to make El Carrizo a winner. His partner Mario is also a winner. David probably will suggest a steak, perhaps **punta trasera** (tip: this steak often is part of a daily four-course luncheon special.) Steaks usually come with two sauces **(guasacaca)**, mild green and red hot. Hallacas serves as the vegetable for most dishes. Another recommended dish is **pollo deshuesado** (boned chicken). Say hello to

NOTE

This award-winning restaurant (for the best criolla food) is understandably packed on weekends thanks to the food, moderate prices, and the popular five-piece combo, specializing in Venezuelan folk music.

NOTE

The 12 tables are comfortably snug in the intimate brick-floor dining room and the aroma of burning charcoal emanates from the kitchen.

David for us, whom you will invariably see working the spotless kitchen. Informal dress.

■■■■■■ TARZILANDIA
Final Av San Juan Bosco
10a Transversal Altamira
(Altamira District)
Noon - 11 pm Closed Monday
Phone: 261-8419
Moderate

TIP

Turtle steaks are the house speciality and delicious.

In a jungle-like outdoor setting, the Tarzilandia owners have created an outstanding eatery that specializes in steaks, especially turtle steaks. Fantastic. Besides the turtle delicacies (soup too), you should sample the pepper steak. Appropriately, stuffed animals, spears, and tortoise shells adorn the rear wall of this double-level restaurant. Late evening breezes can be cool. Be sure to bring a sweater or jacket with you. Since the restaurant is 10 blocks from the main avenue, have your waiter arrange for a cab when you are ready to go. Informal dress.

■■■■■■ EL CANEY
Av Pichincha
At Avenida Casanova
(Chacaíto District)
Phone: 71-8754
Noon - 1 am (daily)
Inexpensive

NOTE

Similar to El Carrizo.

This award winning restaurant with beamed ceiling features superb beef and a pepper and onion sauce (**guasacaca**) which compliments all the meat dishes. Try the **parrillada Mixta**, (a mixed grill), the **Cordero** (lamb chops), or the **Chuletas de Cochino** (pork chops). For openers, try the **guacamole** salad or the hearts of palm (**palmito**). El Caney is located at the border of the Chacaíto District and the El Rosal District.

Per Person:
Expensive $30+
Moderate $20-30
Inexpensive   below $20

LOS PILONES
Av Venezuela at Calle Pichincha
(El Rosal District)
Phone: 7188367
Inexpensive

NOTE

Similar to El Porton.

A pretty comfortable restaurant, Los Pilones centers around its steaks, soups, pabellon and stuffed avocados.

There is occasionally live music. The restaurant is well located.

POSADA DEL LAUREL
No. Pastor a Misericordia
(Parque Central District)
Noon - 12
Phone: 575-1135
Inexpensive

TIP

The bass (Mero) is
most bragged about.

Small, loud, local and happening, Posada del Laurel is at the end of the park, walking away from the Hilton. The interior is shiny wood, and glass, but the local people pack the place for a evening drink and a hearty meal.

THE BEST ITALIAN RESTAURANTS

A major minority group in Caracas are the Italians who as customary throughout the world carry with them their great restaurant tradition. Italians live to eat and reasonably enough love to cook. We have selected the most authentic Italian restaurants in town.

DOLCE VITA
Av Juan Bosco
Edifico El Torbes
(Altamira District)
12 - 4, 7 - 12
Phone: 261-5763
Expensive

NOTE

For decorations there are heavy-set flowers, hassocks at the bar and gardens right outside the restaurant.

An exciting atmosphere wrenches diners out of their seats, occasionally, as live music blares, and the tiny dance floor lures. The twitching head is expected, dance or eat, dance or eat, dance or eat?

The food is excellent, with all kinds of pizza and the speciality being **canejo cazador** (rabbit). All in all, it is a fun place to dine.

■■■■■ **IL PADRINO (The Godfather)**
Plaza Sur Altamira
(Altamira District)
11:30 am - 2 am (daily)
Phone: 32-7684
Moderate

In a straight steal from the Godfather, this huge restaurant features the names of the novel's major characters on each front step. This plagiarism does not extend to the food, which is excellent, which is proved by the masses of people, 400 at times, fighting the spaghetti blues.

NOTE

Strolling musicians (except for Monday) add to the charm, as do the Chianti bottles suspended from the ceiling and walls.

No less than three dozen antipasto variations are on the generous menu which features fine pasta, veal, and chicken dishes. The **veal scaloppina marsala** is an outstanding value, as is the **Saltimbocca a la Romana**. For dessert try the **formaggi misti** (mixed chesses). Party atmosphere nightly. Join in.

■■■■■ **VECCHIO MULINO**
Av Francisco Solano & Los Jabillos
(Sabana Grande District)
Noon - 3:30 pm
7 pm - 12:30 am (Daily)
Phone: 71-2695
Moderate

Per Person:
Expensive $30+
Moderate $20-30
Inexpensive below $20

In consideration of the calorie-watchers of the world, this fresh and cheerful bistro notes the

NOTE

A water mill in the back of a rear garden justifies the restaurant's name which means "Old Mill" in Italian.

calorie content of its food next to the prices. Mamma mia, what is happening to Italian restaurants! Nevertheless, the food is unusually good, regardless of calories. Waiters in brightly-hued shirts and vests move briskly beneath the Cathedral ceiling lined with light blue beams. The floral pattern is carried through on the chairs and benches, and you almost feel as if you're in a small town in Austria. But the fare is definitely Italian. Menu items we like include **saltimbocca**, **escalopas de ternera al marsala** (veal scallopine) and the many pasta specialties. Jacket and tie at night. Violin music is a bonus.

FRANCO'S
Av Francisco Solano
& Av Los Jabillos
(Sabana Grande District)
Noon - 3, 7 - midnight
Phone: 72-0996
Moderate

This first class restaurant, brilliantly conceived as a cloister-like luxury dining station, is rich in arched brick columns that blend into the brick ceiling from which giant prosciuto hams and Chianti baskets are suspended. The reds of the bricks are picked up in the red-hued checkered table cloths.

NOTE

Stained windows, huge murals and subdued lighting create a personal atmosphere.

The **fettuccini**, **cannelloni** are fantastic, and the **zuppa de verdura** (vegetable soup) is a great opening. There is occasionally strolling musicians.

PICCOLO MONDO
Av La Trinidad
(Las Mercedes District)
Noon - 3, 7 - Midnight
Phone: 91-2357
Moderate

Concentrating on its food and not its surrounding, Picccolo Mondo specializes in Rigatoni, Vermicelli for appetizers, and Saltimbocca for the main meal. There are daily specials.

■■■■■■ **PIDA PIZZA**
Calle Bello Monte
(Sabana Grande District)
7 pm - 4:30 am
Phone: 72-8069
Inexpensive

TIP

Bring the Kids

Large cellar like setting, this is a pizza joint, with dj'd music.

STEAK HOUSES

Beef lovers have a meaty choice of either feasting in Argentina-style steak houses, complete with small stoves (parillas) at your table and tangy sauces; or in a U.S.-style steak place with those familiar vegetables and French fried potatoes. We have selected what we consider the best of Caracas' many good steak houses.

Argentinian-Style

■■■■■■ **EL GRAN CHAROLAIS**
Av Principal La Castellana
(La Castellana District)
11:30 - Midnight (Daily)
Phone: 33-2723
Moderate

NOTE

Named for the famed cattle, this choice restaurant offers only the best quality steaks.

Per Person:
Expensive $30+
Moderate $20-30
Inexpensive below $20

Set in a handsome private house, Charolais serves an excellent **parillada mixta**, Argentine-style (mixed grill). Also recommended is the **baby beef**. Try the tomato and onion salad with your meat and you're in Buenos Aires. Manager Antonio Alvarez will tend to your every whim. Highly recommended. This is the perfect spot to sample the parillada. Served on parillas (stoves) at your table, the mixed meats are succulent and tender, and will truly highlight your meal.

SHORTHORN GRILL
Av Liberatador (Near La Florida)
(El Bosque District)
Noon - Midnight (Daily)
Phone: 71-1052
Moderate

Large, with stone archways, and bedecked with gaucho paintings, the Shorthorn is noted for fast service and superb beef. If you are rushing to theater or a film, this is the place to dine. The two best dishes are the **churrasco** (sirloin steak) and the **parrillada mixta Argentina** (mixed grill of beef, liver, sausage, and kidneys) served on a small barbecue at your table. Too, you will like the **baby beef** (T-Bone steak) and the **brochette de lomito** (beef chunks ala brochette). Tossed salads are crisp and fresh and deserve your attention. Informal.

LA ESTANCIA
Av Principal de La Castellana
(La Castellana District)
11 am - 1 am (Daily)
Phone: 33-1937
Moderate

For a feeling of outdoor dining, stop in at the quiet La Estancia where the ambience and food are both recommended. While there is a roof, the sides are open and the greenery and breezes contribute to the airy atmosphere. The **churrasco Martin Fierro** and the **T-Bone steak** are top recommendations. Before dinner, stop at **La Tapera** next door for cocktails around the piano bar. Informal.

LA MANSION
Av Tamanaco
(El Rosal District)
11:30 am - Midnight (Daily)
Phone: 951-2562
Moderate

For garden dining as well as for the best empanadas (meat pies) in Caracas, La Mansion is the place to dine. After the empanada appetizer, try the **punta trasera** and any of the chicken dishes. For dessert, it's definitely the **panqueque de banana** (banana pancake). Informal.

U.S.-STYLE RESTAURANTS

These choices will leave a bit of nostalgia lingering with your empty dishes.

CITY ROCK CAFE
*Centro Comercial Chacaito
Av Francisco Solano
(Chacaito District)
Open until very late
Phone: 71-6352
Moderate*

Sharing this category with the restaurant bar Weekends the City Rock is older. Very much an American set-up, with a sprawling complex of booths, bars and tables. The atmosphere is hip, and videos dominate the walls and ceilings, the music blares, rock of course, the chatter is incessant, excited and indomitable. Like the Hard Rock, it sells itself with t-shirts.

The food is strictly American too, with hot dogs, burgers, roast beef, chicken salad leading the fare. There are even peanut butter and jelly sandwiches.

For a touch of Caracas' American hipness, a place overloaded with cool people and pretty people, come here.

WEEKENDS
*Av San Juan Bosco
(Altamira District)
Noon - 1:30 am
Phone: 261-4863
Moderate*

A huge tri-level eatery with excellent burgers and sandwiches reminiscent of home. While primarily a nite spot, the food is tasty and the atmosphere excellent.

LEE HAMILTON
Av San Felipe corner of El Bosque
(La Castellana District)
11 am - 11:30 pm
Phone: 32-5227
Moderate

TIP

The lettuce is all home grown.

Begun by an American from Maryland, Lee Hamilton's is the best known U.S. eatery in Caracas. Its popularity is justified since the filet mignon is tender and prime, and served with garlic bread, baked potato, tossed salad and coffee. It is a meal back home. Reservations necessary on the weekends.

THE BEST SEAFOOD RESTAURANTS

DENA-ONA
Av Tamanaco #52
(El Rosal)
Noon - Midnight (Daily)
Phone: 33-7658
Moderate

TIP

Choose any of the small dining rooms or ask for a table in the open-air area in the rear.

If seafood sets your palate tingling, plan a meal at this delightfully attractive restaurant which serves no less than 2 dozen house specialities. We particularly enjoy the trout (**trucha**) dishes and bass (**mero**) platters. The Spanish colonial setting adds to the decor.

RIAS BAJAS
Edificio Artelito
(Los Palos Grandes)
Noon - 2 am (Daily)
Phone: 283-3580
Inexpensive

Lobster is the dish here and the **langosta al thermador** and **langosta al whiskey** are both highly regarded by regulars who relish the extensive Spanish-English menu. Owner-host Manual (Manolo) Cordero is likely to stop at your table to review the day's specialties. In addition to langosta, a shellfish casserole called **cazuela de mariscos** is in demand as is the **Langostino al ajillo** (scampi). Here too is your source for exotic dishes such as **squid** and **eel**.

Good solid seafare in comfortable surroundings. Tie and jacket.

PORLAMAR
Plaza Chacaíto
(Chacaíto District)
11 am - 1 am (Daily)
Phone: 32-1666
Inexpensive

Labeling itself "a corner of Margarita Island" (Venezuela's weekend retreat), this charming restaurant specializes in dishes such as **pargo habanero** a seafood casserole topped with a cheese sauce, and consome **de chipi chipi** or de **guacuco**, clam soups that set Margaritans aflame. Other recommended dishes include **arroz a la marinera** and **paella Valenciana**.

Straw baskets, shells, and boat replicas-all from Margarita cover the walls.

BOGA VANTE MARISQUERIA
Av Venezuela
(El Rosal District)
Noon - Midnight
Phone: 71-8624
Inexpensive

Per Person:
Expensive $30+
Moderate $20-30
Inexpensive below $20

Resembling an old whaler's inn, this large restaurant is, in our opinion, probably the most attractive of the seafood restaurants in Caracas. The fare has won several gastronomic awards. You can't miss the large sail in front of the restaurant.

MARISQUERIA RESTAURANT
Centro Ciudad
Comercial Tamanaco
Phone: 92-9034
Moderate

A ship like atmosphere, with the waiters in sailor outfits, the restaurant serves good fish meals.

THE BEST SPANISH RESTAURANTS

Many first time visitors here think that Venezuelan food is typical Spanish or Mexican fare. By now you know that Venezuelan cuisine is distinctive and if you want Spanish food, you have to dine in a Spanish restaurant.

HOSTAL LA CASTELLANA
Plaza La Castellana
(La Castellana District)
Noon - Midnight (Daily)
Phone: 33-4260 33-3111
Moderate

The Spanish vibes here are almost overpowering. From the Don Quixote and Sancho Panza replicas just outside the entrance to the colonial Spanish decor to the pounding Flamenco music, you do get a sensuous sense of Spain. Three formal dining rooms are on the upper level where the armor and spears stare down at you from the walls. A wishing well of all things too. For more informal dining, try the main level tavern where the Flamenco music starts at 8:30. As for the food, you can't go wrong with the **gazpacho soup** or the **paella**, **trucha** (trout), or **pierna cordero castellana** (leg of lamb).

CHOCOLATE
Av Tomanaco
El Rosal District
Noon - Midnight
Phone: 951-7575
Moderate

Also following the pedigree of old Spain, Chocolate is on a busy street and is just as busy inside. There is live music, either in a group or a duet of piano and singer, and there is a huge bar, revving up the festivities.

Try **camerones al Ajillo**, **cazuela de mariscos** or the **pargo provencal**.

CAMILOS
Av Francisco Solano
& Av Los Jabillos
(Sabana Grande District)
Noon - 3 pm, 7 pm - Midnight
Phone: 72-5995
Inexpensive

NOTE

The bar is designed as a recreation of a rural house in Southern Spain.

Camilos is a deliberate recreation of a 15th century Madrid restaurant, according to the owner. Arched doorways, wrought iron lanterns, large simulated window, high white walls, and the ever-present Flamenco music lend a Spanish ambience to this attractive and intimate bistro.

You should stop for a cocktail before dinner. The **paellas** are recommended here along with the **arroz con pollo**. Coat and tie.

EL CASARIO
CCCT (Shopping Center)
Phone: 92-9034
Moderate

Per Person:
Expensive $30+
Moderate $20-30
Inexpensive below $20

Not as blatantly reproduced as the other three restaurants, El Casario specializes in Spanish food and not necessarily Spanish look. In the great shopping mall, El Casario is a fun place to eat because of its liveliness.

THE BEST CHINESE RESTAURANTS

■■■■■■ *EL DRAGON VERDE*
Av Maturin (Cine Paris Building)
(Los Cedros District)
Noon - 3 pm
6:30 pm - 11:30 pm (Daily)
Phone: 71-8404
Moderate

NOTE

Without question, the egg rolls, sweet-and-sour pork, shrimp, and chicken, and the spare ribs are as good as any in memory.

We have eaten in Chinese restaurants in New York, Paris, Mexico City and throughout South America. Never yet have we encountered a better Cantonese restaurant than the Green Dragon, which understandably is an oasis for Asian diplomats here, as well as for North Americans.

In service and food, this restaurant is absolutely first class. You enter past the bar with its imposing water-spouting green dragon on your way to the upstairs dining area where green Chinese lanterns hang from the ceiling. Menus are bi-lingual and the waiters are impeccably courteous and efficient, an appropriate complement to the food. Gracious dining indeed. Informal.

■■■■■■ *EL PALMAR*
Plaza Lincoln
(Bello Monte District)
Noon - Midnight
Phone: 751-4442
Moderate

Typically set up in Chinese style, El Palmar has excellent food, particularly its lo mein and pork dishes.

MEE-NAM
Av Luis Roche
(near the Third Transversal)
(Altamira District)
Noon - 11:30 pm (Daily)
Phone: 262-1685
Moderate

Resembling a large pagoda, this brilliantly colored and decorated mini-palace even features a small bridge over a stream housing a fiery dragon of papier mache. The huge bi-lingual menu includes over 50 dishes and we recommend to you the **sweet and sour shrimp**, the **roast pork** (cha sui ding) with almonds and vegetables, and the **boneless duck.**

MR. CHOW
Av Rio de Janeiro
(Las Mercedes District)
Noon - Midnight
Phone: 752-6335
Inexpensive

Frequented, busy and active, Mr. Chow is good for a faster less complicated Chinese meal. The food is good, and Mr. Chow is a good short stop in the middle of a touring day.

A KOREAN RESTAURANT

RESTAURANT SEOUL
Av Francisco Solano
(Sabana Grande District)
Noon - 11:30
Phone: 72-1519, 72-0971
Inexpensive

Per Person:
Expensive   *$30+*
Moderate   *$20-30*
Inexpensive below $20

A relatively small restaurant, Seoul is nonetheless a good place for dinner. The menu is in both Korean and Spanish, obviously because many Korean come here, which is a good sign about the food. Dishes like **tang soo yook** (meat in sweet and sour sauce), **yook ge jang** (spicy soup), **mas ji bog um** (octopus) and **saeng sun gu i** (baked fish) are all safe and delicious bets.

SWISS-BAVARIAN RESTAURANTS

LA PETITE SWISS
Calle La Trinidad, Calle Madrid
(Las Mercedes District)
Noon - Midnight
Noon - 7 on Sundays
Phone: 91-2357
Moderate

As the name implies, the restaurant is an attempted recreation of the tiny country in the Alps, so quaint in its style. With a chalet, Calvinist feel, flags of the Swiss regions and the milk-maid checkered cloths, La Petite Swiss is at least microscopically Swiss. Fondue is, of course, the main delight, with cheeses and potatoes and other Swiss delicacies abounding.

EL CHALET
Hotel Crillon
Av Liberatador (Corner Las Acias)
(Sabana Grande District)
Phone: 71-4411
Moderate

For a touch of Switzerland in Caracas, head for the main floor of the Hotel Crillon where you can taste a bit of Switzerland in an authentic setting.

GERMAN RESTAURANTS

DIE HUTTE
Av Tamanaco
(El Rosal District)
Noon - Midnight, Closed Monday
Phone: 951-5327
Inexpensive

Munich-like in atmosphere and food, the Die Hutte serves excellent **sauerbraten**, **wienerschnitzel** and **eisbein** (pork) as well as a fine **goulash soup**. Gemutlich ambience with good use of wood in the beamed ceiling, benches and tables. Try the German beer in a chilled stein. Hearty, filling portions.

EL RINCON DE BAVARIA
Av Gamboa corner Pantero
(San Bernardino District)
Noon - Midnight
Phone: 51-8562
Moderate

Much like Die Hutte, the same fare goes. This is a long time favorite of ours, and one of the best restaurants in the San Bernardino area.

A PERUVIAN RESTAURANT

EL TIZON
Centro Comercial Bello Campo
(Bello Campo District)
Noon - 3, 7 - 11:30
Phone: 31-6715
Inexpensive

Stick to the Peruvian fare.

A small restaurant that specializes in both Peruvian and Mexican food. Stick to the Peruvian platters. Specialties include **ceviche** (marinated fish) and **anticuchos de corazon** (heart). **Pisco sours**, the popular Peruvian drink is a must. A touch of Lima, in Caracas.

AN ARAB RESTAURANT

KIBBE
Calle Madrid
(Las Mercedes District)
Noon - Midnight
Phone: 91-0519
Inexpensive

Per Person:
Expensive   *$30+*
Moderate   *$20-30*
Inexpensive below $20

With **cous-cous** the top of the sand dune, Kibbe has all kinds of Arabic dishes, **felafel**, **humis** and others. Take-out is possible. The food is excellent.

SUNDAY BUFFETS

Sunday evenings when many Caracas restaurants are closed, you should consider the buffets at the **Hotel Tamanaco** and **Caracas Hilton**. Both offer great variety in beef, lamb, and seafood at about $15 a person. All you can eat. The Tamanaco buffet is held on the Panorama Terrace (top floor) which offers a stunning view of the city. Music and dancing make for a pleasant evening. The Hilton spreads its food sumptuously in its Cota 880 Club, located on the 15th (top) floor of the hotel. Two bands make the dining easy.

OUTDOOR CAFES

Informal and open all day and evening, these cafes are perfect for a restful break during sightseeing or shopping. Service is leisurely and the menu ranges from espresso to beer to cocktails and from ice cream to double hamburgers.

■■■■■■ *THE FORUM*
Edificio Centro Capriles
Plaza Venezuela

TIP

These are perfect meeting places

On the ground floor of this modern office building is the Forum which has good food and drink at modest prices and as a bonus offers live music in the late afternoon and evening. The place grooves between 5 and 7 most evenings as the young office singles gather en masse. Shoe shine boys are at the ready here. Two other splendidly-slow service cafes where you can relax with a rum cocktail or espresso are **Papagallo**, Centro Comercial Chacaíto, Chacaíto District and the **Cafe Piccolo**, Calle Real de Sabana Grande near Los Jabillos,

Sabana Grande district. The Piccolo's impromptu music keeps the place jammed.

There are other outdoor cafes spread all over the city.

A VEGETARIAN RESTAURANT

■■■■■■■ **EL BUFFET VEGETARIAN**
Av Los Jardines #4
(La Florida District)
7 pm - 9 pm (Closed Sunday)
Phone: 74-7512, 74-7490
Inexpensive

NOTE

For health food fans

A long time favorite among Caraqueños longing for macrobiotic food and other dairy dishes, you will enjoy eating here. Particularly recommended for lunch or if you happen to be in the La Florida area.

FAST FOOD

The **Cada** supermarket chain, with units throughout Venezuela, features fast food outlets attached to each market. You can get from a snack to a full meal.

NOTE

Just like home

From America are **Burger King**, **McDonald's**, **Dunkin Donuts**, **Kentucky Fried Chicken** and **Pizza Hut**. Natively produced are **Tropiburger**, **Pizza King**, **Arturos** and **Plaza Broadway**.

The **Plaza Broadway** at the end of Sabana Grande (nearest to Chacaíto) is a complex featuring **Tropiburger** (hamburgers); **Pizza King** (pizza); **Lung Fung** (Chinese) and **La Alemanita** (hot dogs and sausages). Don't forget to bring the kiddies!

Per Person:
Expensive $30+
Moderate $20-30
Inexpensive below $20

NOTES:

limate is a blessing in Caracas; its perennial autumn weather is an engine for any sightseeing. Because of this, just walking is an option. And old Caracas should be walked through, to enable you to soak in its past.

A STROLL THROUGH OLD CARACAS

The city's historical center, since colonial days, has been El Silencio, a wonderful name, and in within an hour's time you'll be able to cover the 10 block area of Caracas' roots.

Plaza Bolivar

Originally called Plaza de Armas, Plaza Bolivar is the site of Caracas' birth, over 400 years ago. This is the natural starting point for any walk in El Silencio. It is a tranquil one-square block area that is surrounded by the **Cathedral** of Caracas, the **City Hall** and the **Congress** building.

Plaza de Armas was the original blueprinted center of the new city Caracas, the beginning stone of Diego de Losada's vision. Today busy Caraqueños and shoe shine boys ply the Plaza.

As monumental father of the city, Plaza Bolivar, still de Armas, was at the heated center of the independence fight. And, after independence, was the spot where the Constitution was read aloud. But it was still not until 1883 that this atavistic square was officially devoted to Bolivar.

It was actually under President Guzman Blanco, serving in the 1860's, that the Plaza was made into what you see today. The iron work, fountains, lamp posts, bandstand and equestrian statue of Bolivar were all his doing.

On that statue, of Bolivar riding high, is chipped out several statements. On the front it says, "Libertador de Venezuela, Nueva Granada, Ecuador y Peru y Fundador de Bolivia."

NOTE

It is quite a touching site, if you are able to transpose yourself into a Venezuelan's frame of mind. This is their great man, their founding father, and, at the right time, the whole honorarium is moving.

On one side, it says "Born in Caracas 24 July 1783 died Santa Marta 17 December 1830. Remains transferred to Caracas 17 December 1842."

On the other side, it says, "Nation in honoring its Liberator erected this statue Monument in 1874."

The plaza is crowded most afternoons and there are Thursday evening concerts. The **Lectura Salon,** behind the statue, exhibits the works of young Venezuelan artists.

Leaving the Salon, on your left, is the famous **Cathedral** of Caracas, which was completed in 1595, and later destroyed by an earthquake and, of course, reconstructed. The Cathedral houses famous art works, gold altars, chandeliers and beautiful stained glass windows.

The yellow building facing the plaza is City Hall (**Concejo Municipal**) which is the home to historical paintings and documents of the independence war.

EL MUSEO CRIOLLO RAUL SANTANA

Inside City Hall, this museum has miniature in-scale representations of colonial and pre-colonial implements, furniture and wood art. Scenes of old Venezuela are recreated, and there are enormous blow-ups of Caracas street scenes circa 1950.

To reach the museum, enter the City Hall at the side, and walk up a narrow and twisty wooden stairway. The hours are: Tuesday and Thursday 9 - noon, 3 - 6. Saturday and Sunday 9 - 6. It is free.

LA CASA NATAL

As you leave the City Hall from its main entrance, head east, (right) one block to Calle Traposos, a narrow cobblestoned street that is closed to traffic. On this block is La Casa Natal, birthplace of Bolivar. Not the original house of his birth, it is a recreation. In the front room are a series of paintings by Tito Salas depicting the landing of Columbus, the rape of the Indians and the Bolivar-led uprisings. The family chapel and the bedroom are almost truly authentic versions of the original.

The hours are 9 - noon and 2 - 5 daily, except Monday. Admission is free.

EL MUSEO BOLIVAR

On the same street with the Casa Natal, the museum is a pink-hued building that houses revolutionary memorabilia, documents, rifles, swords, military uniforms and battle paintings. You will come away with a better understanding about the era in which Bolivar lived by browsing through this museum.

Museum hours are: Tuesday - Friday, 9 - noon and 2 - 5; Sunday 9 - noon, 2 - 6, closed Saturday and Monday. Admission is free.

MORE OF EL SILENCIO

From the museum walk back to the Plaza and just beyond the City Hall is the gleaming white **Capitol Building** with its outstanding gold dome. In the rear is a magnificent fountain in a garden setting.

NOTE

In 1813, Bolivar was given his title of El Libertador in this church.

Around the corner is the **National Library**, which houses volumes from the 15th century. Heading a block south you come to the famous **San Francisco Church**, completed in the 16th century with an exquisitely etched wooden altar.

At this point you have two choices, either return north for five blocks uphill to the **Panteon Nacional**, where Bolivar and other leaders are interred, or to continue south three more blocks to the **Centro Simon Bolivar**, the twin 32 story office towers that are the commercial center of downtown Caracas. Underground passageways, lined with shops and restaurants, connect the two buildings.

The Pantheon, situated at the end of a narrow cobblestoned street, was built in 1874 by Guzman Blanco, the same president that decorated Plaza Bolivar. In some ways the interior marble designs resemble the Jefferson Monument in Washington D.C. The hours are: Tuesday - Saturday, 9 - noon; 2 - 5; Sunday 9 - noon; 2 - 6; closed Monday.

CARACAS BY CABLE CAR (TELEFERICO)

There may be a more spectacular sight in this world than gliding into Caracas from the 7,000 foot Mount Avila peak via cable car. Particularly at night. But we haven't come across it'yet. However, this is getting ahead of the story. After all, we must first get you up to Mount Avila before we can bring you down. Fortunately that's simple.

The cable car ride takes you into the "lungs of

Caracas" which are the mountains that surround the city and give it its majestic air. From the pit of the city, it is easy to point out Mt. Avila, at 7,000 feet because of the hotel that sits upon it. It is to this peak that the cable car will take you.

The whole mountainous region was declared a National Park, and the circumference of the park extends down to the Caribbean as well. There are 160 miles of hiking that can be done in the park, and if feeling in a particularly ripe mood, you could climb up and take the cable car down.

The terminal is located in the Mariperez district of Caracas, on its north side. The cable cars are large, and will give ample vision for photos, if desired. The ride is 15 minutes even allowing for a stop or two en route and is spectacular; the best views are from the rear of the car. The city recedes, and the vegetation changes visibly.

Although the sun will be blaring just as loudly, you'll feel the change in temperature as you rise.

Once on top of the mountain there are many things to do. Firstly, you can just walk aimlessly. As we noticed, the mountain top, at nearing dusk, is a sort of lover's lane, and many couples will frequent the mountain. But there is also an ice skating rink, many small shops selling souvenirs and a coffee shop and several stalls of food sellers, particularly men selling strawberries and cream.

You might want to visit the Humboldt Hotel, which has 14 floors, making its already high foundation, 7,000 feet even mistier. The hotel is a 5 - star, with pool and disco. If you are into the splurge, go ahead, it will be fantastic.

Hiking in the park is not only a possibility but recommended. There are many trails twisting

TIP

Allow a full day for the trip.

TIP

Oh, yes the car can jiggle in the breeze. Ignore it.

TIP

The cable car ride also descends to the Caribbean side, taking you down into the beach town of Macuto and highlighting the vast panorama of the Caribbean. But now it is out of service, not for good but for a while, with no definite date of reopening.

through the mountains and the changing terrain and vegetation. If feeling strong, as mentioned before, you can hike up the mountain, but you must feel confident in your strength because not only is it long and arduous but for the first 3,000 or so feet there is no shade. If just hiking around on top you need a hiking pass, which can be obtained from the Parques Nacionales (National Park Institute) which is located next to the parking lot of Parque del Este. Overnights are also possible.

The cost of the cable car is $1 for adults and for children from 3 - 12, 50 cents. The cars leave regularly from 8 am to 10 pm with maybe a half an hour between each. There is always a crowd, and it is wise to be early, or even make a reservation.

THE BEST MUSEUMS

MUSEO DEL ARTE COLONIAL
Quinta de Anauco
(San Bernardino District)

NOTE

Bolivar was a frequent visitor to this house, which he loved, and actually spent his last night in Caracas there.

The museum is actually in an old and famous colonial house with particular significance for Venezuelans. Called the Quinta de Anauco, the house was originally built in 1797 by a Spanish captain. In 1821, when loyalists were fleeing the city, Bolivar's friend, Marques del Toro, began renting it. He eventually bought it, at Bolivar's urging.

In 1861 the Anauco was purchased by the Eraso family, and almost 100 years later given to the city of Caracas. In 1961, it became the Colonial Art Museum, replacing the older one and getting much of the other museum's treasures.

In what was the slave's quarters is now the Carlos Manuel Moller Library, which specializes in colonial art and history.

The rest of the house is a reasonable representation of its original design and style. The furniture is obviously colonial, and the house is adorned with art from the period. The kitchen is worth looking at, and the bathroom has a sunken rectangular bathtub which was fed by a cold water stream that flows through a channel in the bathroom floor.

The gardens around the house are nice to walk through, with many tropical plants and orchids, the national flower.

The hours are: Tuesday - Saturday, 9 - noon, 2 - 5; Sunday 10 - 5; closed Monday. The entrance fee is 10 cents for adults and 5 cents for children.

MUSEO DE BELLAS ARTES
Los Caobos Park
(El Conde District)

NOTE

On the weekends, the Museum has a couple of cultural events. On Saturdays there are musical event and on rotating months there are dance and theater performances.

Located near the Caracas Hilton Hotel, in Los Caobos Park, the Fine Arts Museum features varying exhibits of Venezuelan artists, representing all eras, and display major collections of Egyptian art, Latin American art, cubist, international sculpture and a large and fine collection of Chinese Art.

The hours are: Tuesday - Friday, 9 - noon, 3 - 5:30; Saturday, Sunday 10 - 5.

MUSEO DE CIENCIAS NATURALES
Los Caobos Park
(El Conde District)

NOTE

The second floor is devoted to highlighting the tribes of the Amazon. Don't miss it.

Dedicated to the natural sciences, the museum has exhibits of paleontology, archeology and taxonomy. Finds from Venezuela, the rest of Latin American and Africa are exhibited, as well as animals from Africa and birds from Venezuela.

The hours are: Tuesday - Saturday, 9 - noon, 3 - 5:30; Sunday 10 - 5.

■■■■■■ GALERIA DE ARTE NACIONAL
Plaza Morelos

Dedicated to showing and preserving the history of Venezuelan art, the National Art Gallery has many rooms devoted to native artists, throughout Venezuelan history, and sculptors. There are some permanent shows of contemporary art. Guided tours are available.

The hours are: Tuesday - Friday, 9 - noon, 3 - 5:30; Saturday and Sunday, 10 - 5.

■■■■■■ MUSEUM DE ARTE CONTEMPORANEO (El Conde District) (near Hilton Hotel)

Founded in 1974, the museum is obviously dedicated to contemporary art, with permanent works as well as temporary exhibits. From the museum a fantastic view of the Parque Central complex is had.

The hours are: Tuesday - Sunday, 11 - 7.

■■■■■■ MUSEO ARTURO MICHELENA
Esquina Urapal (La Pastora)

NOTE

The museum is in the house in which he lived until his death, and the original furnishings are intact.

Probably Venezuela's most internationally famous artist, Arturo Michelena was born in Valencia and trained in Paris. He was the student and prodigy of Juan Paul Laurens, and was widely viewed in Europe as well as his own country. He died when he was 35 but not without bringing much acclaim to himself and his country.

Little of his work is actually in the museum although many of his sketches are; much of his work is in the National Gallery.

The museum is closed on Monday and Friday, and open from 8-noon and 3-5 on the remaining days.

PARKS AND MONUMENTS

El Paseo De Los Proceres (Av de Los Proceres)

As is true throughout much of South America, the famous Revolutionary War battles of the early 19th century are marked in Caracas by monuments, memorials, and designations of streets and plazas. However, Caracas is unusual in one respect. Most of the monuments are to be found on one avenue, called logically enough the Avenue of the Leaders (Avenida de los Proceres), which is actually located in a lovely park (Proceres Park). Fountains, benches, and flowers line the main walk as you approach the monuments which are in the form of huge concrete slabs, each with a battle noted on it. Statues in front of the slabs are of famous Revolutionary War generals who fought under Bolivar. Looking beyond the monument you will see grandstands, used for reviewing military parades. At the far end of the park is a military officers club, situated on 20 acres, complete with its own theater and pool. You can walk the grounds for a small fee.

Parque Del Este

Fairly resembling Central Park in New York, Parque del Este is great for a day's outing. Wide spread, the park has basketball courts, volleyball courts, a small zoo, mainly featuring seals and crocodiles and snakes, and much picnicking space. The park is jammed on the weekends, and you get a real sense of how Caraqueños spend their free time. Like any public park, all classes of Caraqueños share its relaxing atmosphere.

Come for the day and take the Metro which has a stop marked Parque del Este, and lets you out at its entrance. It costs 10 cents to enter the park.

TIP

By the way, Proceres Park is lovely for an evening stroll since it is well lit.

NOTE

There is actually a Planetarium (Planetario Humboldt) on the grounds, which is free. There are special shows on the weekends for about $1.

Next to the park is the **Museo del Transporte** (Museum of Transportation). Its hours are: Tuesday - Sunday, 9 - noon, 3 - 5:30, closed Monday.

El Pinar Zoo
(Plaza El Pinar - El Paraiso District)

Featuring a childrens zoo area where kids can touch small goats and the like. El Pinar is fun for a family outing. There are more ferocious animals for older children. Lots of fun.

The hours are: 9 am - 6 pm daily (Closed Monday)

Munilandia

Munilandia is a small amusement park in Centro Comercial Chacaíto. Lots of rides, lots of fun. Bring the kids.

UNIVERSITY OF CARACAS

Known, really, as University City, the 400 acres of Caracas' University is locally renown as well as internationally. What gives the University its reputation internationally is its art and architecture. Its design is not a rehashing of classical academic structures – Gothic towers, Ivy-plaqued dorms – but a contemporary twine of building and art works that parallel the climate and modern thought – in essence, a modern campus. There are 49 murals, 10 sculptures, four frescoes, and four works in stained glass. All these works are integral components of the campus, not just exhibits.

The campus can be reached by taxi, of course, metro, and public transportation. It is located south of the Plaza Venezuela.

CARNIVAL

It you are lucky enough to be in Venezuela for the five days before Ash Wednesday, you are in for a

TIP

The campus is also a center for sports events. In addition, there is a botanical gardens on the premises.

festive treat. Each city has its own way of celebrating with day time costumes and parades.

In Caracas, although not of the world caliber of Rio de Janeiro, we enjoyed the costumes of the children marching along the Sabana Grande. They fling confetti, and the atmosphere is unanimously ecstatic.

FLEA MARKET

If it is your thing to spend hours intimately circling silver items, used clothing and exotic foods, then the Mercado Libre de Chacao, off Avenida Francisco de Miranda, is the place. On Thursday mornings from 8:30 to 1 pm and all day Saturday the streets are lined with booths selling exotica as well as fine junk.

SPORTING LIFE

Venezuelans revel in sports. Whether it is the ponies, beisbol (baseball), futbol (soccer), or bull fighting, Caraqueños flock to the arenas. There is also good golf. Boxing is also big; and bowling, skating, basketball and swimming are also popular activities.

Horseracing - El Hipodromo La Rinconada

Located in the scenic suburb of El Valle, a 20 minute ($5) taxi ride from the center of the city, the race track is open Saturdays and Sundays and Thursday nights all year round. The track holds 48,000 spectators, and has a 1:00 post time. The minimum wager is 25 cents and there is a 25 cent admission fee.

Venezuela was made most famous in the horse racing world when a home-grown horse won the Kentucky Derby in 1971. The horse's name was

Canonero II, and has since given Venezuela international respect and admiration.

There is a Sunday only competition that takes place all over the country, and hence is possible to do from home. Called the "cinco y seis" (five and six), the competition involves selecting winners of five of the last six races.

NOTE

The small cost is nothing compared to what can be won – almost a million dollars was won by a security guard in Guarico

Betting places all over town close at 11:30 am on Sunday.

Boxing - Poliedro Stadium

Venezuela boasts some of the world's finest boxers, and a great fighting ring, that was inaugurated in 1974 with the Foreman-Norton championship fight. Located near the racetrack, matches are usually held on Saturday nights. Prices depend on the quality of the fight. Check the Daily Journey for schedules.

Golf

NOTE

Weekends are jammed, and visitors are not allowed.

There are four first-class 18-hole golf courses in Caracas, each one attached to a private club that admits guests from the better hotels usually on weekdays only.

The clubs are: **Country Club**, **Lagunita Golf Club**, **Valle Arriba Golf Club** and **Carabelleda Golf Club**. The first three clubs are within city limits and can be easily reached. The Carabelleda is near the beach. You can rent equipment. Green fees are about $10 and a caddy is about $5. Make arrangements through your hotel.

Bull Fighting - Plaza de Toros - Nuevo Circo

Bull fighting is held in this stadium in the El Silencio district on Avendia San Agustin del Norte. Prices are usually about $2.50 for bleachers and $3 for shaded seats. When fighters from Mexico and Spain are in town, prices are higher. Check the newspaper for schedules.

Baseball - Estadio Universitaria

Between October and February is the Venezuelan baseball season. Baseball is followed seriously and intensely, some people saying it is Venezuela's major sport.

The best ball is played at the University stadium, and games are at night, except on Sunday, which is in the afternoons, and Monday, on which no games are played. A reserved seat is about $5.

Soccer

Soccer is also played at University stadium. The soccer season is from December to March, and the most popular games are Saturday nights. Venezuelans are not as crazed about this game as are Brazilians and Argentinians, but it is still popular. Tickets run from about $2 - $4.

Participant Sports

For participants instead of spectators, there are several sports that are accessible. The easiest and most popular is basketball. There are basketball courts all over the city, with great games going on in Parque del Este. Volleyball is also popular, and in Parque del Este.

There is ice skating at the Mucubaji rink, located in Parque Central. The rink is open Monday - Friday 3:30 pm - 10 pm and weekends from 10 am - 11 pm. The cost is about $1 for 90 minutes of skating and about 75 cents for skates. The phone is 54-3557.

There is also skating on top of Mt. Avila at the Pista de Hielo, as mentioned before.

TOURS AND EXCURSIONS

The Candes tourist agency, on Av. Fransico de Miranda, El Rosal (phone: 339346), Caracas Hilton, and Tamanaco, offers many tours of the city, and short excursions to the suburbs. There is a half day city tour, which covers El Silenco and other major sites, or there is a half day tour of the city's modern sites. There is a whole day, more intensive tour of Caracas, and a night tour of Caracas' jumping night life. Candes also provides a whole day tour of Colonia Tovar, a German village deep in the mountains, and a whole day tour of the Caribbean coast.

In the Caracas Hilton, their phone numbers are 571-0987, 571-1709, 572-4410, 572-4308.

COLONIA TOVAR

One hundred years ago a band of southern German immigrants landed on Venezuela's Caribbean shore. Finding that area too warm, the elders decided their band should push on into the mountains quite visible from the shore. They settled in a forest, which they soon cleared, 35 miles west of Caracas high in the state of Aragua. Relatives and friends joined them over the years. Industrious and shrewd, these Bavarians built a self-sustaining largely agricultural community that was accessible (until 1955) only by donkey.

Today the homes, restaurants, and shops all resemble chalets with peaked roofs (to shed non-existent snow). A steady tourist stream drives up the 6,000 foot elevation, passing along the way a number of charming towns, each with its open air fruit market.

Entering town you will know you have reached Colonia Tovar by the archway leading into the village and by a huge multi-colored vase that stands

NOTE

Because of its inaccessibility, the town was shielded from Venezuelan influences and thus retained its century-old Southern German village traditions in dress and food. The road changed all that.

TIP

*Stop at El Junquito,
virtually hiding in the
Humboldt Valley,
and if it weren't for
the palm trees you
could take an oath
you were in Austria.
We are not camera
happy but this is one
shot you should take.*

TIP

*Pick up homemade
preserves and bread
at the outdoor stalls.*

there as a symbol of the town's only industry, a ceramic factory. The road peaks and then edges down toward a church and a hotel and restaurant in the village center. Even if you're not hungry, stop in at the hotel, appropriately named Selva Negra (Black Forest) for at least a stein of excellent German beer. The sauerbraten will set your appetite aflame. A hearty 3-course lunch is about $5. After that respite, stroll along the main street of **Avenida Bolivar**; stop in at the local museum, which visually traces the town's history; the lovely black and white church (marred by a modern exterior clock); and the shopping arcade. By the way, as you walk around, note the fair skin and blond hair of the residents who contrast markedly with most Venezuelans. Yes, they speak Spanish, if you're wondering.

Other restaurants, in addition to Selva Negra, are **Café Edelweiss**, serving the best German sausage (wurst) in town, located behind the church; and the **Kaiserstuhl**, facing the church, which is justly celebrated for its homemade strawberry tarts. If you have a second meal in town, for contrast you might like a **Parrillada** restaurant on Avenida Bolivar.

Most shops in town seem to specialize in typical tourist souvenirs but one, **Casa Benitz**, located above the Café Muhstall, has an interesting display of cuckoo clocks and beer mugs that we liked. Still, homemade preserves–blackberry, strawberry, and peach–are your best buys.

Staying Overnight

If you have time, remain till morning either at the **Selva Negra**, **The Hotel Alta Baviera** or at any of several clean guest houses. **The Selva Negra** (Phone: 51415) charges $30 for a double, with private bath and meals. A rustic cabin for two is moderate. Owner Wolfgang Gutmann speaks English. Prices at the Alta Baviera (Phone: 51333) are comparable. Guest houses run less but you might have to share the bath. For after dark entertainment, there is one cinema (with U.S. films sometimes) and one discotheque, the basement-level **Bedegon de la Bruja**, (Phone: 51145) on the main street.

Getting To Colonia Tovar

TIP

Bring a sweater. It can get cool.

Either rent a car or go via an organized tour. **Candes** will make reservations. Cost is about $30. for a day tour, including lunch.

LOS ROQUES

Another fun day trip you might consider is to the **Archipielago de Los Roques**, 100 miles from La Guaira where the lure are the white sand beaches where you can swim, dive snorkel and fish. Actually there are over 40 coral islands. The main island is **Gran Roques** where there is a landing strip and boats for hire. **Cayo Frances** is a short boat ride away, but remember there are no facilities so prepare yourself with food and drink (and mucho sun protection). It is windy but there is no shade. You can get there only by small aircraft from Aeropuerto Metropolitano or Aeropuerto Caracas and the twin-engines out of La Carlota Airport. Flight time: 35 minutes. If you have the time, you can also find sailing boats for small groups leaving from the port of La Guaira.

NOTES:

CARACAS AFTER DARK

Caracas is very much a town for night people. This is no place for a hot Ovaltine and early-to-bed routine. The restaurants, night clubs and sidewalk cafes remain open late, often well into the early morning hours. The reason is simple. Caraqueños still maintain the centuries-old tradition of the mid-day break, which extends usually from noon to 2 or even 3 pm.

Thus office workers finish work about 7, head home for a drink, shower, throw on the fancy duds, and head out for a 9 pm dinner. To ready yourself for this style, we recommend a nap. At the end of your stay in Caracas, if you have kept up with the Caraqueños, a long rest will be provided in Margarita or Merida, whichever place you hit next.

We have listed theaters, movie theaters, opera houses, concert halls and night clubs. We have nine categories of clubs, ranging from singles spots to jumping Mariachi places to strip joints to cocktail lounges.

THE THEATER

We start sedately with theater and in Caracas that means the **Teatro Teresa Carreño**, a new cultural complex, similar to New York's Lincoln

TIP

A ramp over the highway connects the theatre with the Caracas Hilton. Use it.

Center. Modern and attractive, the complex is the hub of cultural events for the city. Rotating with opera, plays, music and dance, Teresa Carreño is a great place to experience Caracas and its own culture as well as how it plugs into international culture.

Teresa Carreño was a pianist, and the statues of her and Vincente Emilio Sojo, outside the entrance, pay homage to two of Venezuela's cultural heroes. I saw Bellini's Norma here and it was first rate.

There are no bad seats in Teatro Teresa Carreño, and with the $10 orchestra seats you can't go wrong. The theater is across from the Caracas Hilton Hotel.

In the El Silencio district is **Teatro Municipal**, the center of activity before Teresa Carreño. Working on a slightly less active schedule, losing many of its customers to Teresa Carreño the theater still is host to visiting operas, ballets, symphonies and theater groups.

Both theaters have schedules that are listed in the Daily Journal.

English theater can be seen occasionally at the **Caracas Playhouse**, Calle Chivacoa in San Roman near Las Mercedes. Established in 1945, plays as various as Sleuth, Waiting for Godot, Fiddler on the Roof and Prisoner of Second Avenue can be seen. Performances are in a 400-seat theater, with shows usually on the weekends. Check the Daily Journal.

CINEMA

Movie Buffs will not have to miss a single U.S. release since film houses here stay current and thus far have resisted dubbing (except for children's films). Thus U.S. movies are available in their pristine Hollywood state. The Daily Journal has

NOTE

Films are not dubbed and are surprisingly current

complete listings, reviews and times. Prices are about $2.00. North American exhibitors might do well to imitate the **Multi Cine**, a quadri-theater in the Abeco Shopping Center, near the Chacaíto Shopping Center, which offers the same film in four adjoining theaters, with starting times a half-hour apart. Films are rated by age groupings, and admission restrictions are enforced. Note: Films are half price on Monday.

THE NIGHT CLUBS

If you have come to Caracas for a rest, skip this section because Caraqueños love to dance, loudly and with vigor. As is common throughout Latin America, most clubs have a couples-only policy, we have noted the exceptions. Minimum drinking age is 18 unless otherwise noted. Jacket and tie are suggested, as the clubs tend to be more formal. We have surveyed intimate cocktail lounges, singles places, student hangouts, gay bars, and clubs where entertainment is the draw.

CLUBS WITH MUSIC

FEDORA
Calle Madrid
(Las Mercedes District)
7 pm - 3 am (Closed Sunday)

Designed in the motif of a ship, with the accouterments that go with it, Fedora has both a disk jockey and live music; jazz. The live music is upstairs and usually starts about 9:30 on weekdays, 10 on weekends. Fedora has a huge bar that stretches throughout the entire club. Hopping and sweaty.

NEW YORK NEW YORK
Centro Comercial Concresa
Local C1 (Downstairs)
9 - 3 am, 4 am on weekdays
Phone: 979-7778

In homage to New York, with pictures of the city and its skyline, this club is actually private but will admit people it feels are well dressed enough and fit their bill. Noisy and dark and multi-leveled and large, New York New York, despite the name, is a good example of how Caraqueños party.

▬▬▬ LA MIRAGE
Av Principal de las Mercedes
(Las Mercedes District)
7 pm - 4 am
Phone: 7522434, 7518909

NOTE

The club draws a well heeled clientele who dress to the hilt.

With no cover, La Mirage is a happening place. Very formal, with people in tuxedos, the club is crowded, has two levels, big dance floor and excellent videos as diversion. Next to Mamma Mia pizza and close to the Tamanaco Hotel, La Mirage is centrally located.

▬▬▬ CAFE L'ATTICO
Av Luis Roches
(Altamira)

Very European in style, L'Attico has video discs that thuds the place and makes it hop. There are pop posters that line the walls and a large bar in the center of the dance floor. Food and drinks are served. There is a Sunday brunch, occasional Ladies night where second drinks are free. This is a good place to meet single guys and gals.

▬▬▬ COTA 880
Hotel Caracas Hilton
(El Conde District)
8 pm- 2 am (Tues - Thurs)
9 pm - 4 am (Fri - Sun)
Phone: 54-7001

On the top floor of the Hilton, dancing to the two orchestras with the city lit up and layed-out in front of you gives good vertigo. There is Sunday Buffet here.

■■■■■ HIPOCAMPO
Centro Comercial
Chacaíto (Shopping Center)
No. 215
(Chacaíto District)
Live Music
Open 10 pm - 5 am (daily)
Phone: 72-5096

Hipocampo has live music that staggers Latin, French, English and American tunes. The dance orchestra is of the old jazz sort and fun to even watch, if dancing is not in your plans. The Salani brothers–Rentao and Julio–lead the main combo, but there are alternating combos for soft rock and Latin music.

A COUPLE OF PRIVATE CLUBS

■■■■■ 1900 MY WAY
Ciudad Centro
Comercial Tamanaco
9 pm - 4 am
Phone: 921010

TIP

Have your concierge make a reservation for you at the private clubs.

A private club that is dauntingly plush, with a winding staircase that leads into a latticed ceiling hall with purple chairs surrounding the pedestalled piano, chandeliers illuminating all. There is also a disco, card games and a huge bar.

■■■■■ LE CLUB
Centro Comercial Chacaíto
(Downstairs)
9 pm - 3 am

Also a private club, Le Club is as plush as 1900 My Way, and considered the most exclusive club in Caracas. Elegant and dark, try and get invited.

■■■■ LA LECHUGA
Los Caobos
10 - 7, Thurs - Sat

A private club that allows non members, La Lechuga is downstairs and is a great place to meet singles. With videos giving the visual sensation, the dancing will provide the rest. $5 entrance fee.

DISCOTEQUES

■■■■ WEEKENDS
Av San Juan Bosco
(Altamira)
12 noon - 1:30 am
Phone: 261-3839, 261-4863

TIP

A good place for a sandwich any time of day

Although not a place to dance Weekends must be considered a premiere night activity. Very hip, with three levels of intertwining booths and tables and bars and videos, Weekends is a magnet for singles as well as couples. With a huge video screen in the center of the bar and little video screens smattered over the rest of the place, Weekends is definitely American in style, a fancy bar that is technologically advanced and chic. Even if it is for an hour, you owe it to yourself to stop by.

■■■■ DOG AND FOX
Av Rio de Janeiro
(Las Mercedes District)
8 pm - 4 am

A pub on the first level with the disco on the second, Dog and Fox is for younger people, not as hip as Weekends but active and fun. There is a large bar, and as much conversation as there is dancing.

■■■■ PIDA PIZZA
Calle Bello Monte
Sabana Grande
7 - 4:30 am
Phone: 728069

Downstairs from the restaurant, Pida Pizza has a cellar like feel to it which is sort of nice. The crowd is on the youngish side.

▬▬▬ STUDIO 84
**Centro Comercial Bello Campo
(Bello Campo District)
8 pm - 5 am (daily)
Phone: 33-7489**

Stark black and white decor with floor to ceiling mirrors and professional looking studio lights.

Deliberately modeled after a TV stage set, Studio 84 is a fashionable late night drop-in spot for the cine and theater set who gossip along the lengthy bar. Tables, with director-style chairs are two steps down on the next level but the bar seems to be the fashionable locale. Two bands alternate, both at a high-decibel level. Jackets are required and turtle necks are fine.

▬▬▬ EVA'S
**Centro Comercial Chacaíto
Shopping Center
(Chacaíto District)
10 pm - 4 am (Closed Sunday)
Phone: 72-9138**

Huge sculptures of the female dancers, glorifying the female and her desired design, dominate the main room. The ceiling above the dance floor is periodically raised and lowered and lights, highlighting the sculptures, attempt to make the illusion of movement. The music is loud, but next door is the Baby Scotch Bar for a more relaxing evening.

▬▬▬ THE FLOWER
**Av Principal La Castellana
Plaza La Castellana
6 pm - 3 am
Couples Only**

You've heard of hearts and flowers. In this discotheque it's music and flowers. You have a choice between hard rock (lower level) and Latin and pop (upper level), but whichever you choose, the petals will follow you. With a flower-shaped bar, flowered walls, flowered vests on the waiters, you wonder for a moment if you've wandered into a hot house. Flower nuts will dig it. As for the rest of you, come in and smell your way around.

▬▬▬▬ LA JUNGLA
Plaza La Castellana
(La Castellana District)
5:30 pm - 4 am (daily)
Phone: 32-2336

La Jungla is for singles, and maybe that is why it is called La Jungla with no references, pictures, designs, or anything referring to natural jungles. This is strongly singlesville but many couples come, perhaps out of a sense of nostalgia, to watch the mating maneuvers.

▬▬▬▬ CITY ROCK CAFE
Centro Comercial Chacaíto
(Chacaíto District)
Open until 2 am

·TIP·

The hamburgers are the best in town.

Caracas' answer to the Hard Rock Cafe is City Rock, a restaurant and watering hole for the city's young beautiful people. If you didn't overhear Spanish patois, you'd swear you were in London or New York. Video screens that encircle the dining area set the upbeat tone and colorfully clad and unusually coiffed patrons add to the lively atmosphere–if you're over 30 you might call it noisy.

MARIACHI CLUBS

Not surprisingly there are good Mariachi clubs here that serve up authentic Mexican music and food. You should try one. The music is loud and boisterous and you will find yourself joining in the festivities. Lots of fun

■■■ LAS TROMPETAS DE MEXICO
Av Venezuela
(El Rosal District)
7 pm - 5 am
Phone: 32-0150

Loud, sprawling and jumping, Las Trompetas is a touch of Mexico in Caracas. Patrons throng the place night after night eager to clap and sing along with the strolling sombrero and sarape-clad Mariachi musicians who start at nine nightly. The ceaseless Mexican atmosphere extends to the food and you should sample the tacos, tamales, and enchiladas. Sip a cocktail. A long passageway extends from the street, leading into the large ranch-like main room, complete with wall decor of saddles, bows and arrows, and sombreros.

■■■ MEXICO TIPICO
Av Libertador (Edificio Iamar)
(Chacao District)
9 pm - 4 am
Phone: 31-4808

A ten-piece band is the central highlight of this club, spurting the music as if it were judgement day, and the wooden benches creak with bodies swaying, the glasses on the table rocking back and forth. Unpretentious in style, made for the music and the dance and the wine, try the loaded drink, only once, "Ay! Chihuahua."

PIANO BARS

■■■ LA RONDA
Caracas Hilton
(El Conde District)

NOTE

Pat hails from Maracaibo and is of Irish descent

Subdued and blue-lighted, La Ronda is for the overworked person that wants to be lulled. Pat O'Brien is at the piano, and, along with the drinks, are excellent snacks. No cover or minimum.

▆▆▆ *PIANO DISCO RED PARROT*
Av Tamanaco
(El Rosal District)
9 pm - 4 am

With a dance floor also, the Red Parrot is somber and classy, with not only a pianist but a live band.

▆▆▆ *BARBA ROJA*
Av Tamanaco
(El Rosal District)
9 pm - 4 am

Similar to Red Parrot, Barba Roja, a few steps away, is not as large. This is a popular, crowded stop for Caraqueños.

COCKTAIL LOUNGES AND PUBS

▆▆▆ *RED COACH BAR*
Av San Juan Bosco
(Altamira District)
7 pm - 4 am

TIP

These are great places to meet members of the other sex

Not far from the Hotel Continental Altamira, The Red Coach features a guitar piano duo.

▆▆▆ *SUNSET BAR*
Av Principal La Castellena
(La Castellana District)
7 pm - 4 am
Phone: 31473

Sunset has a loyal following, but it is not a fraternity, and is open to newcomers. Singles admitted.

▆▆▆ *JUAN SEBASTIAN BAR*
Av Venezuela
(El Rosal District)
11 - 4:30, (Closed Sunday)
Phone: 32-4229

With a jazz trio, Juan Sebastian is slightly more active than the other pubs mentioned because of the music. Also with a regular clientele, the pub has good onion soup. Singles admitted.

A FLAMENCO CLUB

Spanish influence is strong in Caracas and not surprisingly, flamenco is popular.

CAFE DE CHINITAS
Av Tamanaco
(El Rosal District)
Open to 4 am (Closed Sunday)
Phone: 33-1086

Easily the most pulsating Flamenco show in Caracas is at the Café de Chinitas, which was an instant smash upon its 1972 premier. Styled after a Spanish supper club, this cafe offers foot-pounding shows at 11 pm and 4 am. There are few inhibitions from the resident dance troupe. They leave the stage exhausted at 5 am with the audience not far behind. The stage is large so don't insist on an up-front table. Good food too. Between shows you can dance to pop Venezuelan tunes.

FOR UNATTACHED MEN

Many of the places that are open to singles have been mentioned–Weekends, Fedora, L'Attico, City Rock and La Lechuga. All the places mentioned are not geared for bonding. The places mentioned now are. The angle, of course, is for the women to make you buy many high-priced drinks. Nothing is a prerequisite, but then why would you be there.

THE DIPLOMATIC CLUB
Central Comercial Cediaz
Av Casanova
(Sabana Grande District)
11 pm - 5 am (Closed Sunday)
Phone: 72-5964
Singles Admitted

NOTE

Without too much pretext, sex is the name of the game

Continental in style, this popular club creates bright, breezy, fast moving musical shows. Even the strippers show some talent along with other displays. The stage is small so if ogling is on your mind grab an up-front table. And yes, males will find unattached muchachas at the bar. Showtime usually is 1:30 and 3:30 am.

PALACIO IMPERIAL
Av Venezuela
(El Rosal District)
Phone: 718027

With three shows nightly–11, 1:30, 3:30–the Imperial is usually crowded, with gals eager to join you for the price of a drink or three.

WHERE THE GAYS GO

As in all major cities, homophiles here have their own sub-culture, centering about several clubs, each with its own special attractions. Most open about 8 pm and close at 4 am.

IBIS CLUB
Centro Comercial Bello Campo
8 - 4 am

Popular with North Americans, Ibis is small and many of the guests speak English.

GAY BAÑOS TURCOS DEL ESTE
Av Principal Sabana Grande
Corner Torre Miracielo
9 - 4 am

A gay bath that is well-known.

ICE PALACE
Edif. Teatro Altamira (downstairs)
(Altamira District)
9 - 5:30 (Closed Sunday)

For both gay men and lesbians, the Ice Palace is more high-tech than most gay bars, with videos, dance floor and that ever-present neon.

TORREMOLINOS
Pasaje Asuncion
(Sabana Grande District)

Torremolinos is near the Cristal Hotel, on the same street as Bar Tolo.

FOR UNATTACHED GALS

Single women are not viewed favorably in Caracas, a product of ages-old Spanish culture. Although Caracas is way ahead of other Latin American countries in accepting the autonomy of women, it is still a tense thing to do unless you are particularly intrepid. It is not worth getting heated-up over, it is their culture and, as a visitor, you don't necessarily want to clash with it.

Obviously you can meet men in your hotel, which is sort of outside the mores of the country, or at least guarded, and by going to the places that admit singles and subtly reversing the tides. There is the unplanned linking that takes place in all societies no matter what the dominating culture is.

There is a weekly singles gathering at the Hotel Continental Altamira every Thursday. It takes place at the bar on the main floor. Look for the ad in the Thursday Daily Journal.

CERVECERIAS

NOTE

The collective energy in these places is awesome and seems to spill out onto the sidewalks. Many have weekend shows.

There are hundreds of these establishments throughout Caracas. Loosely translated as "beer halls" cervecerias do not resemble what you might find in downtown Munich. It is difficult to generalize since some are earthy, others elaborate, some noisy and crowded, but all are great fun.

SHOPS AND SHOPPING

Shopping centers, called "Centro Comerciales", dot the city, literally combing the place with the bustle of the consumer. The range is as wide as in America, with high-priced international goods, department stores like Maxy's and local stores that are more ragtag.

To simplify your search, we have concentrated for the most part on five key shopping areas: Avenida Lincoln, the main thoroughfare in **La Sabana Grande** district; the **Centro Comercial Chacaíto**, an important shopping center, which virtually is an extension of the Eastern end of the Sabana Grande district. The Broadway Cinema on Avenida Lincoln is an approximate demarcation point between Sabana Grande and the Chacaíto shopping center. The third shopping point is the tri-level **Concresa**, the largest in Caracas, in Prado del Este.

The fourth is the **Paseo Las Mercedes**, part of an attractive shopping complex that includes the Paseo Las Mercedes Hotel in Las Mercedes.

Near La Carlota Airport is **Centro Ciudad Comercial Tamanaco** (usually called C.C.C.T.), the newest of the shopping centers and probably the best. The new Eurobuilding, a five star hostelry is located almost within walking distance.

TIP

The metro has a stop at each end of Sabana Grande

LA SABANA GRANDE

Along a one-mile stretch of Avenida Lincoln (also called Calle Sabana Grande) there are hundreds of shops offering clothing, shoes, toys, jewelry, native crafts and gifts. These shops, along with stores on the streets running perpendicular to Avenida Lincoln, offer an almost infinite variety. You can stroll through here for two days and still not visit all the shops of interest.

CENTRO COMERCIAL CHACAÍTO

This elegant tri-level shopping center specializes in high fashion boutiques where you will find outlets for Pierre Cardin, Yves St. Laurent, Charles Jourdan, and Gucci. But even if you're not looking for a Pucci, the center still deserves some of your browsing time.

CONCRESA

TIP

The New York, New York Disco is in the center.

On a par with the Chacaíto Center is this tri-level structure featuring such high fashion outlets as Charles Jourdan, Carnaby, King's Row and Biki Bou. Located south of the Tamanaco Hotel in Prado del Este.

PASEO LAS MERCEDES

This large and elegant tri-level shopping center houses fine restaurants, (**Il Romanaccio**), popular shops and '**LA CUADRA**', an area on the main level that is a replica of colonial Caracas from its cobblestone streets to its shops.

CENTRO CIUDAD COMERCIAL TAMANACO

Probably the most modern of the shopping centers is C.C.C.T., complete with many branches of fine chain stores. **Marisqueria Restaurant** is here, and the shopping center is usually crowded even at night when the stores are closed. The **C.C.C.T. Hotel**, naturally, also is there.

TIP

Ladies leather shoes are an incredible bargain

Without question, the item that provides the most unique value, low price coupled with fine quality, is shoes. Fine shoes line the windows of many shops at half, and more, off the price you'd pay in America. Also, leather, toys, gold and handicrafts stand-out as items to concentrate on.

Venezuelan paintings are justly in demand.

Boutiques freckle the city, and have excellent clothes (Venezuelan women, even with a minimal income, dress well since it is the custom). Both men and women can order custom made clothing and have it ready within a few days.

Sales personnel might surprise you with their aggressive eagerness. Many will insist on accompanying you while you browse. Occasionally a proprietor might even approach you while you're window shopping. It is their style, less laid back, but you can fend it off, or better, just roll with it–it is not hostile but helpful.

TIP

Most shops are open on Saturday

Stores open at 9 am and close at 7 pm including Saturdays, but they are closed from noon until 3 pm for midday break.

SIZES (TAMAÑOS)

Sizes are different here than in North America. Just to be safe, we recommend that you try on everything first.

The comparison chart on the next page will give you a good idea of sizes in Venezuela vs. North America. First the U.S. size, followed by its corresponding size in Venezuela.

Women

Shoes (Zapatos)			Dresses (Vestidos)		
4	–	34	8	–	34
4 1/2	–	35	10	–	38
5	–	36	12	–	42
5 1/2	–	37	14	–	44
6 1/2	–	38	16	–	46
7 1/2	–	39	18	–	48
8 1/2	–	40	20	–	50

Men

Shoes (Zapatos)			Suits (Trajes)		
6 1/2	–	39	40	–	32
7 1/2	–	40	42	–	34
8	–	41	44	–	36
8 1/2	–	42	46	–	38
9 1/2	–	43	48	–	40
10 1/2	–	44	50	–	42
11	–	45	52	–	44
12	–	46	54	–	46
12 1/2	–	47			

WHAT TO BUY

Shoes

As mentioned above, shoes are a great buy. There are rows of shoe stores on Av Lincoln in Sabana Grande, and there are many in the C.C.C.T. and Chacaíto shopping centers. Venezuela has its own shoe industry and is not merely an importer of European and American designs. All styles have one thing in common, they are sold at great discounts. Here is a brief list of stores.

■■■■■■ *PEOLO VALENTE*
Centro Ciudad Comercial Tamanaco
Phone: 921819

Next to the Viasa airline office, Peolo sells handbags as well as fine shoes. Always crowded with Caraqueño women.

■■■■■■■ **CHARLES JOURDAN**
Centro Ciudad Comercial Tamanaco
Phone: 925405

A huge outlet, with a myriad of choices, both international and domestic, Charles Jourdan obviously carries with it its reputation.

■■■■■■■ **NARDI**
Centro Ciudad Comercial Tamanaco
Main Floor
Phone: 915849

Specializing in women's shoes, with prices starting at about $20 and reaching much higher. Men's shoes too. Bags for ladies in elegant designs.

■■■■■■■ **TREVIS**
Centro Comercial Chacaíto
Phone: 729851

Ladies and men's shoes are bargains here.

■■■■■■■ **MONTAIGNE**
Centro Ciudad Comercial Tamanaco
Phone: 926076

■■■■■■■ **CALZADOR TULIO**
Centro Comercial Chacaíto

This store carries a small selection of high quality shoes. The store will order your size, which will take a few days, if they do not carry it. The fabrics for the shoes are imported but they are made nationally.

Leather

■■■■■■■ **FASCINACIÓN**
Centro Ciudad Comercial Tamanaco
Phone: 261-9022, 261-7998

With fantastic leather goods, ranging from clothes to bags and other accessories, Facinación is a good start for the beginning foray into Venezuela's shopping world.

▬▬ FERRADIN
Centro Ciudad Comercial Tamanaco
Phone: 910664

Near Fascinación, these two shops we consider the best for leather items.

Boutiques

NOTE

These attractive shops draw an upscale clientele. You'll feel right at home.

The boutique is as common to Caracas as to Paris. Yet, wonderfully, the prices seem garage sale in comparison. The shops mentioned stress sports wear, usually imported from France, Italy, Spain and the U.S. The boutiques we have listed are centered around the C.C.C.T. and Paseo Las Mercedes shopping centers and the Sabana Grande, but shops are all over the city.

▬▬ PEOPLE
Centro Comercial
Paseo Las Mercedes
Local N1A2
Phone: 918742

One of my favorites. Trendy items.

▬▬ AQUALADY
Paseo Las Mercedes
Phone: 923108

Racks and racks of super items.

▬▬ SYLVIA S. DENIS
Centro Ciudad Comercial Tamanaco
Phone: 918163

For that special outfit.

BELLOCOTTON
Centro Ciudad Comercial Tamanaco
Phone: 261-7604

Excellent for browsing.

MARIA PIA
Nivel C-1
Centro Ciudad Comercial Tamanaco
Phone: 922770

Emphasis on Italian Imports.

TOKYU
(Next to Cada Supermarket)
Centro Comercial Ciudad Tamanaco
Phone: 928691

Wide selection, friendly sales staff.

RORI 2000
CCCT
Downstairs
Phone: 261-6938, 261-5914

Futuristic in decor and merchandise.

KINGS ROAD BEAT TIME
Centro Comercial Chacaíto
Main Level

Super chic and alive, this high-priced bi-level boutique prides itself on a clientele that includes the daughters of Caracas' wealthiest families

BIKI BOU
Centro Comercial Chacaíto
Downstairs

Mainly selling bathing suits from France, Biki Bou also has pants and tops.

▬▬▬ NOSOTRAS BOUTIQUE
Av Lincoln and Pasaje Recreo
(Sabana Grande District)

Nosotras Boutique highlights Venezuelan designs instead of the international look, and for this reason is special.

▬▬▬ RACHEL'S BOUTIQUE
Calle Union (Off Av Lincoln)
(Sabana Grande District)

French and Italian imports are king here and these are attractively showcased by Rachel who offers as well a selection of versatile costume jewelry, perfect accessories for her nylon dresses and pants suits. Nice shop, a half-block off Avenida Lincoln.

▬▬▬ KUKU
Av Lincoln
(Sabana Grande District)

A long time local favorite.

▬▬▬ CHOPPER
Av Lincoln
(Sabana Grande District)

Good location, fine quality and selection.

▬▬▬ ANGELO MODAS
Av Lincoln
(Sabana Grande District)

The most wild in style and look and design is always in Angelo Modas, and for this reason he is most popular with the younger crowd.

Antiques Shops

▬▬▬ ACD ANTIGUEDADES
Hotel Tamanaco
(Shop 23-Main Floor)

NOTE

There is an incredible selection of fine items here. Prices are high.

The owner and director of ACD Antiguedades is a member of LAPADA, the London and Provincial Antique Dealers' Association, and has spent over two decades gathering antiques, especially in Europe and the Orient. Harmoniously displayed at the Tamanaco locale is a wealth of objets d'art which she has culled from widely varying cultures.

Notable among the American antiques is the collection of pre-Columbian stone heads from the Tumaco-La Tolita civilization of northwest South America. There are wood and ivory sculptures from west and central Africa.

Chinese embroidered silk panel from the last Ching Dynasty covers one of the walls. Also from China are selected examples of cloisonne, blue and white porcelains, jades, and an extensive collection of snuff bottles–beautifully worked in jade, porcelain and many other materials. Japanese woodcuts, ivories and porcelains are among the antiques from other parts of Asia.

ACD Antiguedades is open Tuesday through Saturday from 10 am to 7 pm and does not close during lunch hour. The shop changes part of its exhibit every month, making it a rewarding point for browsing at any time.

MANUEL HERRERA CASE DE ANTIGUEDADES
Av Liberatador
(San Bernardino District)

While the once-abundant colonial and pre-colonial antiques are largely depleted, still by careful browsing you can come up with an occasional nugget amidst the dross. One place to look is Manuel Herrera's, a ramshackle store that is almost impossible to find because there is no sign and no street number. Look for the Red Cross Hospital on

Avenida Andres Bello. The shop is behind the hospital and the only designation is a faded sign that reads: "Cerveceria a Paradero" which tells you only that a brewery once existed there. Bargaining is in here. We are partial to the old brass buried under the debris. The hours are 8 am-6:30 pm.

▬▬▬ A.E. LIMES
Paseo Las Mercedes
(Las Mercedes District)

This fine shop features reproductions of Spanish colonial furniture and accessories. There are also genuine antiques available. Another outlet is located at Gerosa in Prado del Este.

Pre-Columbian Artifacts

▬▬▬ GALERIA CANO
Paseo Las Mercedes
Mezzanine No 110
Phone: 917324

TIP

This Colombian company enjoys a world-wide reputation. You can shop with confidence.

You will find excavated relics, some a thousand years old. Prices start at $50. With its main office in Bogota, Galeria Cano is a special place, and should at least be browsed in.

Tipico Shops (Handicrafts)

Handicraft shops, also known as Tipico shops, are the stores that sell the wide gamut of goods that fall under the title ornaments. From jewelry, folk art, toys, wood pieces, all those items that make up the bulk of shopping, are the vast mall of small consumerism, and are fun.

▬▬▬ TIPICO
Hotel Tamanaco
Phone: 911413

A fine range of painting, hand-made rugs, pottery and pillow covers.

■ TIPICALIA HILTON
Caracas Hilton

This large shop in the Hilton Hotel is a good place to browse for an unusual gift.

■ EL ARTESANO
**Centro Comercial
Paseo Las Mercedes
Phone: 911224**

More tipico items. Fine shop.

■ ROCIO
Plaza Bolivar

An interesting place to browse in an open air environment. They even sell musical instruments.

■ ARTESANIAS VENEZOLANA
**Gran Av Sabana Grande
Palacio de Las Industrias
(Sabana Grande District)**

Offering a wide selection of gifts, this store has items from paper mache, to hammocks, blankets, wood sculptures, etched ceramic pieces, rag dolls, ash trays and jewelry.

■ CASA DE LAS ARTESANIAS
**Pasaje El Recreo
(Sabana Grande District)**

Operated by the government, this shop sells offbeat items from all over the country, and at the same time serves as an exhibition site for national handicrafts. Selections are limited but you can find first rate handmade rugs and pillow covers, as well as the more common items.

■ EL ARTESANO
**Av Mirador (Near Cine Paris)
(La Florida District)**

Off–the–beaten–track of shopping, this tipico has handicrafts from other Latin American countries as well as Venezuela. Llama rugs and ceramic bulls from Peru, belts and ponchos from Guatemala and Costa Rica are all available.

JOROPO
Calle Union
(Sabana Grande District)

Good shoulder bags and brilliantly colored skirts are the central items here.

ARTE ESPAÑOL
Av Urdaneta (near Plaza Bolivar)
(El Silencio District)

Mainly stocking Spanish imports, the Toledo ware, including small swords, metal toothpicks, letter openers and bookends are good values.

ARTE INDUSTRIA
Av Francisco Solano
(opposite Hotel Tampa)
(Sabana Grande District)

Run by several women who personally design the far out articles sold here. Unusual framed mirrors, embossed notepads, distinctive lamp shades, piggy banks, paper weights, candle sticks and mobiles all stock the shelves.

Venezuelan Art

SALON LECTURA
Plaza Bolivar
(El Silencio District)

Probably stocking the best values in Caracas, Salon Lectura is run by the government, and is an art gallery that showcases undiscovered talent. Exhibitions usually feature one artist.

▆▆▆ *GALERIA DE ARTE SANS SOUCI*
Centro Comercial Chacaíto

A true art gallery in the New York and London sense, Sans Souci features a wide variety of Venezuelan paintings. The gallery is open Sunday mornings.

▆▆▆ *CENTRO DE ARTE*
CONTEMPORANEO (CDAC)
C.C.C. Tamanaco
Phone: 916779

TIP

If serious about an art purchase, try this shop.

This bi-level shop features the best in Venezuelan paintings and art. The selection is enormous.

▆▆▆ *EXPOSICION SURAMERICANA*
Hotel Caracas Hilton
Phone: 5741122
Hotel Tamanaco
Phone: 208-7027

Stop by at either hotel and look. Prices are not cheap–but the quality is high.

Fabrics and Fabrics

Caracas is lined with smart shops that hawk stunning fabrics of silks, wools, and synthetics. And they all seem to thrive for a good reason: constant demand from local women who have most of their clothes custom made from fabrics they select.

▆▆▆ *RAYMAR*
Centro Comercial Chacaíto
(Main Level–Rear)

TIP

Fabrics are sold by the meter, and the salespeople are very helpful. Raymar also has fine linens.

We were told of Raymar by a Caraqueña business woman who insists that this shop has no equal in Venezuela, particularly in silk crepes imported from France and Italy.

▆▆▆▆ SELECTA
Paseo Las Mercedes
Phone: 927364

Similar to Raymar. Compare fabrics before purchasing.

Jewelry Shops (Joyeria)

Gold pins, earrings, pendants and the like are the jewelry items to buy here. Some less expensive pieces made of cochano gold (a way of working gold which results in a low lustre finish) are particularly good values to buy in Caracas. There are many reliable jewelry shops here so don't limit yourself to our few selections which you can think of as a representative sampling of the first class stores. We start with the best.

▆▆▆▆▆▆ H. STERN
Hotel Tamanaco
Hotel Caracas Hilton and Airport

This Rio-based chain, with some 150 outlets worldwide, specializes in gemstones (aquamarine, amethyst, topaz, tourmaline) set in individual settings. Values are good, with a starting price of $25 for pure gold pieces and more for pearl items. There is a full line of pins and earrings in cochano gold and the bracelets and necklaces designed by Venezuelan artists are really fine. Any purchase can be returned within a year at any worldwide outlet. The service is first rate and the shops are conveniently located. Add the guaranty and H. Stern is definitely worth your first choice for jewelry.

▆▆▆▆▆▆ WALTER PETER
Av Francisco de Miranda
(El Rosal District)

This old-line respected jewelry store sells a popular teleferico (Cable car) charm made of 18K gold.

Too, there are gold pins, earrings and an unusual pendant made of 22K Indian head coins. Peter's carries a full line of cochano jewelry and Margarita pearls.

JOYERIA EL ARTE
Av Lincoln, No. 229
(Sabana Grande District)

Well regarded by its loyal patrons, this shop offers cochano necklaces and earrings for good values.

TALLER SUIZO
Av Lincoln
(Sabana Grande District)

With several branches, this store is also a good secure bet for fine jewelry.

ITALCAMBIO
Av Casanova
(Sabana Grande District)

With pieces that are directed towards Italian design and heritage as well as that of Venezuela's, Italcambio has a 22K Mussolini commemorative coin, and many other fine coins that can be set by your own jeweler, and that fit many things–rings, earrings, pendants, etc.

The Gold Market

NOTE

It's hard to distinguish the items from one shop to another.

It's worth your time to visit the Gold Market in the **Casa Francia** building downtown near the Plaza Bolivar. Here you will find 9 floors of shops featuring gold jewelry, watches, bracelets, necklaces, rings, earrings and chains. **It's best for browsing**.

Open from 9 am until 12:30 pm and 2:30 pm until 6 pm (Mon-Fri) The Gold Market is Venezuela's answer to N.Y.C.'s 47th Street.

For Men

VOGUE
(1) Centro Comercial Chacaíto
(2) Av Lincoln, Sabana Grande
(3) C.C.C.T.

For a large and varied selection of both hand-made shoes and custom suits, Vogue is it.

O'LEARY
Av Lincoln (edifico Don Victor)
(Sabana Grande District)

Heavy in French, Italian, Spanish and West German imports, O'Leary offers a wide range of suits, shoes, ties and socks at prices that go from moderate to high in Venezuelan prices.

PHIL DAVIS
Av Lincoln
(Sabana Grande District)

This store sells all men's clothing, including Venezuelan-made Givenchy suits and first-rate Italian shirts. There are other branches in Caracas.

GEORGES
Av Lincoln
Av Las Mercedes
C.C.C.T.

With three other shops, one in the Macuto Sheraton, this was the original men's boutique in Caracas, and still carries weight. It sells probably the most unique outfits.

CARNABY

With five outlets, one in the Centro Comercial Chacaíto, another in the Concresa Shopping Center a third at Calle Real de Sabana Grande, and another at C.C.C.T.

For Children

If you take only one item home with you then let it be a Piñata, a reinforced papier-mache figure of an animal, or sometimes a well-known comic or super-hero, Superman or Popeye for example. These pieces have, obviously, special roles at parties. Tradition dictates that the hollow interior of the piñata is filled with small toys, candy and confetti. Then it is tied to a tree, and with a broom handle everyone takes turns whacking it until it breaks.

▬▬▬ LA PIÑATA
Av Lincoln
(Sabana Grande District)

The largest piñatas we have seen are sold here. The problem with the really large ones is taking them home, it is difficult, but you can try.

▬▬▬ LA GRAN PIÑATA
Av. Jacinto y Traposos
(El Silencio District)

NOTE

An absolute must if you have kids

For the largest piñata selection in the city, stop here. You will find enormous variety, along with the tiny toys you need for the stuffing. Typical stuffers are whistles, noisemakers, animal figures, yoyos, rings and watches.

▬▬▬ JUGUETERIA EL ROSAL
Av Pichincha
(El Rosal District)

After piñatas, you might be ready for a more conventional toy store.

Munilandia in *Centro Comercial Chacaíto is a small amusement park here for children.*

▬▬▬ JUGUETELANDIA
Av Francisco de Miranda
(El Rosal District)

This store has a great variety of toys from all over the world.

Indian Hand Woven Rugs

▬▬▬▬ **TAPICES TERE**
C.C.C. Tamanaco

Drop in to view the exquisite Guajiro Indian rugs which are uniquely woven. Rest assured that no one else has the same design. Designed by Luis Montiel, these brilliantly-colored rugs are handmade in Paraguaipoa, an Indian Village near Maracaibo. Motifs generally stress birds, animals and flowers.

Blown Crystal

▬▬▬▬ **ARTE MURANO**
Urb. Potrerito
Via La Mariposa

In a small town, 20 minutes from center city is this factory where you can watch these hand made figures created before your eyes. A show room offers these attractive figures for sale. Prices start at $1 for small figurines. I purchased a small dog for $7.

Hand-Printed Fabrics and Novelties

The **Tipico** shop in the Hotel Tamanaco arcade carries hand printed T-shirts, hostess outfits and handbags. Unusual Indian items, ceramics and novelties are on sale too. Great for browsing. Cristina, the proprietress, operates a similar fine shop at the Macuto Sheraton.

Smoke Shop

▬▬▬▬ **HUMOLANDIA**
Paseo Las Mercedes
Centro Comercial Chacaíto
Phone: 918119

With many pipes, some in unique designs, and many tobaccos, Hurnolandia can be shopped in for the tobacco fiend or for unique gifts for the friend at home.

Music

TIP

The items on sale in these shops make great gifts.

Two huge record stores are Don Disco,Chacaíto Shopping Center, lower level, and Musical Magnus, Edifico Arta, opposite the shopping center in Chacaíto. Both offer a wide choice of Latin tapes and records, and have good prices for guitars. Another good record store is Disco Center in the C.C.C.T. Their Phone: 924278.

Books

All the deluxe hotels have bookstores that sell books and magazines in English. Other bookstores are Las Novedads, C.C.C.T., Phone: 922055, and Lectura, in the Chacaíto Shopping Center.

CARACAS ETCETERA

To speed your understanding of Venezuela and Venezuelans, we have compiled a glossary of tips, notes and basic data that will aid you in your travels.

AIRPORTS

Apart from the International **Simon Bolivar** airport at Maiquetía, serving Caracas, there are other airports for smaller planes. Inside the city of Caracas is **La Carlota**, a military base, in current use for twin engines only. (It helped the last dictator, Perez Jimenez, on his get-away). Then, one hour's drive outside Caracas to the south, you have **Aeropuerto Metropolitano** and **Aeropuerto Caracas**. Both are the home of private planes.

AMERICAN EMBASSY

Located in La Floresta on Avenida Francisco de Miranda in front of Edificio Mobil. Phone: 33-8661, 284-6111

AVENSA

The largest domestic airline is Avensa which runs a first class operation. Phone: 563-3366 (Caracas) (031)55-15-55 (Airport).

BABY SITTERS

Your hotel will arrange for a reliable sitter (probably a chamber maid). Establish rate in advance at the desk. Too, U.S. baby foods and paper diapers are available in local markets. Drug stores carry a good selection of U.S. over-the-counter medicines.

BOOKS

Most deluxe hotels have bookstores that sell books and magazines in English as well as other languages. Major bookstores with international press materials and books are: **Libreria Lectura**, in Centro Comercial Chacaito, **Liberia Las Mercedes**, in Centro Comercial CADA, Las Mercedes, **American Book Shop**, Plaza Àltamira-Norte, **English Books Shop**, at Centro Comercial Concresa, **Liberia Centro Plaza**, at Centro Plaza Altamira, **Steeles Book Store** at Ave. Casanova corner at Calle Baruta, Sabana Grande, and **Libreria Washington** in the old center near Plaza Bolivar, Torre Veroes No. 25.

BRITISH EMBASSY

This is located on Avenida La Estancia, Chuao District (Phone: 91-1255)

CADA

This chain of supermarkets is located in shopping centers throughout Caracas. Originally launched by an investment group headed by the Rockefeller family, these stores are uniformly clean and well stocked with North American as well as Venezuelan products.

CANADIAN EMBASSY

Located in Edificio La Estancia, Avenida La Estancia, Chuao (Phone: 91-3277).

CHOCOLATE

Savoy is Venezuela's major chocolate and candy manufacturer with shops scattered throughout the city. A major outlet is on Sabana Grande at the corner of Los Jabillos.

CHURCHES

Catholicism is the predominant religion in Venezuela as it is throughout Latin America. Your hotel clerk will have a list of nearby churches with mass times. Many Protestant churches conduct services in English. Check the Daily Journal for listings.

COFFEE

TIP

Bring back some coffee, it's excellent. Pick it up at any supermarket.

Venezuela grows its own which is somewhat stronger than Colombian coffee. Main brands are **Imperial and Fama de America**. International hotels started to offer American type soft brewage, but normally Venezuelans have it very strong: Served in small cups it is the "**negrito**" (no milk) or "**maroncito**" (little milk) or "**con leche pequeño**" (milk coffee). You also can order your choice in big (normal) cups: Order the **Negro Grande** (no milk) or **Marron Grande** (little milk) or the **Con leche Grande** (milk coffee). Finally, if you prefer the light coffee in a typical Venezuelan place, order a "**cuayoyo**". They will add enough hot water to your cup.

COSTUME JEWELRY

The word "fantasias" means costume jewelry.

CUSTOMS

There is no duty on personal belongings (cameras, cigarettes, liquor, etc.) brought in for your own use.

NOTE

Sears, an old time favorite, has closed in Caracas.

DEPARTMENT STORES

These are a new phenomenon for Venezuela. Maxy's has a Caracas branch in Bello Monte and **Beco** is in Chacaíto.

DRUG STORES

These are quite common throughout the city. All are stocked with U.S. cosmetics and drugs and toiletries. Pharmacies rotate Sunday openings so that in each district one store is always open.

ECONOMY

Oil dominates, of course. Venezuela is the number one exporter ($3^{1/2}$ million barrels daily). Other exports are iron, coffee, cocoa, diamonds and sugar.

ELECTRICITY

Venezuela operates on 110 AC (identical to North America) so you will not need an adaptor.

FLAG

Venezuela's colors are red, yellow and blue.

GASOLINE

Quite inexpensive here, less than 13 cents per gallon for regular, 16 cents for premium. Gas is sold by the liter (slightly more than a quart).

GOVERNMENT

Venezuela is a Democratic Republic of 20 states and a Federal District. The President and Legislature (Senate and Chamber of Deputies) are elected.

HECTARES

Land areas here are measured in these units which

are the equivalent of about 2.5 acres.

HOT DOGS

Vendors are almost as common as in New York. For 12 cents you get a good frankfurter with mustard, cole slaw, onions and relish.

ICE CREAM

High quality local brands are EFE and Tio Rico which in our judgment are better than most U.S. brands.

JAMS AND JELLIES

Pick up a jar of Nina or La Vienese fruit jelly at any grocery store. First rate.

KILOMETERS

Instead of miles, kilometers are used here. They equal .62 of a mile (or about 3/5ths of a mile).

MAGAZINES

Most popular is the Latin American edition of Time (in English), available at newsstands for 75 cents on Wednesdays. You can also buy all sorts of American and European magazines and books, which are sold in most major book stores and Hotel shops throughout Venezuela.

MAPS

Huge revolving maps of Caracas are in the Centro Capriles, Plaza Venezuela. Another is in Centro Comercial Chacaíto, near Papagallo. Maps on Caracas and the country are available in bookstores and sometimes gas stations along the way. Make sure you have one before you leave on a trip with a rented car; street signs outside Caracas are rare.

MAYOR Y DETAL

This sign over many shops simply means wholesale and retail.

MEDICAL CARE

U.S. trained doctors and dentists advertise on page 2 of the Daily Journal.

METERS

Instead of feet and yards, the standard measure is a meter (3.28 feet).

PAN AM

Phone: 284-5411

PASTRIES

For Middle Eastern baked treats try the Pasteleria Siria, near Plaza Venezuela on Sabana Grande.

NOTE

The population of Venezuela is growing rapidly, especially in Caracas.

POPULATION

Caracas has 4 million residents while Venezuela has over 18 million.

PROPIEDAD HORIZONTAL

This sign on many apartment houses means co-operative ownership.

PRESIDENTIAL PALACE

This is located downtown on Avenida Urdaneta and is called Miraflores Palace.

RADIO

Check the Daily Journal for English-language broadcast schedule of the Voice of America and Radio Canada.

SIESTA

Business hours are generally 8 am-noon; and 2-6 pm. But shops may close until 2:30 pm. This results in traffic jams at noon and at 2 besides the normal morning and evening rush hours.

SYNAGOGUE

Surprisingly, Caracas has a large Jewish population.

The main temple is the **Union Israelita**, located one block from the Avila Hotel at Avenida Marquez del Toro, San Bernardino. B'nai Brith has an active chapter in Altamira on Trànsversal 9 and Ave. 7. Another important temple: **Asociación Israelita de Venezuela** (Seferdim) is located in front of Plaza Colon next to Plaza Venezuela.

TELEPHONE

With a fairly good system, Venezuelan phones are easy to use but not necessarily always efficient. When you pick up the receiver you put in Bs and then dial. If you have connected successfully, the amount that you put in will flash on the screen to the left of the receiver. When you hear a tone it means that there are 15 seconds left and you need to put in more money.

TEMPERATURES

Heat is measured by centigrades not Fahrenheit. A chart of temperature equivalencies follows:

Centigrade	Fahrenheit
0	32
5	41
10	50
15	59
20	68
25	77
30	86
35	95
37	98.6

TIPPING

Bellhops expect 10Bs per large bag. Cab drivers are not tipped. Waiters should be tipped 5% over the service charge for satisfactory service.

TOBACCO

TIP

Imported tobacco products are very expensive here. Bring your own.

U.S. made cigarettes in Venezuela. Marlboro and Viceroy are made in Venezuela and sell for about 40 cents. Local brands include Astor and Belmont(30 cents). Pipe tobacco made in the U.S. can cost $3. Try local brands, Bond Street or Caporal (65 cents). Two excellent tobacco stores are **Palacio Del Fumador**, Centro Comercial Chacaíto (Local 168 mail level) and **Todo Para El Fumador**, in Sabana Grande, next to the Broadway Theatre.

TRAFFIC JAMS

Besides the normal morning and evening tieups, the siesta results in additional road clogging at noon and 2 pm. Traffic jams here rival any I've ever seen elswhere.

TRAVEL AGENTS

Our favorite agency is **Candes Turismo**, Edificio Roraima, Avenida Francisco de Miranda, Chacao (phone: 33-9346). Branch offices are at the Macuto Sheraton, Hilton and Tamanaco Hotels, and in Centro Plaza across from the U.S. embassy. They can efficiently arrange day or evening tours of Caracas as well as excursions to all places mentioned in this book. We have received many favorable readers comments about Candes. By the way, its President, Richard Gluski, is a Director of the National Chamber of Tourism. Mr. Richard C. Falsone is Vice-President.

VIASA

Phone: 572-9522

YOGURT

A delicious local brand is **Yoka**, sold in many markets.

ZOO

Besides the Parque del Este zoo, a smaller zoo is located in El Pinar Park, El Pinar district.

DEPARTURE TAX

You will pay a tax when leaving Venezuela by air at the next international airport.

EL LITORAL
THE BEACH

O n the other side of the mountains that dwarf Caracas is the Caribbean. It will, actually, be your first sight of Venezuela, since the airport is located on the Caribbean. The beach, called El Litoral, is readily accessible for day trips from Caracas and is well-equipped enough, with hotels and restaurants, for longer stays. Caracas is only thirty minutes away.

The beaches, while not of the lushness of Margarita Island's, are lovely and relaxing, and of course on the Caribbean. The towns along the beach are slower moving than Caracas, but active and energetic. From the airport, the main beach thoroughfare is Avenida La Playa, which runs through all the major beach towns.

From Caracas, the main route to the beach is a four-lane autopista (you'll probably be taking a cab so the routes won't be of worry to you). But there are several other routes. The Old Road, also connecting Caracas and El Litoral, winds for 16 miles from Avenida Sucre, just east of the autopista, to Maiquetía, the town of the airport.

The Caribbean side of the mountains is much hotter than the Caracas side, and your dress will be much lighter; and because of this restaurants are much less formal than in the city.

Cabs and por puestos, 5-passenger sedans that operate as mini-buses along Avenida La Playa, are the most used and accessible modes of transportation. In each town things are within walking distance, but to get from Macuto, let's say, to La Guaira, you'll need some form of motor transportation.

Even if you are planning to go to Margarita Island or Puerto La Cruz, at least a day should be spent on the beach of Caracas, for both history and beauty.

MAIQUETÍA

This is the town of Simon Bolivar International Airport, and is really of no interest aside from this fact.

NOTE

La Guaira is a major world port

LA GUAIRA

A historically interesting town, founded in 1589 as San Pedro de la Guaira (St. Peter of the Wind), La Guaira was a major defense station from attacks from the sea. Behind the town there are a string of five forts that served as watchpoints for attackers, which triggered soldiers from the forts to warn the city.

La Guaira is now the major port of the country.

CASA GUIPUZCOANA

Built in 1734 as the headquarters for the La Real Compania Guipuzcoana, this building is considered an important landmark in Venezuelan colonial history. The building has wooden balconies, intricately carved doors and windows, and is a wonderful relic of time past.

The company was installed in this La Guaira building to defend Venezuela's shore and spur commerce. It was a trade monopoly approved by

King Philip V of Spain to boost Venezuela's economy, and in its 50 year tenure it did a fairly successful job, although much was skimmed off the top.

MUSEO BOULTON

NOTE

Aside from the building's historical significance, there is an art gallery housed inside and fantastic views of the mountains offered.

In the former house of John Boulton, founder of Boulton enterprises in the country, the museum has the dual aim of chronologizing the history of La Guaira port and to pay homage to John Boulton's business.

The hours are: Tues - 9:30 - 1, 3 - 6; weekends 9 - 1 (Closed Mondays). Phone: (031)25921.

THE BEACH TOWNS

NOTE

Between these towns are smaller communities and many public beaches.

Reaching your beach hotel from Maiquetía airport is as easy as hailing a cab and that's just what you must do. The taxi ride requires only 20 minutes to the hotel furthest from the airport. Heading East from Maiquetía, your cab will travel along **Avenida La Playa**, the main beach road that winds its way through El Litoral's several communities. Your cab will hit **La Guaira**, a port town; then **Macuto**, where the cable car from Caracas terminates; next is Caraballeda, where five of our seven recommended hotels are; then to **Naiguata**, noted for the **Puerto Azul**, a private luxury club; and finally to **Los Caracas**, a community comprised largely of government-sponsored weekend houses for Caraqueño workers.

WHAT TO WEAR

You are in the Caribbean, it's quite warm–85 to 90 in the afternoons, and a sultry 75 - 80 in the evenings. Dress accordingly, keeping in mind that most hotels, restaurants, and clubs are air-conditioned. Too, both men and women will want at least one dressy (lightweight) outfit for that evening in Caracas. Men will not need a tie at any beach hotel or restaurant. But in Caracas ties are generally required.

GETTING AROUND

Cabs are plentiful and they will cost you from 70 cents to $2 depending on distance. Then there are the marvelously handy **Por Puestos**, 5-passenger sedans that operate as mini-buses along Avenida La Playa, continuously picking up and discharging passengers. Cost is 25 cents, a sign in the front window notes final destination. Since most of our restaurants and clubs are within walking distance of Avenida La Playa, you might consider this mode of rapid transit.

BEACH HOTELS

The two premier deluxe hotels here are unquestionably the beach front Macuto Sheraton and the Melia, but there are too a number of first class stops that offer fine accommodations at moderate prices. Most have private pools and good restaurants but none front on the beach.

■■■■■■■ *MACUTO SHERATON 5**
(Caribe District), Caraballeda
600 Rooms Two Buildings
Air Conditioned
Beach and Two Pools
Phone: (031)575-1432, 91801
Deluxe

NOTE

All rooms have terraces.

This self-contained hotel, which is more like a city, is comparable to the Tamanaco and Hilton hotels in Caracas in luxury and service. Whether you seek a beauty salon, cinema, gift shop, boutique, bookstore, airline office, bowling alley, discotheque, gourmet restaurant, or marina, it is all here. Both

NOTE

You do not have to leave the hotel ever, except to go home.

buildings – the newer **"A"** unit and the blue-hued **"B"** structure – offer total contemporary comfort. Adjacent to the marina is a private beach but most guests seem to lounge around either of the two pools, one huge and irregularly-shaped, the other smaller and circular. You have swimming, boating scuba diving, and fishing during the day; cinema and night clubs in the evenings; and fine restaurants open at all hours. True luxury.

■■■■■■ **HOTEL MELIA CARIBE 5 ***
Caraballeda, La Guaira
300 Rooms
Air Conditioned
Pool
Phone: (031)92401-09
Deluxe

TIP

For sports enthusiasts, tennis, golf, fishing and water sports are available.

TIP

Reservations can be made here for the Melia Puerto La Cruz, another of this fine chain's luxurious resort complexes.

Easily on a par with the best Caribbean hotels, the ultramodern five story Melia is an ideal vacation retreat. This spectacular resort complex is only a 20 minute drive from Maiquetía International Airport and 45 minutes from downtown Caracas. All rooms feature color T.V. and terraces offering stunning views of the sea. On the premises are both a grill and an excellent seafood restaurant, as well as a discotheque, beauty salon, gym and sauna.

Meeting facilities, hosting up to 1000 persons, were inaugurated at the hotel's opening in 1977 by the OPEC conference.

■■■■■■ **HOTEL BAHIA 3 ***
(Los Corales District) Caraballeda
40 Rooms 7 Floors
Air Conditioned
Pool
Phone: (031)91440
Moderate

Two miles west of the Macuto Sheraton, and a short walk from the beach, is the comfortable Bahia, which you will remember for its tree-covered breezeway that leads from the pool to a secluded rear area of trees and flowers. Young couples seem to gravitate there for some reason. Too, the bar near the pool is perfect for an evening cocktail. Front rooms overlook the sea while rear units face the mountains. All have terraces. The second floor restaurant (air conditioned) has a good international menu. Fifteen minutes from the airport.

TIP

No beach swimming here, the rocky coast makes that impossible, but the pool is fine.

HOTEL QUINCE LETRAS 3 *
Av La Playa, Macuto
80 Rooms 8 Floors
Air Conditioned
Phone: 45821
Moderate

Thanks to the success of the renowned Quince Letras Restaurant, this modern hotel under the same management won an immediate following. Small and without frills, the hotel's guests enjoy bright carpeted rooms facing the sea. There is a fine seafood restaurant.

TIP

There is a ramp directly from the hotel to the restaurant.

HOTEL PEDIGROTTA
(ROYAL ATLANTIC) 3 *
(Caribe District), Caraballeda
20 Rooms 4 Floors
Pool and Beach Privileges
Air Conditioned
Phone: 91250
Inexpensive

Opposite the Macuto Sheraton, this small hostelry has unpretentious rooms, with air conditioning. There is a pool and a good Italian restaurant. Guests are permitted to use the Sheraton's pool and beach for $2.

■ HOTEL MACUTO 3*
Av La Playa, Macuto
75 Rooms 6 Floors
Air Conditioned
Pool
Phone: 44561
Inexpensive

Nearest to the airport (10 minutes) is the older Macuto, noted for a first rate restaurant and its large salt-water pool. Good service more than makes up for the no-frills furnishings. And, the value is unbeatable.

■ HOTEL VILLAMARE 2*
Av La Playa, Caraballeda
13 Rooms, 1 Floor
Air Conditioned
Pool
Phone: 91691
Inexpensive

This basic choice offers a pool in the rear in a scenic mountain setting. Not many extras, but the price is right.

■ HOTEL FIORE 2*
Av Principal
(front of Macuto Sheraton)
23 Rooms 4 Floors
Phone: 91535
Inexpensive

Our final selection sports an excellent Italian restaurant, and well maintained hostelries with A.C.

BEACH RESTAURANTS

Seafood is the dominant dish here and that's no surprise. But you can find good beef and fowl selections on most menus.

Here is a listing of beach restaurants that are not connected with hotels. The hotel restaurants are very accessible and most of your dining will be there. It is harder to find the good local restaurants, and that is why we have concentrated on them.

A quick review of the introduction chapter will refamiliarize you with dishes, and price ranges are the same as for Caracas.

LAS QUINCE LETRAS
Av La Playa, Macuto
11 am - 11 pm (daily)
Phone: 031 - 44226
Moderate

Considered the best dinner place in El Litoral, this restaurant extends out on a peninsula into the Caribbean within view of the big jets taking off and landing at Maiquetía Airport. In the evening, the sound of waves lapping against the rocks below complete the ambience. As for the food, whether you order shrimp cocktail from the Spanish-English menu, or **cazuela de mariscos (sea food casserole)**, or the **paella,** or any of the beef dishes, you will have a perfect dining experience. Good for lunch too.

TIMOTES
Callejon Liberatador, Maiquetía
12 - 3, 7 - 12
Phone: 22618
Inexpensive

Easily the best "Venezuelan" restaurant in this beach area is Timotes, where the fare rivals that of El Porton in Caracas. Try any of the typical Criolla dishes – delicious. The huge air-conditioned restaurant offers excellent service. Timotes is in Maiquetía, in a shopping center off the main avenue near the airport. Take a cab. Informal.

■■■■■ **PORTON DE TIMOTES**
Av Principal
Caraballeda
11 am - 11 pm
Inexpensive

The sister of Timotes in Maiquetía, Porton de Timotes is more easily reached from the beach, and has the same fantastic food. It's in a private house, with a knight in armor standing in the middle, giving the house a strange aged look. Once again, excellent food.

■■■■■ **COOKERY**
Av Principal
CaribeCaraballeda
Air Conditioned
11 am - 11 pm (daily)
Phone: 031 - 91866
Inexpensive

TIP

Piano bar most evenings.

Ideal for light lunch, the Cookery serves a small but tasty filet mignon, and has a range of pastas. We are partial to the **langostinos al ajillo** (scampi). Within walking distance of the Macuto Sheraton, this restaurant offers dining either outdoors on the terrace or in the air conditioned dining room.

■■■■■ **PIDA PIZZA**
Av Principal
(Caraballeda District)
11 am - 11 pm
Inexpensive

Next to the Cookery, Pida Pizza is obviously the choice for pizza and Italian food. On the sea, and relaxing.

■■■■■ **EL BODEGON DE LINO**
Av Principal
(Caraballeda District)
11 am - 11 pm
Inexpensive

Across from Porton de Timotes, El Bodegon specializes in Spanish food and seafood. Small but good.

■ HONG KONG CHEF
Av Principal
(Caribe District)
11 am - 11 pm
Phone: 91299
Inexpensive

For tasty Chinese food head for the Hong Kong Chef. Dine al Fresco at one of the front tables. We particularly enjoyed the **shark fin soup**, and the sweet and sour dishes. Bi-lingual menu.

■ RESTAURANT NEPTUNO
Av Principal
(Caribe District)
11 am - 1 am
Inexpensive

Across from the Macuto Sheraton is this combination seafood - Italian eatery. Dine at one of the outdoor tables. Try the **Espaguetes con salsa chipi chipi** (spaghetti with clam sauce) or the **pargo.** If pizza is your dish – no problem here. Informal and inexpensive.

■ TOMASELLI
Av Principal
Caribe(Caraballeda District)
7 am - 3 am (daily)
Inexpensive

A fun place for burgers, pizza and desserts is Tomaselli, which attracts the under 21 set in large numbers. Good milk shakes too. This is where you will find crowds of people no matter what time of the day or night. An excellenet meeting place for young people.

HOTEL RESTAURANTS

▬▬ *GRILL SEVILLA*
Hotel Macuto Sheraton
(Main Floor)
7 pm - 11:30 pm
Moderate

TIP

Despite the elegance, men need wear neither a jacket or tie.

Easily the most elegant restaurant in El Litoral is the dinner-only Sevilla which resembles a Spanish colonial villa. Plush carpeting, formal highback chairs, and expensive china and water goblets provide the proper backdrop for the splendid food. Definitely try the **gazpacho** soup, the **churrasco** (steak), and/or the **red snapper**. We flipped too over the **fondu bourguignonne** and the crisp fresh pastries. Next door is **El Torero Discotheque**, which should cap your evening.

▬▬ *GALEON*
Melia Hotel
8 pm - 12 midnight
Moderate

Almost as fancy as the Grill Sevilla, Galeon has great French-leaning food. With **smoked salmon**, **pate de foie**, **steak tartar** and **prawns in whiskey**, dining is as exotic as it is lush.

TIP

Another hotel featuring excellent Italian dishes is the Restaurant Fiore in the hotel of the same name. Definitely dine on the terrace. We recommend the ravioli and calamares.

▬▬ *LA GRAN PAELLA*
Hotel Fioremar
7 pm - 2 am
Inexpensive

Small, with high wooden chairs, La Gran Paella serves Spanish food, and does it well.

▬▬ *LA FORCHETTA*
Pedigrotta Hotel
12 - 3, 7 - 10
Inexpensive

A true Italian restaurant in this area is La Forchetta, located on the main floor of the Pedigrotta Hotel. Pasta, veal, and chicken dishes, with wine provide for a great meal. Both outside and inside dining is available.

QUICK SNACKS

Tropiburger, a MacDonalds like eatery has an outlet on the main street a few blocks from the Macuto Sheraton. Try the **Guapo**, the Venezuelan answer to the Big Mac.

DAYS AT THE BEACH

Aside from beaching it and dawdling at pool side, what is there to do in El Litoral before dusk? For a start, check in at the marina near the Macuto Sheraton. You have a choice of fishing, boating, or water skiing at reasonable rental rates. For information call the hotel, extension 846.

FISHING

You can rent a launch, complete with a crew and fishing gear, that holds six passengers for $90 (half), and $130 (full day). The $15 per person half-day rate is fairly reasonable since the captain throws in lunch and drinks as well as equipment.

BOAT RENTALS

A sunfish or catamaran runs about $10 an hour. Boats are in good shape and you should be able to get a special half-day rate.

WATER SKIING (Esqui Acuatico)

For $15 an hour, you can rent a boat, a driver and water skis at the marina. Share the cost with friends.

TENNIS enthusiasts need go no further than the Macuto Sheraton which accommodates non-guests and guests for the same $5 per hour rate. Rackets can be rented for $1 but there is a deposit required.

NOTE

Never on Saturday or Sunday

GOLFERS can tee off at the 18-hole **Caraballeda Golf Club**, a short ride from the Macuto Sheraton. Green fees are $10 and you can rent clubs. Most hotels have arrangements with the club for guest privileges but on weekdays only. Ask your hotel clerk to book you.

BOWLING

Club Sheraton offers bowling for about $1, including shoes. The four alleys are open from 11 am - midnight. There is a snack bar and air conditioning.

OTHER BEACHES

El Litoral has many fine beaches along Avenida La Playa. The most popular by far with North Americans is the **Playa Sheraton** next to the Macuto Sheraton hotel. Venezuelans tend to use the **Macuto Beach** nearer to the cable car terminal. A third beach in a visually stunning area is **Los Angeles**, about three miles beyond the Macuto Sheraton Hotel. The buses marked"Los Caracas" pass Los Angeles.

TIP

*The closest beach to Caracas is the popular **Marina Grande**.*

Probably the best beach for tourists is **Camuri Chico Balneario** located about one mile from the cable car terminal. The beach is free and you can rent lockers and chairs. There is a cafeteria and showers on the premises too.

NIGHTS AT THE BEACH

While night life in El Litoral will never compare to the upbeat cabarets, boites, and clubs in Caracas still there are discotheques, cocktail lounges and live entertainment clubs here as well as a cinema that shows U.S. films in English (no Spanish dubbing).

FILMS

The attractive air conditioned Macuto Sheraton Theater (in the hotel) shows a new film every night at 8:30, most of them from the U.S. Too, there's a new children's movie (in Spanish, usually) daily at 5. Non-guests are welcome. Buy your tickets at the front desk.

CLUBS AND CABARETS

Unlike in Caracas and elsewhere in Latin America, clubs here generally welcome singles but this is hardly heaven for the unattached since couples seem to predominate at beach hotels.

EL TORERO
Macuto Sheraton Hotel
Discotheque and Live Music
8 pm - 3 am (daily)

A sensational rum punch gets you in the proper mood quickly in this zinging music club which alternates soft rock discs with a good combo. Comfortable leather chairs ring the tables, floors are carpeted, and the motif is Spanish. Perfect for an after-dinner drink.

DON PEPE
Melia Hotel
10 pm - 4 am

As exciting as El Torero, Don Pepe is structured the same way, and has live music as well.

PIANO BARS

For relaxing music along with your cocktail you can try the **Bar Almirante** at the Melia Hotel and the

NOTE

Singles seem to congregate at the lengthy bar with occasional dance breaks.

bar at the **Cookery Restaurant**. Both are open from 6 pm to 1 am. Nightly. Enjoy.

A DAY IN CARACAS

If you are centered at the beach, you will obviously want at least a day in Caracas.

After breakfast and perhaps a morning swim, hop a cab to the city. The ride will run about $8. Ask the driver to let you off at Plaza Bolivar, the historical part of the city, where you can stroll around and see the Bolivar Museum and the Casa Natal, where Simon Bolivar was born. Stop in too at a marvelous toy store, La Gran Piñata, near the museums.

When you have had enough of old Caracas, head to new Caracas represented by the Centro Comercial Chacaíto, a shopping center. The quickest way is by cab. Once there head for City Rock Cafe, the Hard Rock Cafe of Caracas, for an exciting meal. Stroll around the neighborhood, do some shopping.

Then look for the Broadway cinema. Walk toward that movie house (you'll be heading west) and just beyond it is the start of the Sabana Grande shopping district. Avenida Lincoln is the apex for great shopping.

By this time you should be ready for either an early dinner or at least a cocktail. Check our restaurant guide for recommendations and take a cab. After dining, if you still have not reached the envelope of your energy go to some of our recommended clubs.

Then it is a cab back to El Litoral.

Margarita

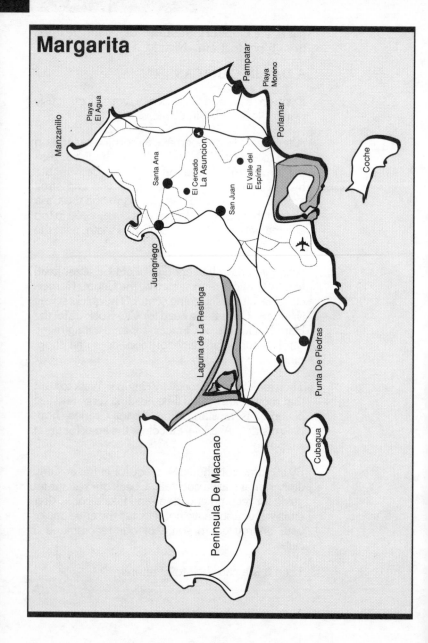

MARGARITA ISLAND
BEACHING IT

I have visited Maragarita Island frequently since 1968 and the incredible thing to me is the rapid evolvement of this once rustic holiday island – an hour by air from Caracas – into an alive tourist find. At one time, and not too long ago, the island was little known outside of Venezuela which was fine with the Caraqueños who thronged the main town of Porlamar every weekend and holiday.

Now Maragarita apparently has been discovered by North America. How do we know? Well on our last trip I spent some time with a New York psychiatrist and his wife who were exulting over a double-lot purchase "for retirement". When psychiatrists discover an island, can the rest of us – patients all – be far behind?

Helping things along was a shrewd government move in 1975 to establish a free port (Zona Franca) which means travelers have one more reason, in addition to the endless beaches, superb seafood and pearls, to journey here.

ISLAND OVERVIEW

Margarita is the largest of three islands that form the Caribbean state of **Nueva Esparta** (New Sparta), so named by Simon Bolivar because of the valor of the residents during the 19th century revolution that overthrew Spanish domination. Today, Margarita has a population of some 125,000 but the other two islands – **Coche** and **Cubagua** – are sparsely settled. Coche has only about 5,000 residents, mostly in the village of San Pedro which boasts a rich salt mine and prime pearl beds. Cubagua, abandoned in 1550 after two tidal waves inundated the island, was discovered by Columbus in 1498 and it housed Venezuela's first foreign settlement in Nueva Cadiz. Today mostly fishermen set foot on the island.

BACKGROUND AND HISTORY

To repeat, Margarita is actually the largest of the three islands that form the Caribbean state of Nueva Esparta. The other two islands – Cubagua and Coche – are the original sites of Venezuela's modern history.

Columbus discovered the islands in 1498. It was an insignificant discovery at the time, but a year later Cristobalde la ·Guerra and Pedro Alonso Nino found a hidden bed of pearls off Cubagua, and eventually went back to Spain with 80 pounds of them. This spurred the settlement of the small island, which became the first in South America. The mad frenzy for pearls drove the Spanish to subjugate and enslave the native Guaiqueri Indians as pearl divers, killing off many young males by incessant diving. The abuse was so intense that eventually it ignited a revolt, and the Spanish were forced off the island in 1520. Years later, December 25, 1541, Cubagua's civilized history came to an end because of a massive tidal wave and earthquake; the island has been empty of people since then.

On March 8, 1525 Margarita was given by the Crown to Licenciado Marcelo Villalobos and his family. They were entrusted to begin a society there. He died before actually reaching the island, but his wife, Doña Isabel Manrique, governed the island until 1535. The Villalobos' governed the island until 1593, when the last of the family died. It was then reinstated under the Crown.

Nueva Esparta, which means New Sparta, was the name given the islands by Bolivar for the valor and loyalty in the Independence War. When the first troops from Spain, 15,000 soldiers, landed on Margarita in 1815 to quell the revolution a spurious peace was made with them by Generals Juan Bautista Arismendi and Jose Francisco Bermudez. Aware that they couldn't defeat them, the Generals stayed submissive until their departure. Immediately afterwards, the truce was broken and the people of Margarita once again began fighting for independence. Bolivar used Margarita, in 1816, as the launching pad for his third expedition into Caracas. On Margarita, in Santa Ana, he declared the 3rd Republic and was proclaimed Commander-in-Chief.

Margarita is the Greek word for pearl, and pearls are the subhistory of the islands. Providing Spain with shiploads of wealth, pearls were frantically searched and dived for. They were the reason for Cubagua's initial settlement and the near decimation of the Guaiqueri Indians. The overmining resulted in a hiatus in the 17th, 18th, and 19th centuries, but in the 20th century it was restarted. At that time, the export was predominantly to Paris. But then again, because of conservation, pearl diving ended, this time outlawed, in 1962.

Margarita was a sleepy fisherman's island until January 8, 1975 when it was declared a free port. The island, particularly at it's main city Porlamar, became a shopping mecca. Venezuelans seeking international goods flock to the island, although for

Americans the prices are not as appetizing as they are for natives. Porlamar has 100,000 people, and although the future seems clear, cranes and hollow tall structures bully Porlamar, the rest of the island is still subdued and quiet; the beaches dominate.

CLIMATE, TERRAIN AND INDUSTRY

Unlike most other Caribbean islands, Margarita has a gently rolling terrain that gives it a distinction lacking in nearby Aruba and other level vacation islands. Perfect for strolling or motoring. The weather is predictable all year round, warm, sunny days offering 12 month swimming and boating. The evenings are cool and breezy, the humidity low. A true island gem, and not only for the excellent pearl buys here. Ideal? I think so.

Today Margarita's principal industries are fishing and tourism. Water understandably dominates the island which is 43 miles long. Officially, there are 18 beaches but I've counted a least a dozen more. You can swim year-round and the waters range from pond-like to North Sea-like. In short, you can choose your wave. More about the beaches later.

A PERSONAL NOTE

Over the centuries, the once spartan nature of the people here has apparently softened for today they are extremely warm and open with strangers. On one visit in Porlamar I tried to buy a soft drink from a passing delivery truck. The driver happily turned over a couple of bottles but refused payment, explaining that he only delivers, he doesn't sell. Later that day, a por puesto driver waived my fare when he was unable to change a 20B note. Good people here. And no surprise that there's not a prison on the island. I'm sure you will share my warm feelings for Margarita.

When I discuss Margarita with friends in New York, invariably I'm asked: "Okay, it can't be all plusses, what are the negatives?" If you consider it such, the negative is the absence of night life. The town is quiet after dark but as the development booms ahead, that problem should rectify itself. I suggest you knock off early, your day will be full enough.

ORIENTATION

Margarita is 43 miles long and 300 square miles in all. Margarita island is actually two islands connected by a narrow isthmus. The second island is called **Peninsula de Macanao.** Largely unpopulated, the island is used for local fishing, and has many isolated beaches.

Peninsula de Macanao is at the western end of Margarita, and Porlamar is south-east. **Aeropuerto Internacional del Caribe** is on the southern rim of the island, and is a half hour to 45 minute taxi cab ride ($3) from Porlamar. The islands' thick section is a three quarter circle from Porlamar to Juangriego, which is center-north. On that near full circle are Margarita's finest beaches, and a ride between the two towns is spectacular; twisted, cliff-hanging roads that have the sea layed out in front of it, and have the green rolling hills behind it. **La Asuncion**, the capital, is the nose of the fat face formed by Margarita's east side, and Santa Ana, a historical city, is the bridge of the nose. **Pampatar**, another wonderful colonial site, is a curve east of Porlamar. And finally, **Punta de Piedra**, the dock for the ferry to Puerto la Cruz, is located in the south-west part of the island, very near to Peninsula de Macanao.The infrastructure of the island is in mint condition, and no ride is longer than an hour.

The flight from Caracas is under an hour, and the ride to Porlamar is another half hour. There are actually two distinct sections of Porlamar. As your cab first enters the city limits the small, crowded somewhat rusted apartment buildings of the residents are visible. That huge dome you see dominating the skyline is part of **St. Nicholas Church**, site of lovely candlelight processions on Christmas Eve and on other religious holidays. The streets are jammed with stores, houses, dogs, and humans. Moving east on either **Calle Zamora** or **Calle Igualdad**, you pass several pedestrian thoroughfares that are strictly for shopping. Then, suddenly, you come to Hotel Bella Vista, and the streets become dotted with tourists, much less crowded, the rusted apartments become glass, shiny clothes stores, and you've reached the tourist section of Porlamar.

The tourist part the of city is dominated by two streets: **Avenida Santiago Mariño** and **Avenida 4 de Mayo**. They are crowded with stores selling international goods, fast food joints and restaurants; off of one of these streets will inevitably be your hotel. Stores selling Nike, Ralph Lauren, Polo, Finlandia, Lindt, line these streets and give it a real 5th Avenue texture.

Avenida 4 de Mayo, east, leads to Pampatar, and the north-east rim where Margarita's best beaches are located.

THE BEST HOTELS

The island, blessed with beaches, is devoted to tourists. Yet it has, I think, now, a shortage of hotels because the island is getting more and more popular. But the contruction and growth of the island is apparent all around the Porlamar area, with small cranes sitting monstrously in the sky, and in other corners of the island., Juangriego being one. Porlamar, at the moment, has just enough to handle the strain, although planning ahead is necessary because it gets saturated quickly. There are two five-star hotels, huge complexes, and one four-star hotel, also stuffed. The rest of the hotels on Margarita are three-stars or two-stars, all are nice and clean. The overwhelming majority of hotels are in Porlamar or right outside, although there are a few others scattered around the island.

▬▬▬▬ *MARGARITA CONCORDE 5**
Bahia El Morro
526 rooms, 24 floors
Phone: 61333
Telex: 95218 Resha Ve
Deluxe

NOTE

The Concorde on Aruba is part of the same chain.

Margarita's first five-star hotel, on a beach of its own, looks as new as it is. The white cement is sparkling, the tower, and its two baby brothers of six floors, proud. A mixture of tropical design and high-tech Americana, the Concorde has a lobby of reed furniture, light green shades, ceiling fans and bright colors, and has a mini-mall of shops and games arcade. The hotel has a gamut of facilities, with a pool, gym, sauna, several restaurants and the services that a hotel of this caliber provides. Its main attraction is its own marina on the sea; with boats and water-sports available. Isolated on its own beach on the end of the road behind Porlamar, the Concorde is a special hotel.

▬▬▬▬ *MARGARITA HILTON*
INTERNATIONAL
Calle Uveros
Playa Moreno
291 Rooms, 11 Floors
Pool & Tennis Courts
Phone: In Caracas - 574-1122
Deluxe

NOTE

The inauguration date for the Hilton is April 1989.

Brand new and magnificent, offering balconied rooms facing Playa Moreno, the Hilton is a welcome addition to Margarita. Amenities include lighted tennis courts, a health club with sauna and steambaths, 2 restaurants, a lobby bar, discotheque, game rooms and fine shops.

All rooms are air conditioned, of course, and the staff has been specially trained to provide excellent and prompt service.

The G.M., Rafael Riquelme, is an old friend of "Venezuela Alive" from his days as G.M. of the Residencias Anauco Hilton in Caracas. We wish him well.

You cannot go wrong here.

▬▬▬ HOTEL BELLA VISTA 4*
Av Santiago Mariño
309 Rooms
Phone: 611813, 614157
Telex: 95123
Expensive

TIP

This is a wonderful place to stay, especially in the newer wing.

For years Margarita's only luxury hotel, the Bella Vista has now lost that status to the Hilton andConcorde. But that has not tarnished it's style and own luxury. With a huge wide lobby that reeks of action and excitement, the Bella Vista is done-up with the excited mess of a padded hotel, with shops, paintings, couches, games, travel agencies, mosaics on the wall, bell boys rushing, waiters with drinks. The lobby is the Bella Vista, and the Bella Vista is still the hub of Porlamar, with all the travel agencies and rent-a-cars and government tourist offices here.

The hotel has several restaurants, a fine pool with a bar and restaurant adjacent, and its own beach. There are occasional pool side films, a nightly (9-12) barbecue, and the lady chefs at poolside prepare the island's special seafood dishes for lunch that are not to be missed. The Concorde and

Hilton may be more regal but the Bella Vista is full of hubris and is the center pin of tourist activity, the banner hotel on the beginning edge of Porlamar's main strip.

███████ **HOTEL FOR YOU 3***
Av Santiago Mariño
85 Rooms, 6 Floors
Phone: 31995
Moderate

Hotel For You is a stone's throw from the main strip, on a street that is perpendicular to it. With a small lobby and a majestic spiralling marble stairway, Hotel For You has no fringe benefits but the rooms are clean, comfortable and thoroughly air conditioned. There is one restaurant in the hotel.

███████ **HOTEL LOS PINOS**
Calle Los Pinos and San Francisco
90 Rooms, 5 Floors
Phone: 611301, 612021
Moderate

On a street that parallels the strip of Avenida. 4 de Mayo, the Los Pinos is on a block to itself and has that tropical serenity that only a few other hotels on the island have. The entrance is hung with palm trees, and the bar, on the patio, is clinking with drinks and soft conversation. The hotel has a truly relaxing feel to it, and aside from its comfort, this is the main attraction. There is Budget Rent-A-Car outlet here.

███████ **HOTEL GUAIQUERI**
Av Raul Leoni, via El Morro
64 Rooms, 3 Floors
Phone: 31346
Moderate

In my mind the most interesting hotel on the island, Hotel Guaiqueri has the colorful playfulness which is contagious when you are on the beach with temperatures in the 90's and on vacation. All pink and in a Mexican hacienda, with a central courtyard and fountain, this hotel is minutes away from the beach, has its own pool, has large spacious rooms, and has a fine restaurant and disco.

■■■■■■ HOTEL FLAMINGO 3*
Av 4 de Mayo
24 Rooms
Phone: 616301,616375
Moderate

New and clean, Hotel Flamingo is in the impressive row of stores and other hotels that line this strip. In the midst of all the action of Porlamar, Hotel Flamingo has a bar and restaurant, and provides good tourist information.

■■■■■■ REAL FLAMINGO 3*
Av 4 de Mayo
34 Rooms
Phone: 22984
Moderate

A bit further away from the action than its other named hotel (I don't know if they are connected) and less new, Real Flamingo is pleasant and clean and near the popular bowling alley.

■■■■■■ HOTEL COLIBRI 2*
Av Santiago Mariño
58 Rooms
Phone: 32567
Inexpensive

Not far from the Bella Vista, this little hotel is right on the beach. It has a familiar atmosphere, since it is run by a family, with home cooking and the television blaring. The rooms are air conditioned. There is a personal touch to the atmosphere here that brightens things a bit.

HOTEL MARIA LUISA 2*
Av Raul Leoni via El Morro
42 Rooms
Phone: 617964, 610564
Inexpensive

Near Hotel Guaiqueri, this is a small hotel located on the beach. The hotel has a bar, air conditioning and a gift shop.

HOTEL LE PARC 2*
Calle Guillarte
Phone: 31239, 32545
Inexpensive

Right outside downtown Porlamar, near Plaza Bolivar, Hotel Le Parc has a pool, playground and piano bar, restaurant and air conditioning. A popular place.

HOTEL IMPERIAL 2*
Av Raul Leoni
Phone: 616420, 614823
Inexpensive

A squat clean building with pleasant rooms, the Hotel Imperial is a little off the strip.

HOTEL EUDAMA 2*
Av Bella Vista
Inexpensive

Just like a roadside hotel in America, Hotel Eudama has that quick overnight feel to it. The rooms are air conditioned.

There are more hotels in Porlamar and its immediate surrounding – we haven't listed all of them. The rest are in the range of the last several hotels listed, all functional with no extras. Depending on what kind of traveller you are these hotels are fine, being clean and air-conditioned – not much time is going to be spent in them anyway, you'll be at the beach.

Here are a few hotels outside Porlamar.

███████ **HOTEL CLUB PUERTO**
ESMERALDA 3*
Porlamar-Pampatar Road
109 Suites
Phone: 4416187
Inexpensive

Built as condo apartments, the hotel is located at the end of Playa Moreno, a few miles outside of Porlamar. The rooms are suites, with couches, tables, refrigerators and wet-bars. There is a pool.

JUANGRIEGO

███████ **HOTEL CLARY 3***
Calle Martires
Phone: 54037
Inexpensive

A family run hotel in the quiet western town of Juangriego, the hotel is relaxing and wonderfully clean. There are seven individual apartments for rent. The hotel has the out-of-the-way sereness of Juangriego's great sunsets.

There are other hotels around the island, all small and functional and mainly ignored by the tourist monopoly Porlamar has. If it is your style to stay away from the crowds, try Hotel Clary, but you will be able to find any of these small places easily.

FOOD AND RESTAURANTS

You would be deficient in good sense if you neglected the food from the sea in Margarita. Whether you gorge yourself on lobster (langosta) or oysters (ostras) or shrimp (camarones), you will rarely find this quality at these modest prices. Sauces are unusual and piquant. Too, there are dishes not easy to find elsewhere, such as choice turtle steak called **filet de tortuga** and Maragrita's prize gift to gourments – a clam consomme called **consomme de chipichipi**. Other must dishes are **arroz con mariscos**, a rice and shell fish platter that usually comes with fried plantain (banana); **hervido de pescado**, a fish stew, and our all time favorite **cazuela de langosta**, lobster chunks baked with a creole sauce. The island's favorite drink is a rum punch, pink and potent.

Porlamar is where most of the restaurants are located, but there are some on Playa Agua (listed in the beach section), Juangriego and the interior cities. Again, most of the restaurants are located, in Porlamar, on the strips of Av Santiago Mariño and Avenida 4 de Mayo.

International and French

L'ETE
Av 4 de Mayo
Open 7 - 12
Phone: 616586
Moderate

NOTE

A restaurant of this caliber was unheard of 10 years ago on Margarita

Very formal and soft, the restaurant is the only French one on the island. The design is the elegant coolness of high style, with the colors mainly peach and yellow. With a classic French menu, pates and mousses head the list of hors d'oeuvres, while the main dishes range from **langosta brunetiere** (shrimp with dark sauce) to **tuite farcie au champagne** (trout in champagne) and **escarago**, and **filet migon**. Fine dining is what is offered here.

LA GRAN PIRAMIDE DE LA BUENA SUERTE
Calle Malave con Patino
Open 6:30 - 11
Phone: 612964
Expensive

Built like a Madison Avenue restaurant with large windows and smooth brick, this restaurant is warm inside, with antique guns hanging on the walls and other weaponry ornaments. With red snapper and steaks headlining the menu, the dishes range in a typically international way. Reservations are necessary.

EL YATE
Calle Jesus con J.M. Patino
Open 12 - 3, 6:30 - 11:30
Phone: 618708
Expensive

Next to Hotel For You, El Yate is a fancy plush restaurant with live music. Spacious but intimate, the restaurant is centered around the bar and stage. The design is nautical, and the food is international, with steaks and fish dominating the menu. Serving excellent drinks, it is suggested that you make reservations.

BRASAS
Frente Al Bco. Provincial
Open 12 - 3, 7 - 12
Phone: 619956
Moderate

A modern white large windowed restaurant located near Los Pinos Hotel, Brasas has a continental menu that leans towards American tastes. Meats dominate, with steaks and chops and barbecued dishes the centerpieces. Modern and personal, there is a very American feel to this place. Brasas also has a good variety of wines and champagnes. You will enjoy dining here.

VIRREY
Hotel Concorde
Open 7 - 12
Phone: 727744
Expensive

Fancy and formal, the Concorde's restaurant is European dining, with the formalities that come with it. The food is excellent, and its service is fantastic.

Venezuelan/Seafood

■■■■■■ *EL CHIPI*
Av Santiago Mariño

El Chipi was the preeminent seafood restaurant on the island, with lines as long as an hours wait. It was large and wild and noisy, and the food was superb. It, unfortunately, burned down, and is now in the midst of being repaired. Check it out when you arrive to see if it is open again. It is located between the Bella Vista Hotel and Hotel For You. Ask anyone.

El Chipi features a pargo dish that is a must – **Filet de Pargo Pampatar** – red snapper stuffed with ham and cheese with a delightful marisco sauce. Excellent. Also popular are **the mejillones marinera** (mussels) and the **calamares** (squid). Specially recommended for lunch or a quick bite anytime is the remarkable **chipi chipi soup**, in constant demand.

■■■■■■ *DA GASPAR*
Av 4 de Mayo
Open 12 -3, 6 - 12
Phone: 613486
Expensive

German and Austrian in texture, Da Gaspar is mainly a seafood restaurant but with patches of German and Italian dishes on the menu. It is loud and communal in atmosphere but that does not negate the fine service. Try the lobster, and some of the German dishes. The restaurant attracts an international crowd and is usually crowded. I've never had a bad meal here.

MARIA GUEVARA
Hotel Bella Vista
Open all day
Phone: 22695
Moderate

Large and thatched and by the sea, Maria Guevara is in the back of the hotel and has fine fish dishes. Juggling elegance and informality, the restaurant can supply both. Try the clams here.

MARTIN PESCADOR
Av 4 de Mayo
Open 11 - 3, 6:30 - 11
Phone: 24364
Moderate

TIP

The chipi chipi soup here is a must

With a huge neon sign announcing its presence, Martin Pescador makes a show of its meats, stacked up on racks, and its fish. A deli type setting, the restaurant has the panache of a restaurant proud of itself. Steaks and shrimp dishes are great.

BAHIA
Av Raul Leoni via El Morro
Open 5 -12
Phone: 614556
Expensive

Large wood and glass restaurant with a small flower garden in the back, Bahia has an old-standing institution of the island. Its lobster is outstanding.

LOS TRES DELFINES
Calle Cedeno
Open all day
Phone: 617557
Moderate

With a piano bar and large neon entrance, Los Tres Delfines is another seafood restaurant with fine food.

███████ **LA LOBA**
Av 4 de Mayo
Open 6 -11
Moderate

On the main strip, La Loba has good shrimp and clams, as well as steak.

███████ **LA COTORRERA**
Av Santiago Mariño
Open all day
Inexpensive

A wide and large open-air restaurant on the main strip, Cotorrera has a real touristy beachy feel to it. Packed for lunch and dinner, and the last restaurant open for late snacks, their meat dishes are really great, cooked on an open fire.

Italian

███████ **LA ITALIANA**
Av 4 de Mayo
Open 12 - 3, 6 - 11:30
Inexpensive

NOTE

Venezuela has a large Italian population and these restaurants are very popular.

A small Italian restaurant on the main strip, right after the bowling alley, with an old fashioned Italian setting, with pictures of Italy on the wall. The food is excellent, overshadowing the somewhat blase setting. The pastas, particularly the bolonaise, is fantastic, and the four-spiced pasta is otherworldly.

███████ **O SOLE MIO**
Calle Cedeno con Molave
Open 6:30 - 11
Phone: 611220
Moderate

O Sole Mio is a large restaurant with couches spread around the place and red sparkling table-cloths. There is a piano bar attached and large photos of Italy on the walls. The Italian-styled fish dishes are fantastic, with their shrimp the star.

EL CANATELE
Av 4 de Mayo
Open all day
Phone: 613275
Moderate

A trailer structure, with wood walls and quilt table-cloths, El Canatele has the typical Italian fare, with pastas and fish heading the bill.

EL PINERO
Av Raul Leoni
Open all day
Phone: 619079
Moderate

Popular and tasty, El Pinero has a trilingual menu and specializes in shrimp, pizza, and exotic drinks.

Chinese

DRAGON CHINO
Av 4 de Mayo
Open all day
Phone: 618253
Moderate

NOTE

Dragon Chino has a large following

Dragon Chino has a huge menu, pages long, and a flashy Hong Kong entrance. It serves typical Chinese dishes, with, once again, fish being the best. Chop suey and egg rolls (lumpias) are fine too.

Spanish

CLEMTINA
Calle Cedeno
Open 12 - 3, 6 - 11:30
Moderate

Paella and snapper and rice dishes are the main

fare at Clemtina that is in an open air setting with inside seating also available. Portions are rather large so hold down on the appetizers. Good restaurant.

Fast Food

 ### *CREAMIS*
Calle Cedeno

Open setting and green colors, Creamis has pizza, ice cream, and hamburgers.

LA ISLA
Av Santiago Mariño

A fast food complex with Chinese, burgers, ice cream, shakes, and cookies all available. Crowded and a big hang-out, La Isla is great for the late-night snacks.

CAFE DE PARIS

Next to Hotel For You, Cafe de Paris has the street setting of a Paris Brasserie, but serves fast food – burgers and ice cream.

Restaurants in Juangriego

RESTAURANT CLARY
Hotel Clary
Open 8 - 12
Inexpensive

With just a few tables, Restaurant Clary has great snapper and parilla. It has a nice serene setting for a quiet but informal dinner as you watch the sunset.

RESTAURANT JUANGRIEGO
Calle La Marina
Inexpensive

On the beach and plain, seafood is again the main dish.

ONE MORE IN LA ASUNCION:

If you are sightseeing in the city and get caught during lunch time you should try **Restaurant Federico**, next to Bolivar Square that has good Italian food.

A FINAL NOTE:

There are restaurants on some of the beaches (the ones on Playa El Agua have been mentioned earlier) that are available during the day as you swim. You will find them as you go.

SUNUP TO SUNDOWN

Aside from exploring the endless sands – two dozen or so magnificent beaches encircle the island – you will wish to poke around the out-of-the-way fishing villages, old Spanish forts and Catholic shrines. Since highways for the most part are first class – as is true in most of Venezuela – and distances are short it makes sense to rent a car. Review our discussion on auto rentals below and make your own arrangements or have the hotel do it for you. Or you can hire a taxi. Establish in advance the rate and time period.

Around the Island

The city of Porlamar is worth exploring on foot (in the cool part of the day, that is), particularly the main streets – Calles Igualdad and Guevara. Calle Igualdad runs from the Bella Vista Hotel to the Plaza Bolivar, the city's largest plaza, a 6-block stretch, which is the site of tremendous building activity. Seven story apartment buildings and ubiquitous Zona Franca shops are everywhere. As elsewhere in Venezuela, the Plaza Bolivar is the social center of the city. Friends meet on its benches, hard fought chess games are played and guitars and banjos are popular. At one end stands

TIP

Margarita is the best place in Venezuela to rent a car

St. Nicholas Church whose huge dome is visible throughout the city. It is as the main church here, the site of religious festivals, particularly on December 5 and 6 (The Feast of St. Nicholas) and at Christmas.

A pleasant stroll along Calle Guevara (in front of the church) for five blocks will put you at Porlamar's outdoor market on the sea. Along the way are jewelry shops and Zona Franca stores. The market which runs for five or six short blocks, offers avocados, oranges and pineapples, plus fish and soft goods. Watch the women maneuver the baskets perched atop their heads. By the way, an indoor market is under construction.

Worth exploring too is Urbanizacion Bella Vista on the Punta El Morro beach. Fishermen live on the strip closest to the sea. Their anchored boats are festooned with colorful balloons and they are extremely friendly to strangers. Goats, donkeys, pigs and assorted fowl seem to have free rein and they wander in and out of the homes. Many families sleep on hammocks with double sized units for couples. Stroll a block or two off the beach and you will find yourself in the city's most attractive residential area with colonial style homes and fashionable cars. Quite a contrast.

Beaching It

TIP

It is best and advisable to swim in the early part of the day

Yes, the beaches here are virtually endless as they ring this enchanting island. Your only problem will be to find enough time to explore even half of them. One general rule: the best swimming in most areas is the early part of the day. By 3 p.m. or so, the waters can get formidable at the open beaches, sometimes rather suddenly.

The beaches are the reason for coming to Margarita, why else? What makes Margarita different from other Caribbean islands is that it is much cheaper, being based on the Venezuelan monetary system and not a European or American one, and that it is less blatantly tourist. The majority of the beaches are quiet sun-catching white lines of sand and are not riddled with attractions such as the food stalls, wind-surfing outlets, scuba entrepreneurs, etc.

TIP

Margarita's best beaches are not in Porlamar

If you are immobile you'll be shackled to either Bella Vista beach or El Morro beach. Bella Vista beach is not wonderful. The sand is less fine and more dirty than Margarita's other beaches, and the activity a bit too jostly. El Morro is a blur of activity, with families of humans, goats, donkeys, pigs and chickens dominating the beach. It is absurd to make yourself static; renting a car, or hiring a taxi, for a day, is about a quarter of what it would cost in the U.S.

Striking off on a northern curve from Porlamar very quickly you come to **Pampatar**. The beach here is nice, calm and tranquil and dominated by a cluster of fishing boats. The setting is also majestic, with the beach shaded by Pampatar's castle and fort. But, again, you are not going to want to spend your day here if your priority is tanning and swimming.

Climbing north from Pampatar you eventually will come to **Playa** (beach) **Guacuco**. This beach is the starting line for a row of beaches that are Margarita's best, and are fit duelling partners for any in the Caribbean. Playa Guacuco is the longest stretch of beach on the island; it is almost perfect, with the surf rough enough for playing but not over-powering, and the sand as soft as a mattress. There is not much shade on the beach, so a healthy dose of sun protector is necessary so as not to fry. There is a restaurant/bar on the beach, as well as showers and restrooms. The beach here never fails to impress newcomers..

Playa Guacuco ends at the little town of **El Tirano**. And right past El Tirano, and a rocky promontory, is **Playa El Agua**, Margarita's finest beach. The beach is matchless, with great waves, palm trees and soft sand. The beach includes several restaurants, on the road, with each place renting out chairs and umbrellas for about $2 for the day. Here is a list of the restaurants in order of best to worst.

■■■■■ LA DORADO
Moderate

All the restaurants have the same set-up: terraced open dining, with a central bar. All play American rock music. All specialize in fish dishes. The snapper here is fantastic, so are the chicken dishes.

■■■■■ A TORTUGA
Moderate

Lobster and shrimp are available here, as well as exotic drinks.

■■■■■ MOONLIGHTING
Moderate

Moonlighting specializes in **Paella de Mariscos** for near $10. And Mussels at about $7. They don't always have what's on the menu, and the waiter will try and bully you into getting the dishes he wants you to have.

El Agua has a beach house with showers and bathrooms. Clothes and souvenir stalls are on the road behind the restaurants.

A squirt north from El Agua is **Playa Manzanillo**, which is only slightly less wonderful than El Agua. Playa Manzanillo is a departure point for fishermen, and the back of the beach is lined with huts, boats, nets, and other fishermen's tools. In the morning, Manzanillo's activity is great, and is a sight worth watching.

The twist around Margarita's northern spur, **Cabo Negro**, and the ride south to Juangriego is inexpressibly spectacular. The road curves and narrows like Big Sur, and you rise to see the fat face of northeast Margarita. The mountains sway and nap behind you and the water engulfs you. Below is a litany of beaches that look abandoned. Fixing your eyes south from the beach opposite Manzanillo, you can see: **Los Morros de Constanza**, **Puerto Viejo**, **Puerto Cruz**, **Bahia Pedrogonzales**, **Playa Caribe**, and **Bahia La Galeria**, the most modernly built up beach of the bunch. All of the beaches are quiet and somewhat isolated.

Finally, at Juangriego, which is on the bay, with stiller and cooler water, the sunset will glaze you.

There are numerous other beaches around the island. There is a beach at **Laguna de la Restinga**, which is only reached by a boat through the Lagoon. There are beaches near **Punta de Piedra**, and the even more untouched beaches of Peninsula de Macanao, the island of Cubagua and the island of Coche.

Porlamar

Porlamar is for shopping. From Calle Igualdad, Zamora and Guevara, at the point where they surround Plaza Bolivar, and Avenida Santiago Mariño and Avenida. 4 de Mayo, Porlamar is overheated with consumer goods. This activity is the result of Margarita's Zona Franca (Duty Free Zone), and Venezuelan's rush here with alacrity; for an American it is less enticing.

The Plaza Bolivar is a nice place to siesta if the sun is too hot and shopping has become a noodle-legged bore. The park is a social magnet, with chess games being played and people playing guitars. At one end is St. Nicholas Church.

NOTE

North Americans will not be entranced by the items Venezuelans are rushing to purchase.

At the intersection of Calle Igualdad and Calle Fraternidad is the **Museo de Arte Contemporaneo Francisco Narvarez**, which is a museum begun by and devoted to Francisco Narvarez, a respected Margaritan-born sculptor and painter.

Pampatar

A huge castle converted to a Spanish Colonial museum makes a trip to this seaport, 6 miles from Porlamar, a must. Along the road, take a 5 minute detour and visit Playa Angel, where a rock formation resembles a praying angel.

A small condensed colonial town, Pampatar is strikingly different than Porlamar. The town is largely its fort, **San Carlos Borromeo**. Destroyed in 1662 when Pampatar was burned by the Dutch, the fort had protected the town diligently until then. Rebuilt almost immediately, the fort has a central square, with four towers making a circle around the square. There is a moat, now dry, surrounding the fort, and the fort has the powerful look of hubris. Completely restored in 1968, the fort now has a museum that contains paintings of independence heroes, paintings of war scenes, historical weapons and a replica of Columbus' Santa Maria. Most popular is the **Battle of Matasiete** painting commemorating an important revolutionary battle fought in Margarita. The fort is open every day from 8 - 12 and 2 - 6.

Directly across the street is an old church which contains the **Christ of the Happy Voyage** statue. Originally destined for Peru, the statue was unloaded here because the ship carrying it from Spain couldn't weigh anchor with the statue aboard. Good beach here too.

West of the fort are a row of opulent colonial houses.

Casa Amarilla is the pink neoclassical building next to the Municipal building. It was the seat of the transitory Republican Government during the independence war.

Leaving Pampatar there are two choices. One route is to continue north (as mentioned in the beach section) and take the climbing road to its radius length and Juangriego. On that trip the island becomes visible from most angles, and there are wonderful observatory points of both the Caribbean, the beaches and the interior of the island. Each beach has a slightly different look, some so quiet and abandoned that they seem colonial, some packed with fishermen, some sporting a newly finished Condo community, and some randomly dotted with tanners. The ride is awesome, and should be done.

Museo Artesania El Caserio

Along the route the Museum of Indian Crafts is a mile north of Playa El Agua. Opened in 1978, the grounds are landscaped and manicured, and 10 one-room huts stand as prefabricated examples of life in rural Venezuela a generation ago. The main building is in the style of a hacienda house, and not only exhibits crafts, but sells them. The museum is open everyday from 9 - 5:30.

Juangriego

At this point in time Juangriego is still subdued and lazy, but it is obvious that the town is slated to be another Porlamar. Now, the town has two main streets, one paralleling the beach and the other perpendicular to it, and is quite small. Both are full of shops, and the street leading away from the beach has a white pretty church in the center.

Juangriego is a place for sunsets. The most spectacular spot to see the sun set is from **El Fortin**

TIP

Viewing a sunset from here is an absolute must

de la Galera. It is on the hill overlooking the bay and offers not only a sunset observatory but a great view of the surrounding area. There is a pizzeria on the main highway, **Avenida Jesus Rafael Laeandro**, that leads into Juangriego, right outside the street heading for the beach, and it is called **La Gran Bahia Pizzeria**.

There are two hotels:

■■■■ *HOTEL JUANGRIEGO*
62 rooms
Moderate

Predominantly condos and apartments for rent for longtime residents or tourists, 62 rooms of the large modern building are available for short-term hotel use. The rooms are as modern as the structure, and there is a restaurant and swimming pool on the premises.

■■■■ *HOTEL CLARY*
Av Jesus Rafael Laeandro
Inexpensive

A nice small family run hotel right around the bend from Juangriego's main street, Hotel Clary's rooms all have refrigerators and kitchens and air conditioning.

El Valle Del Espiritu

Inland, this town should not be missed. The original capital of Maragarita, the town was founded in 1529 by Isabel Manrique, the first governess of the island. It is a mini-Mecca for Margaritans, fishermen in particular. A fisherman, the story goes, had his leg deeply cut open by a shark. He prayed to the Virgin, offering her a pearl, to save his leg. His wound healed, and the fisherman's first pearl to her was in the shape of a tiny leg. (The pearl is displayed in the parish building across the street.) This legend still holds power for the present local residents; and they, if anatomically suffering, will pray to the Virgin; if healed, will have a piece of jewelry molded in the shape of that part of the body saved or cured as a gift.

The Virgin (the statue of the Virgin is said to have been discovered in a cave by a Guaiqueri Indian), flamboyantly dressed, is in a glass case above the altar. She receives a multitude of gifts, with many of them displayed.

The parish house is open everyday from 8 - 6.

La Asuncion

NOTE

La Asuncion is the capital of Nueva Esparta housing the government buildings

Six miles from Porlamar is the city of La Asuncion where the imposing Santa Rosa Fortress dominates the skyline. Asuncion, an authentic colonial town, is a find for history buffs.

The city is a fine example of colonial architecture and style, and is the capital of Nueva Esparta. Inland from Porlamar, the highlights of La Asuncion are mostly centered around the central Plaza Bolivar. The **Nueva Señora de la Asuncion** dates from the late 16th century. The facade is plain, almost sterile (this may have been a security precaution because of Margarita's constant attacks from pirates) except for its door. The inside is as streamlined as the outside; what makes the church interesting is that it was one of Venezuela's first – the left lateral tower is the oldest in Venezuela dating from 1599.

The **Museo Nueva Cadiz** is a potpourri of colonial and pre-colonial items. Displays vary from pre-colonial artifacts to local handicrafts. The museum used to be the Casa Capitular, the seat of the colonial government. It is open from 8 - 12 and 2 - 5.

Also in town are the **Casada la Cultura**, which houses samples of all the varying kinds of pottery in Venezuela, and the **Casa de Juan Bautista Arismendi**, devoted to the Margaritan-born Independence War hero. The government buildings are also worth seeing.

La Asuncions's most special attraction, in my mind, is **Castillo de Santa Rosa** (Santa Rosa Fort). Located high up on a hill, across from the hospital, the fort opens-up most of the island for viewing.

Begun in the late 17th century, the fort's obvious strategic value is its observatory prominence and that fact that it was inland. The fort was built with a tunnel that led to the Governor's house, the convent of San Francisco and the church. Castillo de Santa Rosa's most famous prisoner was the wife of Juan Bautista Arismendi, Luisa. The cell in which she languished with her newly born dead baby has been kept almost the same as it was when she was in it. The inscription above the door reads "Luisa Caceres de Arismendi for her virtue and valor and martyrdom for her husband and country as prisoner in this jail at 16 years of age."

The fort has several rooms that contain colonial weaponry, knights in armor, paintings of Bolivar, iron balls that were attached to prisoner's legs and a bottle dungeon. It retains, with eyes closed, its colonial feel of militarism.

From the fort the view of the island is magnificent, showing-off the mountainous interior and the crevices of flatness by the sea. The fort was obviously efficient in snatching attacks from the east, north and south, but the west part of the island is invisible.

The fort is open everyday from 8 am - 6 pm. A small donation is required.

El Cercado

The village on the west end is where to pick up ceramic pots and vases. Nice gifts and inexpensive. Soft brown or chocolate in color, the vases range in price from $1 to $5. Visit the local factory for the best selection. Recommended.

La Restinga Lagoon

TIP

All in all, La Restinga is very romantic. Bring someone you like

The highlight of your Margarita visit may well be a motor boat ride through this lagoon. Located in the narrow isthmus connecting the two parts of Margarita, the area is noted for thick Mangrove trees, its bird life and oyster beds.

La Restinga is at the Western tip of Margarita. Enroute, from Porlamar, the ride offers a view of the landscape of Peninsula de Macanao. The Lagoon is a maze of channels (named kitschy things like "My Sweet Love Canal", "Garden of Love", "Tunnel of Love") that intersect each other at random, and are shaded by mangroves – the lagoon would be a great place for a James Bond chase scene. The motorboat ride costs about $4 and eventually takes you to the barrier reef that connects Margarita island with Peninsula de Macanao. At the beach on the reef are several open air restaurants. The water is warmer at this end, but the sand is much rockier. Your boat driver will stop as long as you want. From the lagoon there is great bird watching, with hawks and pelicans somewhat common, and a view of **Tetas de Maria Guevara**, two hills resembling a woman's breasts and dedicated to the memory of a local woman, popular with visiting sailors.

From La Restinga you can continue to Peninsula de Macanao, which is mainly unpeopled. This excursion will take about a half hour and is worth viewing for its beauty. The beach is unusual consisting of crushed shells.

Museo Del Mar

At the entrance to **Boca del Rio**, the museum is a model of aquatic life. In a range of exhibits, many fish and crustaceans are displayed, as well as reefs and ocean plant life. The museum is run by the University of the East. The hours are Monday - Friday 8 - 12, 1 - 5.

Ferry

From **Punta de Piedra**, near Peninsula de Macanao, is the ferry to Puerto La Cruz, and boats to the island of Cubagua, which in its unadulterated natural state, is worth the short and interesting trip. On the island are archaeological sites of the islands abandoned civilization.

MARGARITA AFTER DARK

When Venezuela Alive was last written nightlife in Margarita was almost nonexistent. Since that time, a dog track and discos have sprung up, but still the island is not shaking with energy after sunset. Predictably, the nightlife that does exist is in Porlamar. Yet, in a way, Margarita's slim nightlife is not absurd; the sun is so intense and violent that even with competent sun protector your body gets cooked; and, late nights lead to late mornings, and Margarita, it beaches, its nature, its sites are day activities.

Rumors have been circulating for many years that a gambling Casino in Margarita is imminent. But as far as I can learn the rumors are just that and nothing more. Therefore night people here will have to learn to live like day people at least while on this island. For the fact is there's just not much to do here vertically after the sun slips away. I have visited Margarita at least a dozen times and have never felt the quiet nights here to be a handicap.

The Dog Track (Canodromo)

On the road from Porlamar to Pampatar is, quite visibly, an amusement park and race track. The ferris wheel dominates. But make no mistake about it, on Thursday, Friday and Saturday nights the lure are the greyhounds. The dogs race in a lovely open air stadium with purple, blue and orange seating areas. The dogs start chasing the rabbit promptly at 8 pm. Your bet (apuesto) can be as little as 50 cents. There is no admission charge.

NOTE

Apart from the dog races, the only legal gambling in Venezuela involves the horse racing in Valencia (Thursdays), Maracaibo (Saturday and Sunday) and Caracas (Saturday and Sunday).

Next door is a sleek amusement park for the kiddies and a cock fighting area (not for the queezie).

Your best bet is a taxi which will get you to the track in less than 15 minutes.

Discos

DOCE 34
Av 4 de Mayo
Open 10 - 4
Singles admitted

Margarita's numero uno disco, Doce 34 is modern black and very American in style. There is a hint of Studio 54 is the dico's approach and style. The place is large and energetic, and features American and Latin American music.

MAXIMO DISCO
Av 4 de Mayo
Open 11 - 3
Singles admitted

Right next to the bowling alley, Maximo is smaller than Doce 34. It seems less popular, but that might not be true. Also very American in look, Maximo is usually teamed-up with a previous bowl. Why not consider combining a night of bowling and dancing?

PINK PANTHER
Hotel Guaiqueri
Av Raul Leone
Open 10 - 4
Singles admitted

In the wonderfully pink Hotel Guaiqueri is the Pink Panther disco. Lively, and right on the water, the Pink Panther looks like a lot of fun.

Piano Bars

You can cocktail it pleasurably at any of the hotels, particularly as follows:

Hotel Concorde

Piano Blanco
(next to Hotel For You)

Bella Vista Hotel

Hotel Guaiqueri

Another favorite of ours is the piano bar at Restaurant O Sole Mio da Rosetta.

Bowling

Pin enthusiasts can assuage their passion at the 6 lane Margarita Bowling Club on Avenida. 4 de Mayo near the old airport. It is open nightly from 5 - 2. (Sunday until midnight) and a line will cost you $1.50. Shoe rentals are $1. Snack bar in rear.

SHOPS AND SHOPPING

TIP

Local pearls and handicrafts are best buys on Margarita

Margarita is often called the island of pearls and the rich oyster beds yield unusually shaped pearls. However, don't overlook great buys in ceramic, wood carvings, woven hammocks and straw articles which often are attractive works of art.

Shopping, of course, is dominated by the stores selling international goods with no duty; the Zona Franca has squeezed local handicrafts into a corner and made international goods paramount. The avenues of Santiago Mariño and 4 de Mayo are stuffed with stores, and Calles Igualdad, Guevara and Macanao are also brimming with shops.

Pearls

Margarita pearls are primarily pink in color, fairly small and come in unusual shapes. I suggest you buy unset pearls and have them set at home. There are some shops here selling jewelry using Margaritan pearls and we'll discuss those later. Also sold here are cultivated pearls from Japan. These come in whites, grays and blacks and are good buys too.

For pearls try first the **Casa Avila**, Calle Gomez 47 which owner Juan Avila Guerra operates from his home. He has bags of pearls and tosses them out on a green felt table as if they were grains of rice. Both Margarita and cultivated pearls here. Prices start at $10 and go up depending on color and size. Bargaining is advised.

The **Museo Artesania el Caserio**, as mentioned before, sells crafts from all over Venezuela; the items are genuine, well-made and unique.

On the route from La Asuncion to **Tacarigua** there are several stalls selling native crafts and goods, from hammocks to sandals.

El Cercado, a village on the west end of the island, features good pottery. The factory in town is worth visiting. El Cercado is one mile from Santa Ana.

Finally a shop we're usually frequenting is **Los Makiritares** at the end of Calle Igualdad not far from the Bella Vista Hotel. Head up one flight of stairs for a huge selection of local handicrafts.

TRANSPORTATION

Taxis have no meters so fix your price in advance. To most parts of town expect to pay between 50 cents and $1. Por puestos (private autos operating as jitneys) are common and for 12 cents you can get from San Nicholas Church to the Hotel Bella Vista in about 5 minutes.

ETCETERA ETCETERA

AIRLINES

Avensa

Airport 691021; Porlamar, No. 47 Calle Mariño, 31701.

LAV

Airport 23766; Porlamar, Edifico Don Claudio, Calle Fajardo, 32471.

CAR RENTALS

The biggest car rental firm is **Oriental**, which has outlets in the Bella Vista Hotel, Hotel For You, the Concorde and the airport. Their numbers are 22346 at the airport and 24675 in town.

Avis - Airport 691036; Hotel Bella Vista

Budget - Airport 22364; Hotel Bella Vista

Hertz - Airport 691074; Hotel Bella Vista

National - Airport 601171; Hotel Bella Vista

Volkswagen - Airport 22605; Avenida 4 de Mayo 31575

The tourist information office is located in the Bella Vista Hotel.

TOURS

Tours can be arranged from the travel agencies in the Bella Vista Hotel, the Oriental car rental office, and the Concorde Hotel, and Hotel For You.

BAKERY

For delicious pastries stop at Panderia Laura on Calle Igualdad near Casa del Hobby.

BANK

A good bank to exchange money is **Banco de la Construccion** on Calle Guevara corner of Calle Maneiro (open 8 - 11:30, 2 - 4:30 Monday to Friday).

BARBER

We recommend **Barberia Paris** on Calle Santiago Mariño two blocks beyond Hotel Colibri. A good beauty shop is La Capital, Calle Igualdad near the Plaza Bolivar.

DR. SCHOLL

A local branch is at Calle Zamora 18 and is open 8:30 - 12:30, 2:30 - 6:00 Monday to Friday. Saturday am only.

FERRY

Arrangements and information regarding passage from Punta de Piedras to Puerto La Cruz or Cumaná on the mainland can be made at "Conferrys" at Calle La Marina no. 30 Phone: 2687.

NEWSPAPERS

The Daily Journal is sold at the Hilton, Concorde and Hotel Bella Vista's gift shop and at the Heladeria Tiuna downtown at calle Mariño off Calle Guevara. Time magazine too.

OYSTERS

These cost about 60 cents per dozen on the half shell. Local fishermen of Bella Vista beach and elsewhere sell them and your waiter will serve them.

PHARMACIES

These are plentiful and well-stocked with U.S. Drugs and sundries. There is always a drug store open 24 hours.

PIÑATAS

La Isleña on Calle Guevara near Calle Maneiro stocks an attractive variety of these paper mache figures for children.

POST OFFICE

Located at the corner of Calle Gomez and Calle San Nicholas; you can also send radiograms here.

SUPERMARKET

Drop in at Supermercado Ultramar on Calle Guevara for any foodstuffs you might require.

Venezuela

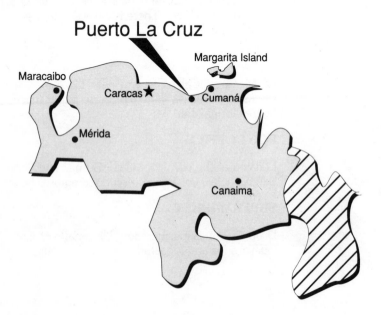

Puerto La Cruz

Margarita Island

Maracaibo

Caracas ★

Cumaná

Mérida

Canaima

PUERTO LA CRUZ

Puerto La Cruz is Venezuela's gateway to the Caribbean, a now well-furnished small city that has the contagious laziness of salt air and the high energy of a vacation spot.

Puerto La Cruz is on the sea, technically the bay, and is not far, separated by water of course, from Margarita. It hugs the larger town of **Barcelona**, and is an hour and a half away from Cumaná, the other beach resort town on the Caribbean.

Puerto La Cruz has fantastic beaches, good hotels and the liveliness of a beach town, with a strip that is brimming with restaurants and shops. It is not too overwhelming, as a large city can be, making you feel small and confused in its presence, and not so small that there is only one restaurant, one hotel, making you feel deserted.

The town, or small city, is growing, with condos and more hotels going up. The city is becoming a stomping ground for weekend tourists from Caracas, and is becoming slightly more popular with an international crowd. It does seem, however, that Canadians have already found the treasure of Puerto La Cruz because they dominate the international population.

Water sports abound, of course, with snorkeling and scuba diving the main attractions. The coral formations off Puerto La Cruz are fabulous and complex, and both these sports are widely practiced here. There is also boating, sailing, fishing, water-skiing and para-sailing. With its fantastic climate, not searing in the day but definitely hot, and warm spring nights, its lyrical promenade on Paseo Colon, the main street, and rejuvenating atmosphere, Puerto La Cruz is a find, and should not be missed.

HISTORY

Oil has a way of bringing attention, and Puerto La Cruz is a recipient of its lust. For close to 400 years Puerto La Cruz treaded in anonymity, languishing as a fisherman's pit-stop. It was known simply as "la playa" (the beach), and it was just that for fishermen from the interior and Margarita, who used it to rest and dry out their catches.

The first transformation, although minor, for Puerto La Cruz was in the early 1800's when the fishing grounds around Chimana were discovered. Instead of stopping for a few hours, a night perhaps, Margariteños now began to spend longer periods of time on the beach of Puerto La Cruz. Eventually, out of pragmatism, some of these people began building homes.

The second bout of growth, more accurately described as popularity, came with Venezuelan tourists, mainly from Caracas, who came here for the beaches and the alkaline waters of the **Spring of the Sacred Cross**.

Finally, in 1937, the first quarts of oil were found in the savannahs south of Puerto La Cruz, and this led to the oil Terminal at the foot of Guaraguao Hill, east of the town. As the fulcrum for oil, the town inflated.

With over 100,000 people today, Puerto La Cruz is the number five port in the world in volumes of oil shipped. This, of course, has made it a thriving commercial center. With its fantastic beaches, Puerto La Cruz has grown as a tourist spot, and the city is responding with great hotels and a tourist oriented structure. The city is still on its first leg of development, with officials eyeballing the future with zealousness and optimism, continuing to push Puerto La Cruz along its path as a central beach destination.

ORIENTATION

Unless you are driving from Caracas, which will soon require only two and a half hours, you'll fly to the city of Barcelona, which is adjacent to Puerto La Cruz. A taxi from the airport to the **Melia Hotel**, which is one of the two main hotels, is about a 20 minute ride. The **Doral Hotel**, the other central place, is much closer. There is a hotel in Barcelona, Hotel Barcelona, but only stay there in a pinch.

The largest structure in the city is the Melia Hotel, which is right on the beach, off Paseo Colon, the central tourist street in Puerto La Cruz. Paseo Colon is the boardwalk of Atlantic City, with the predominance of restaurants, hotels, and night-spots located on it. Activity revolves around Paseo Colon, and unless interested, you will begin to feel that Puerto La Cruz is just Paseo Colon and its tributaries.

On the tourist map that is available in town the only spots listed off Paseo Colon are: a supermarket on Calle Maneiro, which runs perpendicular to Paseo Colon; Plaza Bolivar, in which Calle Bolivar, a block south of Paseo Colon, defines its bottom side and Calle Liberatador its top side; and La Bahia, a seafood restaurant next to the Plaza Bolivar.

Everything else on the map is on Paseo Colon, on its stretch from the Melia Hotel at the eastern end to its western boarder at Calle Anzoategui.

There is a promenade near the public beach, on Paseo Colon, and it is also a nucleus of activity. The promenade is open from 8 am to 8 pm. Between the promenade and Paseo Colon most of Puerto La Cruz's energy and life are enacted.

A few miles away near Barcelona, as a sign of future development, there is the **Complejo Turistico el Morro**, a series of condominium apartments and houses of 5-star quality.

The Doral Hotel is located in this area on the beach.

As mentioned before the Melia and Doral Hotels dominate, and are the only choices for most tourists in Puerto La Cruz.

HOTELS

MELIA PUERTO LA CRUZ 5 *
Paseo Colon
220 Rooms
Phone: (081) 691311
Telex: 81104 MELIA VC
Deluxe

TIP

Some of the cities best restaurants are in this hotel

On the beach, the Melia looks like a first-class hotel, with its sparkling white trim structure. Every room has a terrace, and like many 5-star hotels, it is a city to itself. There is a whole complex of shops, ranging from a newsstand to car rentals to a sports shop. There is a pool, gym and sauna, game room, tennis, laundry service, drugstore, disco and five restaurants. Its crowning attraction are the watersports available:scuba material, sail boats, boat rides, instructors and guides. Lastly, there are conference centers, with the largest space able to hold up to 1,000 people. It is a great hotel.

DORAL BEACH HOTEL 5*
Av Americo Vespucio
Complejo Turistico El Morro
1,312 Rooms
Phone: (081) 87921
Telex: 29425

TIP

The water sport facilities are fabulous at the Doral

The other first-class hotel is the Doral, a huge complex that is on the beach but further out of town. More sprawling than high, there is a huge central pool, tennis, golf and the other things that come with a deluxe hotel. But what the Doral really specializes in is water activities. With **Aquaventura** working out of the premises, the hotel offers para-sailing, aqua rocket rides, water skiing, wind surfing, kayacs, tube rides, water sledding, pedal boats, fishing, sailing, snorkeling, scuba diving and boat excursions. That is a mouthful, but it is all centered at the Doral, and can keep you active for weeks. The Doral's two restaurants offer continental and Polynesian food.

HOSTERIA EL MORRO
Complejo Turistico El Morro
146 Rooms
Phone: (081) 814157, 814335
Moderate

Near the Doral, Hosteria El Morro is a nice small hotel on the beach. It has a pool and serves buffets by its side, and also has a snack bar. The rooms are small, but nice and comfortable and air-conditioned. Unimposing but attractive.

HOTEL GAETA
Paseo Colon
52 Rooms
Phone: 691816, 691817
Moderate

With four floors, Hotel Gaeta is in the thick of things on Paseo Colon. Its top floor restaurant offers great views of the city and sea.

HOTEL SENADOR
Calle Miranda, Plaza Bolivar
34 Rooms
Phone: 22034, 22035
Moderate

Only one block off Paseo Colon, this small but pleasant hotel has the comfort of a good soft bed, a nice hot shower and cool somnolent air conditioning but nothing else outstanding.

HOTEL BARCELONA
Av 5 de Julio
Barcelona
70 Rooms
Phone: 771087
Moderate

In the city of Barcelona, not near a beach, this hotel is good only if the other five are full. It is a pleasant hotel, large and modern in its look, but doesn't have much to offer, and is not on the beach. It is comfortable, however, and clean.

RESTAURANTS

TIP

You should definitely try the Cuajao at least once

Most of Puerto La Cruz's best restaurants are predictably on Paseo Colon, although there are some off the main drag. Prices are not steep, although the fancy restaurants in the Melia and Doral are more expensive than the rest. But even in those restaurants you will pay no more than $15 per person for a hearty dinner.

There are several dishes that are indigenous to the region that you might want to try. **Cuajao**, a dish made with mullet or loach roe, stewed fish, and braised sawfish in round slices are the most common local dishes. Otherwise the fare will be the equivalent of what is served in Venezuelas other cities. However, you can expect lower prices for the most part.

TASCA MAR
Melia Hotel
Open 7 - 11 pm
Expensive

One of the best restaurants in the city, Tasca Mar specializes in Spanish and seafood dishes. The interior parallels the food, with a strange mixture of colonial and nautical design. There is live music, and the dishes to try are the cold fish stew, (**esqueixada Catalina**), and **paella**, **mero en cazuela** (cassarole of bass) and gazpacho soup.

LA PEQUEÑA ROMA
Calle Bolivar
Centro Comercial Mar
Phone: 668624
Moderate

Billed as "A small piece of Italy in Puerto La Cruz," La Pequeña Roma has a homey setting, with couches and lounge chairs, and serves great pizza and ravioli. Giorgio Cherubini is a fine host.

EL DORADO
Calle Bolivar and Carabobo
Phone: 22840
Moderate

El Dorado serves very good continental food. You can eat outdoors, and like La Pequeña Roma is set-up in an informal loungy way, with wicker chairs. Its best dishes are the **filet mero**, **filet mignon**, and **escabeche dorado**, revolving around a meat and fish theme. Take the elevator to the second floor.

LA TARANTELLA
Melia Hotel
Moderate

On the lobby of the hotel, La Tarantella offers formal dinning, with marble floors, green table clothes, organ music and the dim light setting of a hushed-toned eatery. Except for an Italian version of the fish stew the meals are typically Italian and tasty.

▬▬▬ BRASERO
Paseo Colon
Inexpensive

TIP

Some consider this the best in Puerto La Cruz

Also concentrating on fish and meat, Brasero makes it excellently. It's the kind of food that looks the same but itches your taste buds just that extra amount that you think about the food a little longer after paying your bill.

▬▬▬ LA BELLA CHINA
Paseo Colon
Phone: 961985
Inexpensive

Serving good Chinese food at reasonable prices. It's located near the Melia Hotel.

▬▬▬ TIO PEPE
Paseo Colon 11
Phone: 23144
Inexpensive

Very much a Spanish motif with posters of Spain on the walls and waiters dressed in typical Spanish clothes. Try the **Bacalao a la Gallega** and **Calamares en su tinta** (squid in its ink).

▬▬▬ BONASERA PIZZERIA
Paseo Colon
Phone: 24069
Inexpensive

A good Italian restaurant. This place is usually crowded even when others are not. Call for a reservation. I can still savor the excellent veal pizzaola.

LA BAHIA
Paseo Colon
(in front of Hotel Riviera)
Phone: 23752
Inexpensive

A large outdoor dinning room, on a patio, right on the beach makes La Bahia balmy and fun. The food is excellent, with **filet**, **pargo**, **mero** (bass) and **lobster** the highlights.

FUENTEMAR
Paseo Colon
Inexpensive

Similar to La Bahia but not quite as good. Outdoor patio dining, ideal when the weather is right.

RESTAURANT BIG GARDEN
Paseo Colon 91
Phone: 21765

Sharing its space with a disco and dance floor, Restaurant Big Garden specializes in seafood.

TONG SING
Paseo Colon
Phone: 22850

Typically Chinese in style, Tong Sing has great food, particularly the lo meins and seafood dishes.

GITANERIAS
Paseo Colon
Phone: 21439
Inexpensive

Spanish food is the mainstay here, with paella and chicken and rice topping the list. In Gypsy decor that is a bit chaotic but fun. The paella is as good as it gets in these parts and the **arroz con pollo** is good too.

■■■■■ *RESTAURANT COLONIAL*
Hotel Doral
Open 7 - 11:30 pm
Moderate

More formal than most of the restaurants mentioned, this place also specializes in Spanish food, but also serves international dishes as well as local ones.

■■■■■ *CAFETERIA MELIA*
Melia Hotel

TIP

Near the pool scenic and offers fast service

A snack bar that has salads, soups, sandwiches and burgers and is by the pool, Cafeteria Melia is a great place to relax and have a light meal. If particularly hungry there is also heavier meals like pabellon criollo (beef, black beans, rice and plantains) and stewed fish.

FAST FOOD

Tropi

Like Burger King, Tropi has many branches, the closest one in front of the Melia. It serves burgers, hot dogs, shakes, pizza and other tasty but junky delights.

El Paseo De Los Canales

A fast food center, look for a huge green sign that marks the entrance. Housed in the complex is a **Tropi**, **La Alemanita**, which serves sausages and pies, **Pizza King**, **Arizonas**, serving Mexican food, **Chip-A-Cookie**, **Barquilla**, for ice cream, and **Chinatown**. There is even more, if you can believe it. It's a fun place; bring the kids.

SUNUP TO SUNDOWN

Water Sports

The sea is the reason to be in Puerto La Cruz and the water is a haven for athletics whether done with the intensity of a professional to the lighthearted-ness of a dilettante. There are so many sports, that if you have any quest to try them all you'll need either two to three weeks or a week that has no sleep.

The coral formations of the islands are rich and plentiful and should be viewed. There is a plethora of shells that can be looked at in a simple outing. Scuba is of course more complex but safe in these waters since they are never rough. There are a multitude of sights for diving and that information is easily gotten.

Renting local boats for the day is not hard, and is usually done on an hourly basis. Prices should be arranged with the owner before departing.

The **Aquaventura** agency in the Doral Hotel has a gamut of activities to offer. There are snorkeling trips to the nearby islands for either half a day, at about $10, or the whole day at under $20. It is a 20 minute ride to the islands, and snorkeling gear and refreshments are included.

As necessary, Aquaventura also has a full day course in scuba diving for $40. Then, after the course, there are either one dive or two dive trips, at $35 and $50, respectively. The diving trips are at volcano mouths, marine canyons, blue lagoons and coral reefs.

Aquaventura also offers aqua rocket rides, water skiing, wind surfing, tube rides, water sleds and boat trips. None of these rentals or activities is over $15. There is also para-sailing, flying over the water, at $15.

The **Explosub** agency in the Melia Hotel also offers a range of activities. There is a boat ride to a local island, an island hopping cruise to four of the prettiest islands and lagoons and the whole range of under water sports.

Explosub offers a "Pirate Cruise " on the Kanaloa, an authentic pirate ship of an elder era.

There is a "Moonlight Fantasy Cruise" at dusk that is designed for lovers, of course.

And lastly, there is an all-day beach party that is offered. Snorkeling, beach games, frisbee, volley-ball, BBQ, music and floating bar are all on the itinerary. This runs for $20 per person.

Walking Tour

A half day walking tour of the city is a good way to orient yourself with the city and see a bit of its history. The main street is Paseo Colon, the hub of tourist activity. Walking its length, about a mile, starting from the Melia Hotel, you'll take in the beach, and outdoor roving consumer stalls, in which you can buy jewelry, leather goods, belts and other nice items.

On Calle Sucre turn left, south, and in one block you will reach Plaza Bolivar, a nice square. Two blocks from there, off Calle Anzoategui is a pretty church.

You might want to walk back as far as Avenida Municipal to get a real feel for the local life, but Avenida 5 de Julio is a good place to make the turn back to the Melia Hotel, making a wide rectangle of a walk.

Municipal Gallery of Modern Art

A small permanent collection of paintings and sculptures by native artists is exhibited here free of charge. It is located just past the **Alfonso Car-**

rasquel **Stadium** in a small one-story building.
The hours are Tuesday - Friday 9 - 12, 3 - 6 and
Saturdays and Sundays 3 - 6.

Ferry To Margarita

NOTE

*The ferrys are
conveniently located
in town*

There are ferrys from Puerto La Cruz to Margarita.
You can use the ferry as a means to get to
Maragarita for a longer stay or merely a day's trip.

The **Gran Cacique** is a ship that only takes
pedestrians and takes two hours and a half to reach
Punta de Piedras in Margarita. It is a two-level ship
that costs $3 for a first class ticket. The Gran
Cacique has two sister ships, the **Gran Cacique II**
and **III**. Departure times are 7 am and 2 pm from
Puerto La Cruz and 10 am and 6 pm from
Margarita.

The **Conferry** takes automobiles and is a four hour
trip. The cost is $6, and it has many departure
times:

From Puerto La Cruz - 4 am, 7 am, noon, 4 pm,
7 pm and midnight.

From Margarita - 7 am, 10 am, noon, 6 pm, 10 pm
and midnight.

El Morro Tourist Complex

The Complejo Turistico El Morro is a massive
project that would see the construction of 500 one-
family homes, each with a few acres, 1000 house-
boat lots, a large shopping center, modern docks,
condo apartments, hotels and a golf course.

Obviously the desire is for a real estate push for
both foreigners and locals hoping to have a beach
resort home. Very Floridian in concept, the El
Morro Complex is a huge venture and should be
seen.

It is near the Doral Hotel and about 3 miles from Barcelona.

Amusement Park

On the Paseo Colon is **Guayaneven** which has bumper cars, ferris wheels, and other rides.

Los Altos Lookout

TIP

Obviously you will need a taxi or auto rental to get here

About 11 miles out of Puerto La Cruz is the fantastic 2925 foot natural observatory. From this point you can see the beaches, bays and islands that make up the shore of Eastern Venezuela. The view is limitless and stunning, giving one the feeling of eternity and nature that is only stirred by the salty winds.

The road also continues on past the lookout into highlands that are interesting to see.

Bring sweaters if you come at dusk.

SIGHTS IN BARCELONA

Barcelona is about 20 minutes from Puerto La Cruz and offers more historic sites.

Casa Fuerte

With a strange and exciting history, Casa Fuerte started as a Franciscan hospice, **Convento de San Francisco**, and later became a military stronghold only to be run over and pounded by Spanish troops in the Independence War.

The monks who owned the hospice in the 18th and 19th centuries were the pupils of the Franciscan with austere values that saw their role as caretakers of the poor and sick and alienated. The hospice housed the residue of Barcelona, and the monks also used the house as a departure point for missionary action down south.

NOTE

*Another date
that has lived in
infamy*

Refusing to accept the constitution of Venezuela during the independence battle made them lose Casa Fuerte. It was transformed into a fort. It had immediate success, but that was brutally ended in a battle that took place on April 17, 1817. General Jose Adama grounded-out all his enemies in a forceful attack, letting the victory intoxicate him. In his stupor he killed everyone in sight, regardless of age and gender, and, in particular, killed Major Chamberlain, an Irishman from Jamaica who swore allegiance to Bolivar's cause. His death became legend in Europe where tales and poems were written about him.

The ruins became a national landmark, and have stayed that way since the battle.

Museo De La Tradicion

A potpourri of historic items, the Museum of Tradition is more like an antique shop. The house itself is the fourth one built in Barcelona in 1671, and the oldest one standing. It has been recreated in its colonial style.

The museum has about 400 items of Indian, colonial and post-colonial interest. There are statues of saints, old stones, street signs warning against leaning on the lightpost after six pm because of electrocution, and other odd relics.

The museum is open everyday from 8 - 12, 3 - 6.

Opposite Casa Fuerte is Plaza Bolivar, and from the Plaza is a cluster of interesting sights. There is **Plaza Miranda**, **Plaza Boyaca**, the main plaza of the city and government, and the **Cathedral of Barcelona**. These are all in a cluster and are easily taken in by a short stroll. If you allocate an hour or two you can leisurely view these places and savor their history. We recommend it.

SHOPPING

On Paseo Colon is a string of shops and boutiques. But also there are street vendors selling art, leather items, masks, jewelry, hats, belts and tapes. It is the most fun shop on this stretch because it is the most active and alive.

■ LA PRICESA
Paseo Colon, above Hotel Riviera

For jewelry, gold, emeralds, diamonds, rubies and other stones this is a good place to shop.

■ JOYERIA
Av 5 de Julio No. 56
Phone: 21136

Also for jewelry. Good prices.

■ PLAYMON
ARTESANIA Y DEPORTES
Paseo Colon
Phone: 24569

For local handicrafts and souvenirs this is a good place to look around.

NIGHT LIFE

Puerto La Cruz does not have a searing night life, although it is not empty. There are a few good discos on Paseo Colon and in the shopping centers. But there is one great disco.

■ CLUB GUATACARAZO
Paseo Colon

A flamboyant club that was called, on TV, the best club in Venezuela, Club Guatacarazo is a trip.

How about getting married and not worrying about alimony? This club is structured for lovers, for

NOTE

*I have 2 certificates
hanging in my office*

flingers, for one-night-standers. A matrimonial city, you are greeted at the bar with a cup, in the shape of a breast, filled with champagne. With a marriage confession, and Club Guatacarazo, you are hitched. You even get a marriage certificate and waiters singing "here comes the bride". Inside is swinging and wild. Costumed waiters add to the festivities. Don't miss it.

▄▄▄▄ CARIBIANO
Melia Hotel
Open 9 - 3, Weekends 9 - 4,
(Closed Sunday)

A nice hopping place, Caribiano has a large dance floor, with tables surrounding it and couches lining the walls.

▄▄▄▄ LA BAMBOLA
Av Alberto Ravell
Open 7 - 3
Phone: 22968

Behind the amusement park, La Bambola is modern and trim, with black and neon confronting you at its entrance. There is a visible and elevated dj, and a nice-sized dance floor.

▄▄▄▄ SEPTIMO CIELO
Calle Bolivar
Phone: 23642

Across from the Dorado Restaurant, Septimo Cielo has a Hawaiian look to it and is sparkling orange.

▄▄▄▄ DISCOTHEQUE SENADOR
Open 9 - 2, Weekends 9 - 4

Next to Senador Hotel, this disco is fun and pleasant.

IV DIMENSION
Calle Bolivar 32B
Open 9 - 2, Weekends 9 - 5
Phone: 691752

Fast-moving and jumpy, this disco is a good place to meet singles.

STUDIO 99

Near the Doral Hotel. This is another lively disco.

BAR MORICHE
Melia Hotel

For a more relaxed and seated evening, the bar in the Melia is plush and intimate – a good place to meet people. Location: right in the lobby.

ETCETERA ETCETERA

Casa Scholl
Calle Anzoategui
Phone: 23162

For aching feet.

Avensa
Edifico Pepsi
Phone: 663101

Viasa
Phone: 663011

Pan Am
Phone: 22950

Aeropostal
Phone: 691968

PUERTO LA CRUZ TO CUMANÁ

The 50 mile coastal road from Puerto La Cruz to Cumaná is poetic, a link of nature that makes you

TIP

*This is a must trip.
If you staying in
Cumaná drive there.
If not its a wonderful
day trip by taxi or
auto rental.*

feel awed. The viewers are staggered with offshore islands and slightly hidden beaches and coves which hint at the shore's beauty. The ride is eternal in that you feel you can see forever and that it will probably stick with you, maybe even after death.

Along the route are many beaches, of course, and small towns. The first beach is **Arapito**, which has a few small places to eat, and the first town is **Guanta**. Just past Guanta is a turn-off for **Parque La Sirena** (there will be road signs), above the village of **Chorreron**. The park is worth going to because of its river and waterfall, and the natural pools of water that form. In the rainy season these pools are great to swim in, but the park is also nice because of picnicking (there are charcoal grills) and walks.

TIP

*Stop for a taste of
Cachapa, fresh and
delicious*

Also near Guanta is the **Vencemos Zoo**, owned by the Mendoza Cement Company. The zoo was set-up to show native Venezuelan animals, and is in a coconut grove next to the water. To get to the zoo you must turn right off the highway at the Pertigalete sign.

Consistently along the route you will see women making **cachapa**, a melange of ground corn, sugar and salt in a flat cake. It is cooked on a wooden fire, and it is communally done, with the children participating.

The second beach you come to is **Playa Colorado** (Red Beach), which is more narrow than Arapito but more popular. From Colorado you can rent (on weekends) a boat to take you to the parallel islands of **Arapo** and **Arapito**. There are nice beaches on the islands, and some fishing families live there.

The next beach is **Playa Los Hicacos**, a beach for the professors and students of Club Universitario UDO Los Hicacos. You then come upon **Playa**

Santa Cruz, a fishing village 18 miles from Puerto La Cruz. Since it faces west the sunsets are fabulous.

The Valley of Santa Fe, the surrounding area, is a fertile valley that sits upon the gulf and is home to many fishermen. It is the part of South America that was first exposed to missionaries, coming from the island of Santo Domingo.

TIP

Mochima Bay is the highlight of this trip

Probably the most outstanding piece of the stretch between Puerto La Cruz and Cumaná is **Mochima Bay**, 30 miles from Puerto La Cruz. Mochima Bay is a part of an entire region of cliffs and bays and waterways that wind and twist between the mainland and the Caribbean. It is divided into 6% islands, 52% water and 42% land, which gives you and idea of its maze-like beauty. The mainland is composed of narrow valleys and rugged hillsides, and the ecology is aquatic vegetation, mangrove trees, and coral reefs. It is obviously a wonderland of nature, a preservation of time slightly toyed with.

Mochima is designated a National Park and it has become popular with water-skiers and boaters. From Mochima you can get boats into the interior bays and cliffs. It should not be missed.

Through Bella Vista you come to the penultimate town of **Barbacoas**. Barbacoas is famous for its dolls and they are on sale all along the road. They are colorful and imaginative, and even if you are not buying one you should stop and look at them. The next stop is Cumaná.

NOTES:

Venezuela

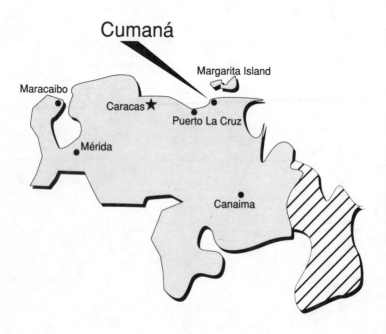

Cumaná

Margarita Island

Maracaibo

Caracas ★

Puerto La Cruz

Mérida

Canaima

CUMANÁ
CASTLE ON THE MOUNTAIN

**I**n this warm Caribbean city of 100,00 a magnificent star-shaped restored colonial fortress towers over the city. And its dungeons and cannon are only part of the reason for visiting Cumaná which – as the Western Hemisphere's oldest city – still retains its Spanish Colonial charm. The red tile roofs delineate the colonial sector with its narrow cobblestoned streets and 18th century churches.

For those of you who like your history in small doses, Cumaná does offer something more – miles of nearby immaculate beaches in use year round. Too, it is a jumping off point for the ferry to Margarita and many Caraqueños combine vacations here and the islands.

A QUICK ORIENTATION

Your flight via **Avensa** or **Aeropostal** will land at Aeropuerto **Gran Mariscal de Ayacucho** in El Piñon, 15 minutes by cab from your hotel. Or you can rent a car at the airport Volkswagen rent-a-car office. In driving into town after settling in your hotel, you will find yourself passing through the San Luis section along **Avenida Universidad**, which leads into center city. The inner city begins at the **Plaza Nueva Toledo** where reposes a statue of a Cumanagoto Indian holding aloft a fish.

To the left of the Plaza is the major street of **Calle Perimetral**, a two-way thoroughfare (unusual here) which houses a number of recommended restaurants. Intersecting Calle Perimetral are the two shopping streets of **Avenida Bermudez** and **Calle Mariño**. **Plaza Miranda**, which marks the beginning of "colonial Cumaná", is across the bridge on the bank of the **Manzanares River** and is the starting point for our recommended walking tour. Keep in mind that the Manzanares River bisects the city, with the areas closest to the river colonial and the modern area furthest from it. The best resort hotels understandably are located on the Caribbean, not far from the airport.

A CAPSULE HISTORY

NOTE

Cumaná was the first settlement founded by the Spanish on the mainland of South America. This alone makes it special.

It was in 1506 that the first true, but unintended, steps towards colonization began. Although the missionaries that arrived had no specific intention to colonize, the foundation was set for a European presence. The first Franciscan missionaries were received benevolently by the Indians, and they were the only Europeans there for a while.

With the discovery of gold and pearls Spanish settlers began to arrive and populate the area. In 1521, the date given as Cumaná's founding Bartolome de las Casas arrived with a community of artisans and farmers.

Cumaná's colonization was quickened by an Indian rebellion a year earlier. With the glut of pearls found on the island of Cubagua, the Spanish periodically swept the coast of Cumaná catching slaves like fish. This spurred a revolt, which in turn made the Spanish more militaristic, building a fort in Cumaná.

In-between these repeating attacks was a unique event. Las Casas, an aristocrat from Spain, became activized by Spain's inhumanity towards the

Indians. As a result of his lobbying the King he was given a tract of land to begin his own community. His vision quickly evaporated as he discovered a coast void of Indians who had gone inland to escape death and to retrench. The final blow to his utopia was inertia; the progress of Spain in crushing its weaker foe was too intoxicating and profitable for anyone, at a time when there was but a few weak alternative visions, for anyone to stop.

Over the next 100 years or so the history of Cumaná was a cycle of warfare and retribution, with the Spanish and Indians trading blows. The outcome is well-known, but happened less as a result of military conquests than religious ones.

Cumaná was not a quick or easy comrade in the Independence War. It accepted membership in the Captains-Generalcy in 1777, but only on its own terms. It reneged on its oath and reversed to the loyalist side; it was a friendly port for General Pablo Morillo, sent from Spain to quash Bolivar.

Eventually, obviously, Cumaná creeped into the nation of Venezuela, and modern time has marked it by its port, fishing, tourism, beaches and being the capital of the State of Sucre.

CLIMATE

The weatherman would have an easy time in Cumaná. Warm sunny days with cooling evening breezes all year round. Average temperature: 80°.

THE BEST HOTELS

As you might expect, the better hotels are to be found on the nearby Caribbean shores. Unless you have a business reason for staying at a downtown hotel, stick to the beachfront. Hotels below are all airconditioned and come with private bath and phone.

■■■ HOTEL LOS BORDONES 4*
Av Universidad
(San Luis Section)
114, Rooms, 8 Floors
Phone: 653783, 653644
Expensive

A mini playland, like all the good international hotels on the seas, Los Bordones is the kind of hotel which keeps you busy, wondering what to do next. Bright colors, as would be expected of Latin American style and being in a tropical zone, the hotel has elegant rooms. It also has a list of features: several restaurants, tennis courts, jacuzzi, two pools, water-sports equipment, and many shops. The hotel has a fun alive feel to it, making your stay even nicer.

■■■ HOTEL CUMANAGOTO 3*
Av Universidad
(San Luis Beach)
89 Rooms, 4 Floors
Phone: 653111
Telex: 93173
Moderate

Cumaná's second hotel, Cumanagoto has a spread of grounds that are neatly tailored and balmy. With a feel that is like a small community's, the hotel is less distinct than the Los Bordones but not less comfortable. The hotel offers a swimming pool, several restaurants, one very formal, tennis courts, a travel agency and some shops.

■■■ HOTEL MINERVA
Av Cristobal Colon
138 Rooms
Phone: 64471, 23902
Moderate

More blase than either of the two hotels mentioned above, the Minerva is, nonetheless, a nice comfortable hotel that has all the needed functions plus more. In front of the hotel is a long promenade that parallels the water. There are two restaurants, a pool, and many of the rooms have terraces.

███████ **HOTEL SAVOIA**
Av Perimetral
47 Rooms, 4 Floors
Phone: 22206, 664379
Inexpensive

A nice relaxing hotel with no extras, Hotel Savoia is a fine place for people on a less hearty budget.

THE BEST RESTAURANTS

Seafood dominates local palates here and with justification for the **chipichipi** (small clams, usually served in a soup), and **pebre de morrocoy** (turtle steak in garlic sauce) are superb dishes. North American restaurant owners would do well to check out this cuisine. You should sample too the **Mejillones** (mussels) and **empanadas de cazon** (shark meat pie).

███████ **POLINESA**
Hotel Los Bordones
Open 12 - 3, 7 - 11
Expensive

A tasty place that is proud of its fish and chicken dishes. The restaurant is large, with beamed ceiling and colonial look. Polinesa has a large menu.

███████ **LOS CASTILLITOS**
Av Cristobal Colon
Open 11:30 - 11:30
Expensive

Across from the Minerva Hotel, Los Castillitos is a glass-enclosed structure that hangs over the water, in which you can view the children swimming around in the water. Specializing in fish dishes, the food is quite good.

▬▬▬ ARAYA
Hotel Cumanagoto
Open 11 - 11
Expensive

Araya, on the second floor of the hotel, overlooks the beach and Caribbean. Not as formal as the hotel's other restaurant, Araya is good for a quicker meal, but without suffering a loss of taste.

▬▬▬ LE CHANSONNIER
Av Universidad
Open 12 - 11
Moderate

Le Chansonnier is a colorful lively restaurant that has an international menu.

▬▬▬ CHEF DINOSOFF
Los Bordones
Open 12 - 11
Moderate

Another good choice for lighter fare. Service and food quality are first rate.

SUNUP TO SUNDOWN

As customary, we strongly urge a walking tour to get the "feel" of Cumaná by day. Start in the old colonial section where the buildings all seem to be red tile roofed. At the **Plaza Miranda**, the so-called right bank of the Manzanares River, immerse yourself in the city's sounds and sights – buses, taxis, fruit stalls, news vendors, shoe shine boys. Follow the river street for 2 blocks, turn left and you will find yourself on **Calle Rivero**, and old narrow colonial street, all of 7 feet wide plus a 2-foot wide sidewalk. Walk through the deserted street (resi-

TIP

Adjacent to the church is the fortress of Santa Maria de la Cabeza which 300 years ago housed a garrison of 250 soldiers. Only the outer walls stand today. Ask the church priest to let you see the inside garden.

dents spend their outdoor time on interior patios, the streets are used only to enter and leave their homes). Just ahead on your right will be the **Santa Ines Church**, the city's main church built in 1572. Note the impressive stain glass windows. The statue you will see is that of Saint Ines, patron Saint of Cumaná.

Half a block beyond the church on your left atop a hill is the yellow-walled **San Antonio Castle**, the city's most important site. Ascend the steps to the castle, which resembles a movie set, and then climb some more to the structure's peak. All of Cumaná will be visible. To your left will be the Cumanagoto strip (look for the hotel) while on your right is Araya Peninsula. Originally constructed in the 17th century and since restored, the castle is shaped like a six-sided star, with the walls made of local coral. A guide (Spanish speaking only) escorts visitors through the dungeons and onto the outer walls. Note the red-tile roofs of the structures surrounding the castle and don't overlook the sculpted lion's heads which are atop the wall. If you're thirsty (we usually are at this point) stop at the snack shop here.

After a respite, retrace your steps back to the Santa Ines Church; at Calle Sucre turn right and two blocks beyond is the **Plaza Bolivar** and the adjoining **Plaza Pichincha**. Here are the Sucre State government buildings, including the governor's home.

A block left of Plaza Pichincha, where Sunday afternoon concerts are held, is the city's main Cathedral. Note the etched wooden ceiling and elaborate chandeliers.

Continue strolling, bearing left, and you will find yourself back at the Plaza Miranda. Just beyond it is the **Plaza Ayacucho** with its statue of General

Sucre, revolutionary war hero who was born in Cumaná. That colonial-style building is the Municipal Palace. On the second floor is a small museum commemorating General Sucre.

Sucre Museum

This museum is dedicated to the Cumaná-born war hero Genral Antonio Jose de Sucre. The General was considered the second most brilliant war mind next to Bolivar's. On December 9, 1824 he won the battle at Ayacucho, which resulted in the independence of Peru, and later beat the royalist forces in alto Peru, culminating in Bolivia's creation. He then became the Gran Mariscal de Ayacucho. His short career spiralled, as he then became Bolivia's first president. But, as a result of sharing Bolivar's vast dream of a united Latin America, he was murdered in the mountains of Colombia.

The museum is located in the Consejo Municipal (Municipal Council Building) and is opened Tuesday - Friday, 9 - 12, 3 - 6, Saturday, 4 - 6, and Sunday, 10 - 12, 4 - 6.

Market

The market of Cumaná is electric and restless. There are foods, from spices, to meats, to fish, arts and crafts and other items. The more special things sold are hammocks, coffee and **cuatros**, a hybrid guitar developed by the local Guaiqueri Indians.

Castillo De San Antonio De La Eminencia

This fort is Cumaná. Its structure sits aperch one of the two mountains that look down on the city, and offers a wide-spread view of the surrounding area and out in the Caribbean.

Its history is Cumaná's. Built originally to spot oncoming enemies, the fort served this loyal purpose for years, preempting Captain Henry Mor-

TIP

The fort offers fantastic views of the region, and should not be missed.

gan's attempt to smash the city. An earthquake flattened the fort and the city in 1684, but the fort was soon rebuilt. In 1853 the fort was again smooshed by an earthquake, and this time, it took almost 50 years to rebuild it. Again an earthquake, doubled with a tidal wave, chopped-down the fort, leaving it stranded. It was minimally rebuilt in 1959 and more sturdily done in 1975.

Araya Peninsula

The main attraction of the peninsula is the effort that is built there and its beauty. The peninsula is reached by Hovercraft or car-ferry from Cumaná or by a jeep road from Cariaco and Chacopata.

The construction of **Castillo de Santiago de Araya** became necessary because of Dutch theft of the abundant salt located off Cumaná. The Dutch would blatantly take Cumaná's salt for their own needs. At one point the Spanish sent out a ship to stop them, which resulted in a battle, and finally a truce. The truce ostensibly kept although the Dutch continued to steal the salt clandestinely. It soon became a necessity to build the fort, which was done in 1621.

Completed in 1665, Araya fort is considered the best one in Venezuela, and of superior quality to any other in the Americas. The fort was able to accommodate 300 men, had 45 cannons and was built in a strange trapezoidal form. It was a huge structure, haughty in its look.

In 1726 a hurricane destroyed most of the fort, and in 1762 the Spanish blew it up to keep it from falling into the wrong hands. But by that time salt could no longer be mined.

The bulwarks still stand today, powerful monuments to good architecture, and salt is now available again.

Mochima National Park

As described in the introduction the route from Puerto La Cruz to Cumaná, Mochima National Park and the Bay are quite special and should not be missed for anything.

Museo Del Mar
Av Universidad

An interesting aquarium, the Museum is open Tuesday - Sunday, 8:30 - 11:30, 3 - 7.

CUMANÁ AFTER DARK

Three film houses in town are the **Paramount**, in the Plaza Miranda, the **Teatro Humbolt** (Calle Bermudez) and **Pichincha**, near the Plaza Pichincha. All are air conditioned and the offerings while not too current are beyond the silent era, if that's any comfort.

Free concerts often are held weekends at the **Universidad de Oriente** (University of the East) in the main auditorium.

The night crowd, singles and young couples, congregate at a few chosen clubs.

■■■■■■ *DISCO CLUB 47*
Hotel Bordones
Open 9:30 - 4

Actually across from the hotel next to the tennis courts, the disco is lively and entertaining and fun. Heated and lighted and wet, it is worth the outing.

■■■■■■ *AQUARIO*
Av Universidad

A small disco that is loud and dark. The music blasts off at 10 pm and continues until 4 am.

▰▰▰ *BAR MOCHIMA*
Hotel Cumanagoto

Next to the pool, this bar is relaxed and very nice.

ETCETERA ETCETERA

AIRLINES

Avensa

Main office here is on Calle Armario 18. Phone: (093) 24 - 505.

AEROPOSTAL

At Calle Bolivar.

AUTO RENTALS

Volkswagen has offices at the airport and on Avenida Bermudez. Rates vary with the model you select.

BANKS

A good one is the Banco Union, Calle Mariño and Calle Carabobo.

BARBER SHOP AND BEAUTY PARLOR

Try the one on Pasaje Tobia, between Calles Bermudez and Mariño (downtown).

BOOKS AND MAGAZINES

Gift shop in the Hotel Cumanagoto carries English-language publications, including Daily Journal (published in Caracas).

BUSES

The red and yellow bus marked San Luis will drop you at your beach hotel. Fare is 6 cents. Last stop is the Cumanagoto Hotel. Pick it up on Avenida Universidad.

CABS

General rate is 70 cents to $1.15. Set the fare in advance. Hourly cost is $4.50.

CADA SUPERMARKET

Wide range of edibles. Located on Avenida Perimetral. Open Sundays 8 am to noon; Saturdays all day, and weekdays all day except from 12:30 - 2:30.

DR. SCHOLL

The foot sore should head to Casa Scholl, Calle Sucre, near Plaza Bolivar; full treatment is $2.25. Closed noon - 2:30 pm. Open Saturdays.

ONE WAY STREETS

Except for Avenidas Perimetral and Universidad, almost all streets have one way traffic.

PHARMACY

A good farmacia, **Virgen del Valle** is on Avenida Perimetral and Mariño. Another one is **Central** on Avenida Bermudez near the Bridge.

POST OFFICE

It is near Plaza Eloy Blanco on Calle Paraiso.

UNIVERSIDAD DE ORIENTE

Among the oldest universities in the Western Hemisphere, its main entrance is on Avenida Universidad. This is by far the most prestigious school in this part of Venezuela.

SHOPPING

Your best browsing is along Avenida Bermudez. You might also stroll through the shops in Pasaje Tobia located between Calles Bermudez and Mariño near the Bridge.

Venezuela

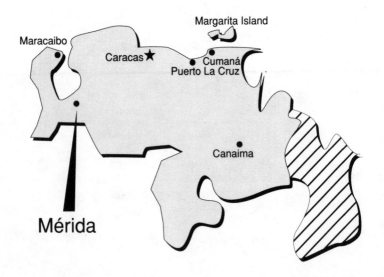

MÉRIDA
WHERE THE
FISHERMEN PLAY

ocals here boast that some of the world's finest trout fishing is to be found in the lagoons in and around Mérida. But that's only part of the story as to why you should journey the 400 miles from Caracas to this town of 110,000 tucked neatly into the Andes 5,400 feet above sea level.

For openers there is the air itself. It reminds us of Vermont in May after the sun has burst forth following an early morning rain. Fresh, crisp, clean. Then there is the charm that can only be found in a colonial-era city – closer in atmosphere to a rustic village actually – nestled on a mountain plateau surrounded by snowcapped mountains that draw experienced climbers. The people – including the students at the local university evidence an openness to strangers that is as welcome as it is rare in this closed-off world of today.

Too, there is the pleasure of strolling the narrow colonial streets in town and the sprawling seductive countryside outside of it. And if all of this is insufficient, there is the world's highest cable car which sweeps up to a peak almost 16,000 feet high. Little wonder we are rather fond of Mérida as are many Venezuelans who use it as a holiday retreat all year round. And why not? Temperatures average 66 over the 12 months. Perfection.

A BIT OF BACKGROUND

Mérida, the base city for the Venezuelan Andes, is built on a plateau, which, from above, looks like a large roof to a small building surrounded by much larger buildings with smaller roofs. From Mérida's roof you can, allegedly, take binoculars and peruse the entire conglomerated Venezuelan Andes. With that image in mind, you can get a sense of Mérida's beauty.

NOTE

Obviously this peak surpasses the Alps by at least 3,000 ft.

The geography around Mérida is similar to that of the Alps. The lower parts of the mountains are treeswarmed, and the peaks are usually snow-capped. The highest peaks are around Mérida, with Pico **Bolivar** at 16,427 ft. The city is surrounded by four rivers – the **Albarregas** and the **Chama** being the main ones, and the **Milla** and **Mucujin** the periphery ones. It is perpetual fall in Mérida, and that is why, with the heavenly peaks in the background, the city is so alive.

NOTE

The streets are clean, ungutted, and the buildings average about five to seven floors high.

The city, though, with a population of 110,000, has grown out of its pastoral colonial look. Although, particularly at Plaza Bolivar, the city retains its architectural pedigree, most of the city has become modernized. Nothing overwhelms, except maybe the University's circular hospital by the airport. There is enough of the colonial Spanish look, intermixed with the psychedelic Indian style to give a hint of Mérida in the past.

HISTORY

Founded on October 9, 1558 by Captain Juan Rodriquez Suarez, the city's birthdate was blackened by crime. Suarez, who was on official business from Colombia (then Nueva Granada), was sent to the Andes to explore and, as then was popular, conquer some Indians. As a tangent he discovered and founded Mérida; but the founding of a city, then, could only be done by Royal Decree;

hence, Suarez, technically committed a crime. His rival Juan Maldonado y Ordoñez was eager to see him arrested, and have him stand trial. If not for the intervention of Bishop Juan Carlos de los Barrios, Suarez would have been drawn and quartered. Suarez was eventually exiled to America.

With Mérida's eventual incorporation into Venezuela, its head has been high. It was the first city to accept Bolivar as El Libertador, and the first city to erect a statue to him, in 1842 (it is located in the Parque de las Cinco Republicas).

Mérida is dominated by youth. It is the location of Venezuela's second largest university, **Universidad de los Andes**, founded in 1810. The combination between the mountain air and unchecked youth prevails in a sort of organic high, and because of it Mérida is very attracting.

ARRIVAL

While many Caraqueños drive here – it takes about 10 hours – chances are you will be flying into modern **Alberto Carnevale Airport** located in the southern part of the city. You can pick up cigarettes and odds and ends at the gift shop and get flight information at the Avensa and LAV (Aeropostal) desks.

A cab to your hotel runs under $2 but if you are traveling on a budget take a por puesto (jitney car) which will drop you downtown within walking distance of several hotels.

A QUICK ORIENTATION

Sometimes called the techo (roof) of Venezuela, the state of Mérida is perched atop the highest part of the Venezuelan Andes. Mérida City, the capital of the state, anchors the foot of the Sierra Nevada range.

Mérida is small and contained. The city is only about three miles long, north to south, and half a mile wide – it is in the width that Mérida is most visibly expanding though.

The city numerically begins at the northern end, but for the traveller arriving by plane, which is the predominate means of transportation, the city will start at the southern end. The airport is at Calle (street) 52, and stretches until Calle 40. The city's most southern point is about half a mile south of the airport, but that part of the city is dominated by parks, eight of them to be exact. Walking north from the airport on **Avenue Urdaneta**, the main thoroughfare, there is initially a quiet residential area, which turns more active at the Hotel Caribay, and, just beyond, the CCCD shopping center. The belly of the city is usually quiet and subdued, and that part can be mapped from **Parque Glorias Patrias**, which is parallel to the Park Hotel. The technical center of the city is **Plaza Bolivar**, which starts at Calle 23 and stretches from Avenida 3 (which was Avenida Urdaneta) to Avenida 2. Surrounding the Plaza are many small shops, the government buildings – wonderful colonial structures – and the imposing cathedral.

Bounded by the **Chama** and **Albarregas** rivers, the Pan American highway runs parallel and west to Mérida, and in the city, is called Avenida Las Americas. The nucleus of the city has narrow colonial streets with high curbs and small squat buildings. Viaducts one and two, Calles 38 and 26 respectively, link up with Avenida Las Americas, and are the routes out of the narrow confines of old Mérida and into the wider and newer streets of the suburbs. Once outside the central part of the city, the buildings become larger and more modern, and the area is dotted by shopping malls, restaurants and clubs. **Avenida Las Americas** is the route to the suburbs and into the northern Andes. The

NOTE

To orient yourself quickly, remember that the avenues – which are the main thoroughfares – run lengthwise, that is North and South. All are one way. Streets (calles) run East-West, between the rivers. At the city's widest point there are only eight blocks and for much of the width there are only five intersections.

avenue also takes you to the important suburb of **Chorros de Milla**, where the zoological park and other important sites are located. The eastern part of Mérida has no construction going on at all, or at least very little, and that is because of natural obstacles; mainly that Mérida hugs a minor cliff.

CLIMATE

Like New England in spring. That's the way Mérida is the year round. Many afternoons are warm enough for swimming with temperatures in the 70's while evenings and mornings are cool and crisp with readings in the upper 50's. Humidity is low. In short spectacular weather.

THE BEST HOTELS

Since Mérida is strongly tourist oriented, it's understandable why the city – for its size – has so many good hotels. These range from 2 to 4 star hostelries to a good number of perfectly acceptable 2 and 3 star standard hotels. There are no 5 star hotels in Mérida.

All hotels noted below offer private baths. Air conditioning is unnecessary here and no hotel offers it.

Hotel prices in Mérida are much less than Caracas, with few more than $25 - $30 per day. Prices can, however, vary because of international monetary fluctuations.

HOTEL PEDREGOSA 4*
Off Pan American Highway in Urb. Pedregosa Norte
75 Rooms
25 Cabins
Phone: 632505
Moderate

NOTE

Aside form the spectacular exterior, this hotel has A-Frame cabins that can handle 6 guests.

Located beyond the Pan American Highway in a largely undeveloped area, La Pedregosa encompasses a lake, a pool, riding trails, tennis courts and a children's play area, on 25 acres that take on the look of a small village. Rowboats, available for rental, dot the manmade lake which is stocked with fish to please anglers. Launch rides are offered too. Rooms in the main lodge all have enclosed terraces that are pleasant indeed. At night there is a good discotheque too.

Although the hotel sounds blissful, reports are not always flattering – anyway, in Mérida, you will probably not be a pool bum.

PARK HOTEL 4 *
Across from Parque Glorias
Patrias at Calle 37, Av 4
125 Rooms
8 Suites
5 Presidential Suites
Phone: 634866 - 63803

A modern white building that elevates like a staircase, the Park Hotel's lobby is bustling and active. With its 6 meeting rooms, accommodating up to 500 people, the hotel is probably the central place for non-residential business. Its stained wood paneling gives it an international look, and during restful moments, its couches are teeming with reclining, cigarette smoking visitors. Attached to the hotel is a mini shopping mall. There is a restaurant, a disco and a travel agency in the hotel. The hotel was recently elevated from a 3 to a 4 star, so that is an indication of its present momentum.

HOTEL CARIBAY 3 *
Av 2 Prolongacion
77 Rooms
3 Suites
Phone: 637431, 636451, 637596
Moderate

The first tall building you'll encounter after leaving the airport, the Caribay has 7 floors. It is a mainstay of Mérida, not overly fancy nor at all squalid. It is a pleasant comfortable hotel that has a restaurant, bar, conference room and English speaking travel agency. Its small lobby is functional. Its main attraction is its **Match Disco**, probably the most popular in the city, with its neon lights and black interior.

████████ *HOTEL PRADO RIO 3 **
Av Universidad, Hoyada de Milla
42 Cabanas (cabins)
2 Suites
13 Rooms
Phone: 520775, 520704
Moderate

As befits a good resort hotel, the Prado Rio has created a holiday air about it – almost like a ski lodge – through creation of an unusual three-tier dining room. The lower level houses a comfortable bar and t.v. area while the middle tier is an informal lounge area with a fireplace and potbelly stove. The grounds, perfect for strollers, house a garden and volley ball area and the pool comes complete with an adult slide. A recreation room draws ping pong addicts. The red-hued cabanas, located a short distance from the main house, are good values for families. This hotel was created for comfort and relaxation and the lobby and lounge have the most comfortable overstuffed chairs and couches we've sat in for a long time. Vivid flower arrangements brighten up the lobby. Private entrance as well as parking.

TIP

On the top is a spacious Swiss-style restaurant with good food to boot.

████████ *HOTEL VALLE GRANDE 3 **
El Valle
30 Rooms
50 Cabins
Phone: 443011
Moderate

Probably the only hotel with a truly rural and country surrounding, Hotel Valle Grande sits in the valley, all alone, peaceful and serene. If being all alone, in the midst of your own dreams is important, Valle Grande is perfect. Like any hotel, though it has a restaurant, bar and disco and travel agency.

■■■■■■■■ HOTEL BELENSATE 3*
Off Pan American Highway
Urb. La Hacienda
63 Rooms
Phone: 630870, 639809
Moderate

TIP

First-rate horses rent by the hour and riding aficionados throng the Belensate on weekends.

The marvelous wooded grounds are spacious enough to house a stable, a children's playground and a brook stocked with trout, as well as ducks and monkeys. If you're traveling in a group, you might consider renting the three-bedroom cabin with private bath – comfortable and private. Suites are posh what with carpeting, sitting rooms, and tiled bath. The Spanish styled main lodge features a fireplace nook that draws yarn spinning sportsmen in the evening.

The Belensate is located across the Albarregas River to the south of colonial Mérida, a 5 minute drive from the airport. No pool. In a country setting. At night you will find it hard to believe you are in a city.

■■■■■■ HOTEL CHAMA 3*
Av 4 Calle 29
63 Rooms
Phone: 521082
Moderate

On Avenida 4, off the main Avenida 3, the Chama is thoroughly entrenched in the center of town, an easy walk to Calle 26 and Plaza Bolivar. Rooms are small yet spotless. There is a bar, snack bar, boutique and pizzeria, which is a loud student hangout and lots of fun.

■■■■■■ HOTEL TERREZA 3 *
Chorros de Milla
150 Rooms
Phone: 448005, 441133
Inexpensive

In the suburb of Chorros de Milla is the hotel, which is a large white and blue building, with a huge parking lot. The hotel is on the edge of the plateau, with the mountains beginning to climb right after it. The Terreza has a desolate feel to it, with such a large lobby that even crowded, it seems roomy with sculptures in the lobby.   The hotel has three restaurants, a piano bar and a disco, that has as its dancing space a caged in chessboard. It also has a conference room.

■■■■■■ HOTEL GRAN BALCON 2 *
Av Pasco de la Ferra
35 Rooms
3 Cabins
Inexpensive

TIP

The front patio to the hotel is wonderful for just sitting and staring at the mountains.

On the eastern edge of town, with the mountainous range as its backyard, the Grand Balcon is a personal, clean, friendly motel. It is on a residential block, and at night it is quiet and serene. There is a restaurant that serves really good Venezuelan food, and a breakfast corner in the lobby which is really good. The rooms are functional, but clean and cool. There are filtered water coolers in the hallway.

■■■■■■ HOTEL PRINCESA 2 *
Av El Valle
19 Rooms
10 Cabins
Inexpensive

Like the Valle Grande Hotel but less spectacular and pastoral, the hotel's unique feature is video. With restaurant, snack bar and playground, you will be happy here.

▬▬▬ HOTEL OVIEDO 2*
Av 3
63 Rooms
Phone: 632009
Inexpensive

On Avenida 3, the main thoroughfare, closer to the airport than Plaza Bolivar, Oviedo has a sparkling new look to it as if it was either just built or newly renovated. An uninteresting white structure, the hotel has a decent restaurant attached to it.

▬▬▬ HOTEL TELEFERICO 2*
Av Parque Las Heroinas
30 Rooms
Phone: 529839
Inexpensive

NOTE

The Teleferico Hotel is the hotel in Mérida nearest to the cable car terminal.

By the teleferico, on the eastern edge of town, the hotel is functional and inexpensive. It contains a restaurant, bar and snack bar.

▬▬▬ HOTEL MUCUBAJI 2*
Av Urdaneta No. 33
63 Rooms
Phone: 443788
Inexpensive

A tall modern building on the outskirts of Mérida, the Mucubaji is clean and friendly. There is a restaurant in the hotel.

▬▬▬ HOTEL NEVADA PALACE 2*
Calle 24 No. 5 - 45
42 Rooms - 3 Floors (no elevators)
Phone: 529931
Inexpensive

NOTE

Good value for the money.

If you're driving you might look at the Palace since it offers underground on-site parking. Beyond that, the hotel is clean and comfortable. Rooms are small and modestly furnished. Bar and restaurant on the main floor.

Within easy walking distance of Plaza Bolivar and the teleferico (cable car).

■ *HOTEL MUNCHEGO 2**
Av Verdanteta
Inexpensive

Near the airport, Munchego is a quiet, family run hotel that has a very hometown feel to it. Smells waft into the lobby from the kitchen, and the family hangs around the lobby in shorts.

THE BEST RESTAURANTS

Mérida is not the kind of city to concentrate on world-class restaurants; and that is by no means a pessimistic remark. The informality of the city is not contradicted by the look of its restaurants – but that, by no means, is a comment on the food. With a vast array of choices, Mérida is jam-packed with restaurants. Once again, Mérida is so small you can stroll the city, pass 10 to 15 restaurants, and then pop into one.

Before we note our recommendations, a few pointers. First, Mérideños tend to dine relatively early in the evening. While a Caraqueño dines comfortably at 9, residents here usually sit down closer to 7:30 pm. A pleasant surprise is the cost for a good 4-course dinner. Nothing is expensive in American terms. Since the area around Mérida is famous for its trout, that fish is a highlight of cuisine for the region, and lives up to its reputation. Any hotel you stay in will have a restaurant. We did not have one bad food experience, so its not a risky game. As for prices, a 4-course meal including tax and service

TIP

Sugar-coated figs called Dulce de Higo are a local delight along with domestic cheeses.

(exclusive of cocktails) should run you less than $10 per person. Again, a sudden change in international monetary values can affect prices.

CASA VIEJA
Av Los Proceres via
Av Los Americas
Lunch and Dinner
Phone: 635885
Moderate

NOTE

The ambience compliments the fine food here

A restored, Spanish mansion, the Casa Vieja is as much a visible experience as a gastronomic one. Specializing in Venezuelan and international meats, the restaurant (mansion) is complex and large. There is a Salon para fiestas that abuts a garden and man made waterfall. It is a large space for dancing, hued by black chandeliers. There is a bar, squashed between the salon and restaurant that is a cowhide masculine watering hole, with old west ornaments. The restaurant is large, and in consistency with its menu has a leather interior. There is, also, a reception area, gift shop at the entrance, and open mezzanine to take in the air.

PRADO RIO
Hotel Prado Rio
Open 7 am - 10 am
Noon - 3 pm, 7 pm - 10 pm
Moderate

TIP

Dine near a window for a nice view of the city and bull ring.

Aside from the superb seafood, this tri-level restaurant offers an informal ski lodge ambience amid gleaming planked flooring, ceiling beams, and original handwoven Indian rug wall hangings. The restaurant on the upper tier overlooks a lounge and the bar on the lower two levels. Try the trout or red snapper (pargo), absolutely fresh and first rate, or the chicken with ham dish. The bi-lingual menu offers a daily fixed price 4-course dinner and it is a bargain indeed. Service is expert and efficient. If you like to linger over your cocktail, order your dinner from the lounge. The maitre will do the rest. Great value.

Italian

IL DUCE
Av Los Americas
Lunch and Dinner
Phone: 632814, 638308
Moderate

TIP

Once again, the fish is fantastic.

Probably the most American in look, with candle-lighted tables, varnished floors, plush seats, fancy silver and plates and soft music, il Duce is new and spotless. Specializing in Italian food, it is located in the shopping mall, with the entrance on the first floor. There is a piano bar and sitting room.

A Mexican Selection

VUELTA DEL ZORRO
Av Las Americas
Phone: 441859
Moderate

Specializing in Mexican food, the restaurant is a haunt for students, and hence is lively, with live music or stereo. The drinks are excellent, and so is the food, with many Mexican variations. The portions are very large, but with some sangria and nachos already in your stomach, you won't need as many burritos.

RESTAURANT GRAN BALCON
Hotel Gran Balcon
Av Paseo de la Feria
Phone: 520366
Open Noon - 3 pm
6:30 - 10 pm daily
Moderate

NOTE

By the way, the restaurant is in a separate building behind the hotel.

With a panoramic view of the mountains, this restaurant could get by with mediocre food. But that isn't the case, as witness two outstanding dishes – **Milanesa ternera** (veal cutlet) and **Chuleta de cochino** (pork chops). Too, there is a paella Valenciana and a nice pargo (red snapper). Aside from the huge glass expanse facing the mountain, the decor could use some sprucing up.

▰▰▰ RESTAURANT CHINO
Av Los Chorros de Milla
(Chorros de Milla District)
Phone: 504508
Open 11 am - midnight (daily)
Moderate

NOTE

The exterior resembles a pagoda and is marked with Chinese characters.

The owner has managed to create and oddity: a first class restaurant featuring Chinese and international food (both recommended) in a Latin country. Restaurant Chino would do well in San Francisco's Chinatown. If you're Chinese hungry, stick to the left side of the huge menu where the dishes range from a delicious **subgum kai tin** (diced chicken with shrimp and almonds) to a marvelous grilled pork and mushroom dish called **mou ku siu pin**. We're hooked on the egg rolls (lumpias) and the perennial favorite, won ton soup. International dishes (right side of Menu) include an outstanding trout with mushroom sauce dish (**trucha con salsa de Hongo**). Any por puesto with a blue top will drop you here, but these stop running about 9:00 pm. A cab is best.

▰▰▰ LA TERRAZA
Av Los Chorros de Milla
Phone: 441133
Open 11 am - Midnight (daily)
Moderate

Your introduction to La Terraza will warm you toward this cozy comfortable restaurant. You dine

NOTE

Located in what was once a private home, you cross a small foot bridge over a brook to enter.

on a roofed terrace with the stillness broken only by the running brook. A must here is the **aguacate con camarones**, an appetizer of avocado stuffed with shrimp, as well as the sugared fig dessert (dulce de higo). In between we like the **trucha meunier** and the **parrillada**.

■■■■■■ LA PAELLERA
Av 5 (near Plaza Bolivar)
Phone: 520519
Open 11 am - 3 pm
6:30 -10:30 pm (closed Mondays)
Inexpensive

TIP

Opt for sitting in the garden area in the rear.

The owners are justifiably proud of the fresh fish served in their Spanish-motif place in center city. After seating yourself in the rear area near the garden (walk past the bar to reach it), feast on the delicious marinated trout (**trucha en escabeche**) or the **paella Valenciana**. Start with the seafood soup (sopa Mariscos). Splendid. For more conventional palates there is a good filet mignon along with a selection of chicken dishes.

■■■■■■ RESTAURANT LOS PINOS
Av Urdaneta. Calle 39
Lunch and Dinner
Phone: 637116
Inexpensive

Los Pinos is an open roofed restaurant that is informal and pleasant. Near the Hotel Caribay and airport, the restaurant is a good place to stop for lunch if you're in the neighborhood. They specialize in meats.

■■■■■■ CHEZ PEPPINO
Av Gonzalo Picon Febres
(near Colonial Art Museum)
Phone: 631259
Open 12 - 3 pm, 6:30 - 11 pm
Moderate

NOTE

A taste of Italy in a medieval setting.

Typically European, with wide Medieval chairs, wine racks and Italian Renaissance paintings, Chez Peppino is a dinner haunt serving good Italian food. Ravioli dishes are in demand along with the pizza pies. The gregarious customers also call for the veal parmesan and paella (the chef sneaked that in when the owner wasn't looking).

RESTAURANT BELENSATE
Hotel Belensate
Open all day
Phone: 691655
Moderate

The rustic dining choice, while not plush, offers good food in a quiet pleasant cabin-like setting. The trout, avocado and shrimp dishes are all good. Nice dining treat.

LA CASITA DE LAS ROSAS
Av Los Chorros de Milla
Phone: 446448
Open 8 am - midnight (daily)
Inexpensive

TIP

Look for the sign in the shape of a house in front.

For a dinner setting more refreshing than La Casita you'd have to look long and hard. Overlooking Chorros de Milla Park, the restaurant offers out-door terrace dining in a quiet lovely area of the city. While the decor is simple, the food is definitely not. Indulge yourself with the Argentine parrillada grilled on a parilla at your table. And the churrasco (steak) a la brasa is recommended as is the trucha.

LA CAMPANA
Via Panamerica
Open all day
Phone: 639834
Inexpensive

Set up similarly to the Casa Vieja, but not as nicely, La Campana is an Italian restaurant with a more noisy atmosphere. Featuring great spagetti, the restaurant is a local favorite.

RESTAURANT MARISQUERIA
Av Julio Febres Cordero (Calle 31)
Dinner only
Phone: 522769
Moderate

Small, cozy and formal, with plush chairs and chandeliers, Marisqueria is a place for fish, all variations, with lobster served here.

RESTAURANT DIAMANTE
Av 3, Calle 34
Lunch and Dinner
Inexpensive

For good, quick Chinese food. Chop suey dishes are first rate as are the egg rolls (lumpias).

Mérida has an abundance of pizza pasta places non-formal much like their U.S. counter parts.

PIZZERIA DA PEPPINO
Av Gonzalo Picon Febres
Open all day

Disco and Cerveceria (beer hall) on premises.

CAFETIN EL BUEN GUSTO
Av 3

Always crowded

COCINA ITALIANA
20 - 65 Bs.
Av Proceres

A student hangout.

D'ANGELO PIZZERIA
Calle Franco Anzil

Best pizza we had in Mérida.

An Arabic Choice

 **KALIFFAS**
Calle 44 (by airport)

Arab food.

For Excellent Ice Cream

CAFE LE GLACE
Calle 29

For ice cream and sweets. Very California setting.

MÉRIDA BY DAY

The countryside here has a beauty all its own and you would be remiss if you failed either to rent a car or to hire a cab for our recommended excursions. Too, the mountain rivers and lakes are stocked with trout and fishermen should make it a point to indulge themselves between March 16 and September 30 (the legal period) when Venezuelans and Colombians throng the area.

On Foot In Mérida

> **NOTE**
>
> *Streets downtown are narrow and generally hilly.*

To get a true feeling for the Spanish colonial flavor of center city Mérida you should stroll through it. As noted earlier, the city is built on a plateau between two rivers and at its widest point is only eight avenues wide but it is long – 44 blocks in all.

> **NOTE**
>
> *Mérida – in contrast to much of tropical Venezuela – has flourishing red plants and trees common to temperate climates.*

A good place to start your walk is at the **Plaza Bolivar** (Avenida 3 and Calle 22) where you might stroll through the gray-stone **Cathedral** (look for the modern clock on it) which faces the plaza. Those buildings nearby are municipal government structures for the most part. Browse in the shops around the plaza, the city's best. On the plaza's south side is one of the many structures scattered throughout the city belonging to the University of the Andes (among Venezuela's largest with 12,000

NOTE

The University of the Andes is Venezuelas second largest.

students). You will notice how young much of Mérida's population seems – most are students. The homes you will see, uninteresting from the exterior are uniformly built with lovely interior patios and red tile roofs, in Spanish colonial style.

From the Plaza, we don't think it matters in which direction you head. To the north (uphill) is the **Plaza Milla,** an after lunch sunning spot, and the Prado Rio Hotel. To the West along Avenida 2 is the city's outdoor market area which you might enjoy. To the south (heading toward **Plaza Glorias Patrias**) is the city's newest shopping center (Todos). Whichever way you choose, we know you will return to your hotel with a better understanding of Mérida.

The many other recommended stops, cannot be reached on foot and you will have to take a cab, go by por puesto or rent a car.

The Teleferico (Cable Car)

Ready for a 2-mile ascent up to Espejo peak? It's on your own head if you fail to take advantage of what is said to be the earth's highest cable car journey, rising well above tundra line and the cloud line to an incredible level of just under 16,000 feet. That's twice the height of Mexico City, three times the height of Denver and 3,000 feet above La Paz, Bolivia, the world's highest capital. You will wind up at the highest point in the Venezuelan Andes.

After packing a warm sweater, sunglasses, a camera (with extra film), hop a cab early any morning, except Monday or Tuesday, to the teleferico terminal on Calle 25 in the Barinitas section.

Once there, you board a trolley-like cable car for the first of four legs to the summit. While at some points your car will seem to be travelling vertically, the average angle of ascent is about 30° – steep enough. It is a ride of extremes, going from sunny and hot Mérida to the icy foggy peak of Espejo; in fact, Pico Espejo is the highest point in the Venezuelan Andes.

There will be no less than a half an hours wait, unless you are the first in line at 8 am. (The ride stops running upwards at 12 noon.) The ride costs $3 for adults and $2 for students.

The first segment, form Barinitas station to **La Montaña** station, is a steep departure from Mérida and its flat plateau. On a sunny day, Mérida recedes and gets reduced to small closely meshed dots, the Chama River becomes snake-like, the sugar-cane and coffee fields become aerially expansive and the other peaks become less tall. Mérida becomes marked only by the airport, the baseball stadium and the bull-fighting stadium. At Montaña you're at 8,000 ft. and the geography is thick and foresty.

From Montaña, board another cable car for the ascension is to **La Aquada** station; it is a two mile rise over deep valley. A few homes are visible while going up, and one is forced to wonder how the residents of these homes get their necessities. The geography becomes less foresty. Mérida, at this point, is now a microscopic dot, if visible at all. This ascent is the most drastic, with its apparent environment changes – the leaves on the trees get thinner and the mist passing through the air is clear.

On the sides of La Aquada are two small lakes which water the area. The mule trail, off to the side, is also quite obvious. But not much more can be seen. On a particularly clear day, however, several peaks can be seen: **Pico Bolivar** and **La Concha** glacier being two.

Now it is time to board a third cable car from La Aquada to **Loma Redonda,** at 13,000 ft. The mist is even thicker, but Lagunas Negra, Colorada and Anteojos are visible – these are the homes of some of Mérida's famous trout.

Finally, Loma Redonda leads to the ultimate stop at **Pico Espejo**. It is cold and windy and icy up there and some people don't acclimatize that quickly so are left breathless – just take it slow. If it is clear you see La Corona, with its twin peaks of Humboldt and Bonpland, the glacier of Timoncitos, and the Virgin of the Snows, patron saint of alpinists, sculptured in marble. The panoramic view will make conversation superfluous as you move about the summit. If the day is cloudless the views will be incredible. That snow-capped peak to the East is **Pico Bolivar**. All you can hear in the looming silence are the clicks of cameras recording a moment at "the top of world". There is an observation area as well as pathways. There is a small cabin nearby to walk to, and you can sun-bathe on lounge chairs during the sojourn at topside. Pico Espejo has an observatory pathway, a small restaurant and food stalls. You can stay on the peak for hours, if so desired.

Ultimately, it's time for the four stage descent. Note once again the changes in vegetation as you move down, the small cascades, mountain streams, the absence of trees, and the Indians who live at each level. Yes, you can remain at any station and pick up the next cable car (perhaps two hours later). In all, the system is 7 miles long and that's why two days a week (Mondays and Tuesdays) are required for maintenance.

Cable Car Departure Schedule

Wednesdays, Thursdays, Fridays – 8 am, 10 am, and noon. Saturdays and Sundays – on the hour from 8 am to noon. Check at your Hotel to make sure the schedule has not changed.

TIP

Warning: You will sunburn rapidly at these heights.

TIP

Depart no later than 10 a.m. to avoid midday haze. Allow three hours for a leisurely round trip. The last return car leaves at 3 pm, but check with the guide. The entire ride is about an hour each way, with a change at each station.

Note: Mountain climbers should hire a local guide – check your hotel clerk – to conduct you up from Espejo Peak down a few thousand feet to a plateau. From here you climb up neighboring Bolivar Peak (Pico Bolivar).

Parque Beethoven
And Museo De Arte Moderno

Amid North American-style homes in the new northern section of Mérida is a park-like Plaza famous throughout Venezuela for two clocks – one planted with fresh red, white, and green flowers, similar to the ones in Interlaken, Switzerland and Viña del Mar, Chile and the other a glockenspiel inside a quaint German house. On the hour the latter clock plays a short Beethoven piece, thus the park's name. Every quarter hour listen for the gong and watch the small Bavarian statues beat time.

TIP

A must visit for art and handicraft lovers

Opposite the park is the **Museo De Arte Moderno** which houses the best in Mérida's modern art – paintings, mobiles and wood cuts, many for sale. Some of the most famous artists in Venezuela studied in Mérida. I purchased a hand-crafted wooden rooster there for $20. The two-story white colonial house is open Tuesday thru Friday, 9 am-noon and 3 - 8 pm; Saturdays 3 - 6 pm; and Sundays 10 - noon. Closed Mondays. Free admission. By the way, this area also boasts the best homes of colonial Mérida.

Plaza Bolivar

A true relic of colonial days, Plaza Bolivar is now becoming isolated in time because of Mérida's rapid modernization. The plaza is so perfect and clean and manicured and outdated that it looks like a model. It is serene and criss-crossed by walking lanes. The nucleus is a statue of Bolivar, and the rest of the plaza is patched with grass and flowers;

there is one dominating coconut tree that looms over Bolivar and the park.

On the southern edge of the Plaza are government buildings, colonial in style and very fitting for the time lapse that sets upon you when in the park. If you were going to stand by Bolivar's statue, facing east, you could possibly, imagine life at that time. Bolivar would be the figure of revolt, not as glorified as he is now. Yet his war meant change and created a split in society – the colonists on one side and the revolutionaries on the other. To the south of the Plaza are the colonial styled government buildings (actually built in the 1950's); trim, neat, and wrought-ironed. They would be the symbols of reactionaryism, the status quo. Then, directly in front of you would be the church, with a statue of Mary on the facade. At night, particularly, this mental time-travelling works well.

NOTE

The church actually took 160 years to complete, slowed by earthquakes and wars.

It was started 1803 and finished in 1958. In the crypt below the main altar are a late renaissance statue of the Virgin of the Apple, and the remains of San Clemente, decapitated because he was a Christian.

Palacio Arzobispal

Next to the Cathedral, this palace was constructed between 1933 and 1951 as the residence of the archbishop. Inside the palace is a gallery that contains portraits of the prelate of Mérida and the **Archdiocese Museum**, a collection of colonial oil paintings. The museum also has what is considered the oldest bell in the world, built in 909 A.D.

Museo De Arte Colonial

Venezuelan religious and colonial art from the 16th, 17th, 18th, and 19th centuries is exhibited here. Works in paintings, sculptures, wood carvings, furniture and gold and silver are all on display.

In a private house on Avenida 3 between Calles 18 and 19, the museum is open 9 - 6 Tuesday-Friday; 3 - 6 Saturday; and 10 - 12 Sunday.

Jardin Acuario

This aquarium museum housed in three attached cottages on Avenida Andrés Bello, in the city's southern section, features the largest Rainbow trout (stuffed) we've ever seen, most of which were caught in nearby lagoons. An interesting feature is the number next to each fish. They stand for the altitude at which the fish was caught (in meters). Two of the cottages display live fish landed in regional lakes and elsewhere. To reach the aquarium look for the park, Andrés Bello, (one of Venezuela's revolutionary heros) and at the end of the park stands the Aquarium. Student often study at the large monument in the park at night. Open 9 - 11:30, 2:30 - 6 everyday. There is a nominal charge.

Parque Chorros De Milla

Right outside Mérida, near the La Terreza Hotel, this park was built on a slight incline in the mountain. Housing a small zoo, which has indigenous animals as well as big African cats, in cages too small for anyone, the park has places for picnicking and barbecuing. There is a ten cent charge for entry.

In front of the park are several gift shops and four restaurants.

Parque La Isla

Off the Pan American highway overlooking Mérida, this park is pretty and pleasant. It is nice either at sunset or in the middle of a lazy day. The park has an orchidarium, and open from 6 - 6.

Jamau Children

An amazing collection of life-like dolls created by Maria Eugenia Dubois and Jane Smith de Garces, who live in Mérida. The dolls are pieced together solely from organic substances – the heads and hands from clay, the bodies from cotton and the eyes from glass and the hair human. Each doll is dressed in traditional Venezuelan costumes. Phone: 3477772.

San Javier Del Valle

In 1950, 27 school boys, students at a boarding school in Mérida were killed in a plane crash returning to Caracas to spend Christmas vacations with their families. Near the site – located in a valley 15 minutes North of the city today stands a memorial (as part of a spiritual retreat) that is a simple and moving reminder of our mortality. The artist uncle of one of the boys has created a masterpiece in the ceiling of the lovely chapel nearby with etched representations of all the professions the 27 young men planned to pursue. Most touching are photos of the lads that are mounted along an exterior walkway. A colonial-style house here is used by an order of nuns as a retreat. It is a moving experience to be part of the hushed beauty with the Venezuelan Andes majestically encircling you and this rememberance of tragedy. (A round trip cab ride will run you $5 and it's worth it. A por puesto is under $1 per person) Open to the public daily from 11 - 12:30 pm.

NOTE

The propellers from the felled two-engine plane are mounted on twin concrete pillars that rise from a lovely pond with a small waterfall on the immaculate grounds.

EXCURSIONS

The regal peaks outside of Mérida are the main attraction of the region. As stated before, the city of Mérida is predominantly a base town for excursions in the Andes. The peaks tempt you, lure you into them as you stare at them from the city. You

NOTE

The Incas are alleged to have influenced the small societies in the Andes, and the Andes is an Inca word for the small communities and farms here.

can see the cold up there, the frost and the dark mist, but it is enlivening, making you beat your chest. The state of Mérida is called Techo de Venezuela (the roof of Venezuela), and it is fitting. Anyplace in the world (the Himalayas, the Alps, etc.) where it looks like you can climb into outer-space is hypnotic and exciting.

Leaving Mérida, travelling north on Avenida Las Americas, eventually you will come to signs for **Barinas** and **Valera**. This is the route to Santo Domingo, Timotes and Pico el Aguila; three highlights of the Venezuelan Andes. The road is a windy groove, with the temperature getting palpably colder with every kilometer. The vegetation is woody and very much like the north-east of America. There are many streams, brooks and small rivers. The architecture becomes more distinct as you climb, moving away from the generic boxes of the modern world and becoming colonially roccoco and colorfully Indian – wooden patchwork homes that look weather-beaten but stubborn. The road is very slim, and the turns, so sharp that it is wise to stay slow, especially if your eyes wander.

On the trip up into the Andes you'll pass many roadside gift shops, and this will be the most unique shopping available in Mérida. Specializing in Indian and Andean handicrafts (leather and wooden utensils, kitchen ware, toys, small guitars, Indian psychedelic sweaters or stanchos, etc.) anyone of these stalls, and there are many, are worth stopping at and browsing – the point is to linger, isn't it? Most are nameless and will appear as you get closer, or turn a corner. **Los Aleros** is one that is named and that is very large; they serve food also.

You'll pass through many small two street towns, where you'll be forced to reduce your speed even further and you'll be stared at by street-hanging men and dogs. **Macuruba** is the first semi-substantial town you'll encounter, with a small central square and a pretty yellow two-tiered church. The **Hotel Macuruba**, with rates moderate, is functional and clean.

The next town is **Mucuchies**, which is larger. It has many small clothes stores, more like cubbies, that are interesting to stop in. **Castillo San Ignacio** is a hotel and restaurant that has clean inexpensive rooms and good food (even in the Andes credit cards are accepted regularly). In town, is also the Hotel Los Andes, with similar rates, and a restaurant.

TIP

A must see, is the Plaza Bolivar

Mucuchies was founded in 1596, and achieved fame for its gift to Bolivar. Thinking of his welfare, the town gave him a boy and a dog for companions. They became so connected with Bolivar that, after years of loyalty, they died simultaneously with him. The boy's name was Tinajaca and the dog was called Nevado. Their statues are in the Plaza Bolivar.

San Rafael, 8.4 miles from Mucuchies, is followed by **Apartaderos**, which is the fork town for Santo Domingo and Timotes. Aparataderos is really just a pit stop. The **Mifafi** hotel and restaurant is clean and friendly and has really good food from $5. Inside the restaurant is a gift shop, small and somewhat tacky. The people are nice, and the food genuinely Venezuelan. Across from the Mifafi is an anomaly, a Tudor styled hotel, with spires and a weathervane; why it was built, I don't know? Called **Hotel Parque Turistico**, it is so European is style, that, in a way, it is repelling; but the rooms are clean and comfortable, and the restaurant serves good food. Prices are moderate.

From Apartaderos to Santo Domingo is a twisty slow drive until **Hotel Los Frailes**. It is so isolated,

NOTE

A monastery, built in 1642, high in the mountains, seen from elevated distances because of its dome and cross, Los Frailes is a time-warping wonder.

and pious, that you become solemn and monk-like in your steps. One storey, the hotel is shaped as a rectangle, has a courtyard and a bell tower. Caught inside, it is easy to imagine yourself a monk in the medieval or renaissance era, controlled by austerity and prayers (we've all read enough historical novels to do this leap). The hotel and grounds are peaceful and beautiful and quiet. There is a game room, library, video and reading lounge, disco and restaurant, which serves food only at allotted times. At night the atmosphere is communal, guests intermingle in the library lounge or disco. Rates are moderate.

Right before the town of Santo Domingo is the **Hotel Moruco**, that has 19 rooms, four suites and eight cabins. Very Swiss in style, with a ski-lodge structure, wood paneling, fountains and gardens, the hotel is spacious and modern. The hotel offers eight secluded cabins, on grounds that have a playground for children. There is a pool table and restaurant. Rates are in the inexpensive category.

In town, there are 2 hotels you can consider:

HOTEL HALCON DE ORO
Inexpensive

The hotel is under expansion, and owner Arnaldo Willdpret, who speaks German, French, Spanish and English says that close to 10 more cabins will arrive in the next few months. Right now, it is still a pretty hotel that has a great view of the valley and mountains.

HOTEL LA TRUCHA AZUL
Inexpensive

With 25 rooms, the hotel is very Spanish, and has its rear end hanging over the cliff into the valley.

The geography at this height in the Andes is called the **Paramo**. It is dominated by the fragrant flower

NOTE

The flower is used variously as wrapping for butter, to stuff mattresses, and as jam.

frailejon, obviously a derivative form Frailes, and rolls across the tarp of the earth like a rug. If the weather is dark and uninviting, the majesty of the Paramo diminishes, but on a clear and transparent day, the Paramo is resplendent and luring.

Near Santo Domingo is **Parque Las Piedras**, which is good for walking and picnicking.

Two and a half miles off the main road, outside of Santo Domingo, is the **Santo Domingo Truchi Cultura El Baho** (trout farm), which is a three-tiered waterfall, that hatches trout, breeds them and ultimately sells them. It is a mainstay business and culinary delight of the area, and Venezuelans are proud of it.

Lake Victoria, invisible from the road, is a beautiful glacial lake. It is reached from the road that leads to Los Frailes.

Santo Domingo Hydroelectric Plant, was opened in 1973, and offers, not only a glimpse into Venezuela's technological capacities but its mountains because of its observatory. From the plant is a good view of the **Paez Dam**. The turn-off is marked by Mirador Complejo Gen. Jose Antonio Paez.

Parque Nacional Sierra Nevada

Parque Nacional Sierra Nevada is Venezuela's second oldest park and covers 190,000 hectares. It was opened in 1952, and is a huge expanse of minimally tampered with natural environment.

The park's highlights are its paramo, its glacial topography and its lakes. The paramo here is overflowing with plants, bright lit hued because of the need to lure in insects for pollination – (insects are less common so high up). There are also a variety of small animals, the fox being the largest, that roam the park freely. It would be wise, if you have any neophyte interest in botany, ecology or, even, gardening, to buy a guide to Andean vegetation.

The park is interspersed with glacial valleys and stretches; and as anyone who has glimpsed glacial wilderness before knows, the sight is sparkling and awesome.

TIP

Laguna Negra can be reached by horseback or hiking. It is an hour by horse. If walking leave early because of fog.

The two most visited lakes are **Laguna Mucubaji,** locally called **Laguna Grande**, and **Laguna Negra**. Laguna Mucubaji is the largest glacial lake in the region and is located near the park's entrance.

The main entrance to the park is on the road between Apartaderos and Santo Domingo, closer to Apartaderos, at the 3550 meter mark. There are, however, other smaller entrances used primarily by fisherman, in their never ending trout search. Some of these entrances are: Laguna Los Patos, La Canon, Laguna Seca, Laguna Sur-America, Laguna El Oso.

Paso Pico Aguila

The highest paved road in Venezuela, the Paso is a steep ascent into the mist-ridden Andes. The vegetation is the paramo, and the gray stuff on the mountains is called Sheep's Sorrel.

NOTE

In 1813 Bolivar passed on this route towards Caracas.

The actual pass, the apex, is Pico el Aguila, at 4077 meters (over 12,000 ft.). There, a statue of a spread eagle celebrates Bolivar and his independence march to Caracas.

Next to the statue is a lodge for hot chocolate and coffee. Across form the monument, and down, is Los Frailes and its proud white tower. Also, from this vantage point, is a view of **Apartaderos Knot**, the highest intersection of the Chama, Mututan and Santo Domingo rivers.

Timotes

Actually in the neighboring state of Trujillo, Timotes is reached by going the opposite route of Santo Domingo at Apartaderos, past Pico el Aguila. The Timotes church, on Plaza Bolivar, is quite unique. It has a four-tiered bell tower, and an artificial marble finish inside. It is somewhat ostentatious, and it stands out with the rugged, hard existence of the Andes. There is a small pre-Hispanic museum right outside the town coming from Apartaderos. It features the artifact collection of Jose Pio Rondon. Watch for the sign "Museo, Visitalo" (Museum, Visit It) on the left side of the road.

NOTE

Founded in 1691 by the Spanish, Timotes is the name of the Indian tribe that inhabited the area before colonization.

Jaji

Reached by leaving Mérida to the west, the opposite way of Santo Domingo, Jaji is a reconstructed colonial village. Completed in 1971, Jaji is perfectly blueprinted for colonial times with its church, government buildings and wealthy residences making up the central square. The work on Jaji was a mixture of fixing up what was there and prefabricating the rest. The doors, windows and grills of the building were just touched up, but the rest had to be built. The Pasada de Jaji is open to the public and is an example of colonial living circa the 16th and 17th centuries. Food, of the times, is available in the house.

NOTE

In colonial times, the square and its immediate circumference was the center of town, the fulcrum for all activity.

NOTE

The restoration of Jaji spurred local residents to redo their own homes in traditional style. Hence, much of the town resembles colonial living, and the effect is interesting.

Jaji is 20 miles from Mérida.

SPORTS

Toreador

If the bulls excite you, then you should spend time at the modern **Plaza de Toros** bullring not far from the Prado Rio Hotel just off the Pan American Highway. Unfortunately the matadors are here only twice a year – in February during Carnival and in September-October. Usually on weekends only. Seats range from $7 to $30. Check your hotel clerk for arrangement's.

Futbol (Soccer)

Between May and October, there are matches held on weekend afternoons at the **Estadio Olimpico** in the Santa Juana district. Prices range from $1 to $4. Your hotel clerk can help with tickets.

Beisbol

During the school year, baseball fans can watch their favorite sport at the **Estadio Universitario** near the teleferico where the University of the Andes and other teams regularly play. Again, check with your hotel clerk for schedules.

THE BEST SHOPPING

While the shops here are not overflowing with unbeatable "native" bargains, still you can find good value wool ruanas that are warm and brilliantly colored. All handmade by Andean Indians.

The most unique shopping in Mérida is along the road towards Santo Domingo. At the roadside stalls are many authentic Andean items and crafts. A stop at anyone of these places is fun and time consuming – the myriad designs on the sweaters are tantalizing and the crafts neat.

In Mérida shops are closed from 12-2 for siesta. Here is a list of some shops and malls.

▬▬▬ CDAA SHOPPING CENTER
Av Urdaneta

Right past the Park Hotel, this mall has a conglomeration of shops that sell Westernized goods as well as local goods.

El Mercado

There are several Mercados (shopping centers) throughout town. A Mercado is one large building packed with stalls and vendors. Usually a Mercado specifies in one item or goods; i.e. food, clothes, crafts, etc. The clothes Mercado is located on Avenida Las Americas and Calle 39.

On Calle 22 between Avenida 4 and 5, near the Plaza Bolivar, is a street devoted to shopping. No car are allowed, and independent vendors sell their goods.

MÉRIDA AFTER DARK

TIP

Schedules are available in the Vigilante, the local daily, or through your hotel.

Current U.S. and British films – fortunately undubbed – are usually showing at one or more of four theaters, all in center city. The cinemas are: **Glorias Patrias** on Avenida 2 (Phone: 3095); **Gran Casino**, near the Plaza Mila (Phone: 4220); **Cinelandia** on Avenida 2, Calle 22 (Phone: 3610); and the **Miranda**, near the Plaza Miranda (Phone: 2923).

THE SERIOUS ARTS

TIP

Check the Vigilante or your hotel clerk for information.

Concerts, plays and occasionally operas are performed on weekends mostly in the city's main cultural center, **Paraninfo**, which is part of the University of the Andes near the Plaza Bolivar.

DISCOS

Not a city of crunching wildness at night, Mérida does have three good discos.

DISCO MATCH
Hotel Caribay

Perhaps the most popular in the city, there is usually a small line to get in. Padded with black leather chairs, stools and couches, Match has a moderately sized dance floor that is shadowed by a circulating light wheel above. There is no beer served, and the action doesn't seem to get going until about 12, continuing until 3 or 4. It costs $5 to get in.

◼◼◼◼◼ LA VIDA NEGRA
Centro Comercial Alto Chama

Vying for top notch, La Vida Negra is also filled-to-the-gills with students. A somewhat generic set-up, the place is lively and hot.

◼◼◼◼◼ EL FIN DEL MUNDO
Centro Comercial Las Tapias

This is another highly regarded disco, popular with the younger set. Not for the inhibited.

BOWLING

If you're restless some evening and you can't get through another moment without a round of bowling, you are in luck.

Oddly enough, this sport might be Venezuela's favorite night time unstrenuous activity. Mérida's alley has eight lanes and is located off Avenida Las Americas on Avenida Los Procerstor. The hours are 2 pm - 3 am Monday-Friday; 10 - 3 pm Saturday and Sunday. There is a disco downstairs.

ETCETERA ETCETERA

AIRLINES

Avensa

Airport: 637737, open 8 - 9:30 am, 3 - 5:30 pm

Plaza Bolivar: 526232, 524152, open 8-12, 2 - 6

AEROPOSTAL (LAV)

Airport: 637798, open 8 - 11 am

Parque Glorias Patrias: 635555, open 8-12, 2 - 6

AUTO RENTALS

Since the roads here are excellent and since we do recommend a number of one-day excursions, you might consider a car rental.

At the airport are several car rental outlets, all offering jeeps also. **National, Budget, Avis, Oriental,** and others. Budget is the best, womaned by an indomitable Alex who is fluent in English and super nice and extremely helpful. A car is about $25 - 30 a day.

BANKING

A good local bank is Banco Union, Avenida 4 near Calle 23.

FOLKLORE

The Andean Indians have a rich folklore tradition. The local dances and costumes vary from town to town. Mérida City's fiesta is called "Feria del Sol" and occurs each February.

LANGUAGE

It is very helpful to know some Spanish in Mérida. While many of the University students understand English, you will have difficulty communicating with the average Mérideño.

MEDICAL HELP

Hospital Los Andes is on Avenida 2 (Phone: 3960). The Hospital de Niños (for children) is on Calle 17.

NEWSPAPER

EL Vigilante is the local Spanish-language daily.
For a few cents you get listings of films and
sporting cultural events. The Daily Journal,
English-language daily published in Caracas, is
often sold here at the major hotels.

PHARMACIES

These are plentiful; a good one is the **Farmacia
Moderna**, Avenida 3 and Calle 21.

POPULATION

Mérida's population 110,000 is one quarter of
the total population of Mérida State.

POR PUESTOS

These jitney-like sedans travel the main streets
only, continually picking up and dropping
passengers. Depending on distance traveled,
the cost is always small. Remember these stop
running about 9 pm. Your hotel clerk can guide
you as to the specific line to take you to your
destination.

SAFETY IN THE STREETS

You need not fear to walk at any time of the day
or night in any part of Colonial Mérida. Even
though it may be quiet and deserted, it is absolutely safe.

DR. SCHOLL

Yes, even in Mérida the good doctor has an
office in the Edificio La Quinta on Avenida 4
(Phone: 2988). A complete foot treatment runs
($2.25). The hours are 8:45 - 12:30 pm and
2:45 - 6:30 pm; Saturday hours are 9 - 5:30pm.

TAXIS

Plentiful in the evening, scarce during the day (when the cheaper Por Puestos are preferred), rates usually up to $1.25 within the city and twice that to reach the Chorros de Milla suburb. Since there are no meters, set the fare in advance.

TOURIST OFFICE

Maps and other information are available at the **Oficina de Turismo**, Palacio de Gobierno in the Plaza Bolivar. The government agency in charge of economic development, **Corporacion de Los Andes**, also has a helpful Division of Tourism located on the Pan American Highway, near the Hotel Pedregosa.

Venezuela

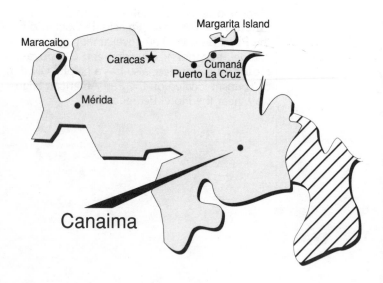

Maracaibo

Caracas ★

Mérida

Margarita Island

Cumaná
Puerto La Cruz

Canaima

CANAIMA
ANGEL FALLS

ot far from Brazil's Border, some 500 miles southeast of Caracas, lies a small community – Canaima – carved out of the jungle for only one purpose: To draw tourists to Venezuela's interior. And what an adventure to experience, including the 2-1/2 hour Avensa flight there, which passes the legendary **Angel Falls**.

The falls, with a drop of 3,200 feet (Niagara Falls has a 200-foot drop), becomes stunningly visible as your pilot guides the jet through a narrow ravine. With only slight urging, the pilot will make a second pass, and perhaps a third. Keep your cameras ready, and sit on the left side for the best shots. U.S. flier Jimmy Angel gave his name to the Falls when he survived the crash of his small plane into the mountain side in 1937 and later wrote an account of his experience. By the way, the Falls are rather narrow but considering the length of the drop, a wider flow of water would long ago have eroded much of the mountain base.

Most flights refuel at the old revolutionary city of **Ciudad Bolivar**, on the Orinoco River (remember those geography courses?). Just before reaching Angel Falls you will fly over the stark **Auyantepuy Devil Mountain**, a towering flat outcropping that thrusts upward from the jungle below. Arthur Conan Doyle used this site for the setting of his story "Lost Worlds".

Ten minutes or so after the Angel Falls fly-by, your pilot will be landing at the surprisingly smooth air strip in Canaima. A jitney will carry you and your luggage (tip: travel light) to your camp. A camp official will escort non-overnight travelers to lockers where they can change and shower. Overnighters will be conducted to either the Avensa or Jungle Rudy camps.

Listen for the muffled roar of the **La Hacha** waterfalls from the right side of the lagoon. These falls are fed by the **Carrao River** which is turn in indirectly fed by Angel Falls well upriver.

What to do in Canaima? One traveler who comes here for a week each year says tartly: "Nothing! This is the only place I know where you can come and do nothing and enjoy it. That to me is what vacationing is all about". For the activists, there is swimming in the lagoon, boating to La Hacha Falls. Fishing and hiking along little-used Indian trails. We find fatigue quickly ebbs and the air and waters act as restoratives to spirit and energy. Wild flowers, lush vegetation, exotic birds and strange scents all tantalize and tease the senses. A few Indian families will offer to sell you their handcrafts – very inexpensive – good souvenirs.

There are no phones and the camps generate their own electricity. Oh yes, on Saturday evenings there might be the Big Movie, usually of Mexican origin, circa 1940. Indian families from 20 miles around view this as the big entertainment of the week and they paddle down in their canoes faithfully each week.

Climate is warm all year round but evenings are pleasant for sleeping. As for clothing, bring only a bathing suit, walking shorts, slacks and a warm sweater. That's all you need. Also remember to bring the suntan lotion.

Your package price – air fare, lodging, includes all meals and you will be pleasantly surprised at the variety – eggs, meat, poultry, fish, vegetables and pastries – and the quality. The bar has a good selection of rum, whiskey and gin as well as cordials and beers.

Come – you will be enchanted.

ORIENTATION

NOTE

Auyantepuy, Devil Mountain, as noted was the setting for Conan Doyle's "Lost Worlds" and is resemblent to the tepuy, rock mountain, in "Close Encounters of the Third Kind".

Canaima is in the State of Bolivar, the second most southern state of Venezuela, bordering Brazil and its attractions are physical and geographical. Canaima is the point of civilization in Venezuela's Gran Sabana, a huge region of wilderness that is actually a mixture of dense savannah and patches of jungle. The savannah is wide and seemingly infinite, but at unexpected moments there appears the dense, overgrown, echoing semi-darkness of a jungle. Also, majestically, the savannah is dotted with tepuys (mesas), large rock formations that are common to Arizona and the Badlands in South Dakota.

What makes Canaima so attractive is that it does still seem like entering an unexplored world, a part of the Earth that man hasn't tread yet. Although it is an illusion, it is not shattered by the reality because Canaima, the Gran Savana, is so isolated, teeming with animal and insect life. Also, the tale of Jimmy Angel, the namesake for Angel Falls, the world's tallest at 3,212 feet (15 times Niagra's drop) adds to the remoteness of the area, and is a dreamy lure to the area.

THE LEGEND OF JIMMY ANGEL

Jimmy Angel was a typical mercenary of pre WW II. He was hired by a wealthy Mexican to fly into the Gran Savana for reasons unvoiced. He was paid 5,000 dollars, then a lot of money. He landed right by Angel Falls, but the mist was so intense then that although the Falls were probably audible they were not visible. The Mexican went into the bush and come out about five hours later with bags overflowing with gold. Angel, a professional, asked no questions. A year later, 1937, Angel with his wife a geologist named Gustav Heny and Heny's gardener, went in again to find the "hidden treasure". We can only assume that Heny and his gardener were employed to make the search efficient and precise. If the treasure were gold the geologist could quickly detect it. As for the gardener, Conan Doyle's most famous creation would probably deduce that he was there to point out poisonous plants. In any event, on this mission Angel crashed, and in their 15 days of being stranded, found Angel Falls. (This story has many versions, it should be noted). Take your choice.

Until 1970 Jimmy Angel's original plane was still on top of the tepuy where he landed it. But now the plane sitting there is a replica and the original in Ciudad Bolivar.

GETTING TO CANAIMA

Canaima National Park is 3,000,000 hectares, and is commonly reached by airplane, although the option of driving is available. If you are rugged enough to drive the way is by route 10 from Ciudad Bolivar through El Dorado and Santa Elena de Uairen.

By plane, Avensa leaves everyday at 10 am from Simon Bolivar airport in Maiquetia, outside Caracas. The flight stops in Ciudad Bolivar for about one half an hour, and thus the whole flight is about 2-1/2 hours. This flight without doubt will linger in your memory long after you have returned home. The views of Angel Falls are incredible.

NOTE

As noted, Canaima is included without additional cost as part of the Venezuela Air Pass, an inexpensive must for visiting Venezuela.

WHERE TO STAY

The Avensa Camp

The Avensa camp is the central lodge, and on its grounds are 57 huts, all with private bathrooms, a central terraced outside dining room and bar. The food is cafeteria style, with long lines and trays. The camp lies on the banks of the **Carrao** river, at a point where it becomes so wide it looks like a small lake. The source for this wide sink of water is the roaring Hacha Falls. The sand is tinted red because of the iron and ore deposits, and is warm and swimmable. At the small beach are beach chairs, umbrella's and a volleyball court.

TIP

The Avensa camp rates high marks from prior readers comments.

Between the airport and the Avensa camp, which is a five minute walk, is a gift shop selling goods that are very touristy, from tee-shirts, sunglasses, to Indian crafts to chocolate bars and postcards.

What To Do At The Avensa Camp

At the Avensa camp are three tour companies, and one company that runs plane flights to Angel Falls. The tour companies all sell different tours but since they are all into the savannah it is not worth brooding over the choice.

All three companies offer half day excursions, about $10, to whole day excursions, about $20, to four day trips to Angel Falls, which go for about $125.

The half day trips are a mixture of driving, boat riding and walking. The driving part is to get you to a point where you can get on a boat and ride through the small dense waterways that the Gran Savana has so many of. The boat ride is fun and exciting for its "Heart of Darkness" aspect. Finally, there is usually an hour walk or so to one of the region's many waterfalls. The walk gets you sweaty and bitten and the pounding waterfall takes it all away. At the waterfall refreshments are served, and on the way back there is a short stop at a tiny little Indian village.

The whole day excursions are extended versions of the half day trips, a bit more rugged and sweaty.

The four day hike to Angel Falls is truly exciting and unique but is only for people feeling confident about their stamina and will-power. From the people we talked to who had made the trip nothing but self-assurance and pride were mentioned, and of course the beauty of the trek is overwhelming.

The plane ride to Angel Falls, in a 5-seater and for $20, is spectacular, as most aerial views are. To see the true windy paths of the rivers, streams and inlets, to get an estimation for the height of the Tepuys, to see how diverse the savannah really is can only be seen from above, and for this reason a plane ride is worth it. The savannah is a myriad of waterways, cutting through the trees like snakes, just parting them enough to move. The trees, from above, look like huge broccolis. You can see for miles if the sky is clear; if the sky is not clear you won't see Angel Falls except for the bottom quarter, and this will obviously be disappointing.

TIP

To insure that you see the falls take the ride no later than 8 o'clock, since clouds are less frequent in the morning.

Jungle Rudy's Camp Ucaima

Two miles up river from Canaima on the Carrao River is a unique experiment in jungle living where a rare tough original named Rudy Truffino has carved a life for himself and his family out of the wilderness. Fortunately for adventurous travellers multi-lingual Rudy can accommodate 16 guests in eight double rooms (half in the main house and the balance in two cottages). How did Rudy – all of 140 lean pounds – wind up in Ucaima, as he calls his camp? The story starts in 1956 when at the mature

age of 27 he decided he had enough of "civilization", represented by his job as assistant manager
of the Hotel Tamanaco in Caracas. Then single,
with a degree in veterinary medicine and with
experience as a mechanic, architect, photogra-
pher, farmer and mountain climbing guide, mostly
in his native Holland, Rudy decided he would live
his life away from the mainstream and that he
would support himself by operating a camp or
jungle hotel for tourists. Simple, right? Hardly, as
Rudy found out when he was flown into what is now
Canaima (downriver) and told by his two partners,
"Scout the area, we'll be back in two days to get
you." They did not return for eight months. Rudy
survived by joining with Indian tribes and foraging
in the jungle for small game and fishing. That was
a blessing it turned out for later when Rudy needed
Indian construction labor he was able to get it. His
partners eventually returned, explaining they had
plane trouble. Rudy flew back to Caracas, raised
funds and returned once again to begin building his
first camp at Canaima at the shore of a serene
lagoon. In 1959, while in Caracas to buy supplies,
Rudy met an attractive blonde Austrian vacationer,
whom he married soon after. Gerty joined Rudy in
Canaima but shortly afterwards the couple decided
that even this camp was becoming too civilized
what with the increasing flow of tourism. Then he
made the decision to establish a new camp two
miles up the Carrao which would be a true jungle
retreat. Thus was born Camp Ucaima, more
commonly referred to as Jungle Rudy's. Still today
it is not accessible by water because of the Hacha
Falls. There is only an Indian foot trail and back
road of sorts that only a hardy jeep can negotiate.
Since Gerty's passing, the camp is run by Rudy and
his daughter.

With the help of Indians, and using locale timber,
the Truffinos built a main house, including .a
kitchen, dining room bar and lounge area, a work

room, and five bedrooms – one for the Truffinos – the balance for the guests.

You will walk at a good clip along the beach toward the Hacha Falls. After 50 yards or so, you will be guided to the right up a narrow Indian trail that more or less follows the Carrao upriver. While not arduous, the path is steep in parts and sneakers will help. In 15 to 20 minutes you find yourself in a small clearing at the river's edge and as Rudy's daughter, Lillie, told us, "Now we wait for the boat". Sure enough a few minutes later, the chug chug of an outboard motor was heard and there was Rudy – who had motored back to Ucaima on the back road – coming for us in a 15-foot canoe. We piled in and five minutes later we were at the camp. Greeting us first was the family's pet curacao, which resembles a turkey. In our group during one of my last trips were five birdwatchers from North America, the wife and daughter of Marlin "Wild Kingdom" Perkins, and a pathologist from Florida who comes yearly to "Unwind". A young Washington couple was working their way through Rudy's "university".

What To Do At Jungle Rudy

Since it's lights out at 11 pm, you are up early for breakfast. After a morning swim, there is a boat trip up the Carrao to explore the lagoons and coves. The birdwatchers in our group provided an education on Venezuelan ornithology. After lunch there might be a hike in the wooded areas behind the camp or another canoe trip, this time to an Indian camp where you can bargain for baskets and other handcrafts. After dinner, try to persuade Rudy to show his film on Angel Falls. Much of it is brilliant. Then a nightcap and to bed. By the way, the food is quite good – hearty and filling and geared for North American palates. For some reason, Rudy prefers to do the serving and he does so with great skill.

Making Reservations and Cost

It is necessary to make reservations for both camps and the flight way in advance. Neither camp has a phone so only certain travel agencies are connected. Each camp is about $20 per person which includes meals and a free trip to Hacha Falls. (It is necessary to show your receipts upon landing, or else your reservations might be disputed.)

Canaima with its overteeming wilderness, beauty and peacefulness is unique and fascinating. **Don't miss it!**

Venezuela

Maracaibo

Margarita Island

Caracas ★

Cumaná
Puerto La Cruz

Mérida

Canaima

MARACAIBO
BOOM TOWN
VENEZUELA

Oil! When that cry echoing from here was heard round the world 60 years ago it transformed Maracaibo virtually overnight from a drowsy village beside a lazy blue lake into Boom Town. What happened here would be familiar to veteran Texas oilmen who witnessed similar urban instant-grow all over that state.

But the difference – ar d fortunately for travelers there is a difference – is that the oil industry is virtually invisible in town. You must drive well outside the city to see your first oil derrick rising dramatically from Lake Maracaibo. Petrochemical plant aromas well known to New Jersey Turnpike motorists are unknown in this tidy attractive town.

What then has happened to Maracaibo in the last half century? For openers, the city now boasts over 1 million residents – all of them it seems city boosters – representing approximately 10 per cent of Venezuela's population, second only to Caracas in size. The rivalry between the Maracucho and the Caraqueño is much like the competition between a wealthy oil-rich Texan and a cosmopolitan New Yorker.

In recent years the city –capital of the State of Zulia –has sprawled out from its original site along huge Lake Maracaibo to encompass comfort-

NOTE

Maracaibo is the capital of the State of Zulia.

able North American-style suburbs. The city by the way is at the north end of the lake which just a shade further north runs into the Gulf of Venezuela which in turn connects with the Caribbean, not far from Curacao and Aruba. Now that's a concise geography lesson! The magnificent 5-mile-long Urdaneta Bridge, which links Maracaibo with Cabimas across the neck of the lake, skims above the lake here and we will guide you on a motor trip across it. A nice town Maracaibo, and not jammed with tourists.

BACKGROUND AND HISTORY

Maracaibo is in the State of Zulia, which is in the western region of Venezuela, bordering Colombia. Its central geographic, economic and historic feature is Lake Maracaibo, which is 93 miles long, 72 miles wide and 3 miles deep, making it the largest lake in South America. The lake was discovered by Alonso de Ojeda on August 24, 1499. Houses were built on piles over the water and people got around by small wooden bridges and canoes.

NOTE

Resembling, to the Spaniards at the time, Venice, they named the settlement Gulf of Venezuela (Little Venice), which eventually, minus the Gulf, became the name for the whole country.

Maracaibo was lost and then refound by Alonso Pacheco in 1570, which is considered the true birth year of the city. Yet, Pacheco's community was destroyed by Indians, and the permanent city was not truly established until 1574 by Pedro Maldonado. The city was then named Nueva Zamora de la Laguna de Maracaibo, and it lasted over 200 years.

The city was repeatedly a target for pirates in its early days. They pillaged the city, almost at whim, until the completion of San Carlos Fort in 1683.

Maracaibo, isolated from the rest of Venezuela until modern times, was the last refuge of the colonial Spanish forces during the independence war. Although Bolivar had declared Venezuela independent on June 24, 1823, Maracaibo, and Zulia, were held by the tyrannical Spanish General Francisco Tomas Morales. Yet, without the help of Bolivar, the independent forces rallied behind Rear Admiral Jose Padilla, forced their way onto the lake, effected a blockade and eventually defeated the Spanish Navy in a famous, and prideful, battle on July 24, 1823.

During the 17th and 18th centuries Maracaibo, as a result of its isolation, held most of its trade with the Dutch Antilles. This interaction led to a marked Dutch architectural influence in Maracaibo's houses, which can be seen in the older part of the city. Physically, Zulia, and Maracaibo, were more a part of Colombia and its culture than a region of Venezuela. For Zulians to reach Caracas, the route was circuitous and time consuming. From the northern tip of Lake Maracaibo, a Zulian would then go to Aruba, or Curazo, then take a ship to Caracas, at times using Margarita as a mid-point.

NOTE

It was only since this century that Maracaibo became connected with the rest of Venezuela by road.

Current recognition and influence came with the discovery of oil in Lake Maracaibo. The discovery launched the state and city to monetary heights, making it the wealthiest in the country, and giving Venezuela a level of prosperity previously unknown. Oil obviously translated into internationalism, and the city is an economic flagship. The money from the oil enabled Venezuela to build the longest pre-stressed concrete bridge in the world, which spans the lake five miles east/west. The boom also spurred a channel, built between 1953-1956, for oil tankers.

Maracaibo, now, has a dual atmosphere. On the one hand is its internationalism, catalyzed by the oil; there are many tall new towers, restaurants and hotels, the infrastructure is near pristine, everyone has a car, the wealthy neighborhood is as opulent as Scarsdale, and air conditioning is omnipresent.

The oil has also led to more visitors. On the other hand is the city's old and uninterrupted history. There is a street-hanging indolence about the city which seems timeless (things are a lot less private than in America, and, even, Caracas). The architecture of the past is preserved widely in the city. And, the indigenous Guajira Indians are the most visible in Venezuela because of their firm resistance to Westernization; they have stayed traditionally dressed, the women in long colorful robes, and the men, outside the city, in loin cloths and cowboy hats. The mixture is exotic and strange.

ARRIVAL

The 400-mile flight from Maiquetía Airport near Caracas puts you in Maracaibo's small modern two-level airport (**Aeropuerto La Chinita**) in under an hour. The white-stone terminal houses a bookshop, gift shop, restaurant and four car rental agencies. Grab a cab from in front of the terminal and in 30 minutes or so you might find yourself at either of our first two recommended hotels the **Hotel Kristoff** in center city or the **Hotel del Lago** on the lake (the fare will run about $5). Economy-minded travelers should use the por puestos which pack five passengers into conventional autos and conclude their run in center city at Avenida 5 de Julio and Avenida 9, not far from the Kristoff Hotel. The charge is $1.25 per person. Remember though you will need a taxi to get to your hotel and the por puestos can only handle limited luggage.

On the way into town via a modern four-lane highway, you will pass a complex of stadiums, the **Polideportivo Stadium** where baseball and futbol (soccer) game are held along with boxing matches. You also pass the University of Zulia, easily the finest academic institution in the state of Zulia.

A QUICK ORIENTATION

NOTE

Streets also retain their colonial names which are noted on street signs.

In general, Maracaibo breaks down into small neighborhoods, but unlike Caracas these sections are rarely used in locating say a restaurant, the street address being enough. The streets (calles) are numbered with the higher numbers in the oldest sections and the lower numbers in the city's newer areas.

KEY STREETS

NOTE

Addresses are explicit. They list the cross street and building number. Therefore, Avenida 4 No. 75-25 means sensibly enough 4th Avenue (Bellavista) and 75th Street (calle), Building number 25. And Calle 78 No. 10-15 translates as 78th Street and 10th Avenue, building 15. By the way, some avenues have both a number and letter such as Avenida 3H or 3Y. This means simply that it is between Avenidas 3 and 4.

Familiarize yourself with Calle 77 (also called **Avenida 5 de Julio**), the city's major shopping thoroughfare particularly the stretch from the **Plaza Republica** (Avenida 3) to Avenida 15. Here you will find recommended shops, restaurants, and shopping centers (called centro comerciales). Avenida 4 (**Bellavista**) is important in that it runs from the lake through the center of Maracaibo. For quick inexpensive transportation along Avenida 4 use the por puestos (jitneys). Avenida 2 (**El Milagro**) which parallels the lake shore homes the Hotel del Lago and its with-it night club and chic restaurant. Further on, near the dock area, are old markets worth exploring. Avenida 8 (**Santa Rita**) is another key commercial street. Oddly, adjacent to Avenida 8 is Avenida 4. Avenidas 5,6 and 7 do not extend beyond the old part of town.

Although Maracaibo is a large city, the nucleus as stated is a congregated circle spreading out from the intersection of Avenida 5 de Julio (Calle 77) and Avenida 4 or Bella Vista. These two streets are the primary ones in the city, and are either the specific street for many of the restaurants named, or the route used to get there. Inside the circle the city is jammed with restaurants, hotels, stores and business buildings. The eastern limit of the city is the lake, of which Avenida 2, or El Milagro, runs parallel. Bella Vista will take you to the lake and

Maracaibo's only 5-star hotel, Hotel del Lago. The southern inner city boundary is marked by **Paseo Las Ciencias** (Science Walk), which is one of the attractions of the city. The north western edge could be said to reach Maracaibo's large and good university, but you will probably not get out that far unless it is to visit the university itself. Travelling north, which is necessary to reach Sinamaica Lagoon, Maracaibo's most exotic sight, you'll have to pass Hotel del Lago, which could, reasonably, stand as the northern end of the inner city. The area is clean, which could be said of much of the city, and quiet, which can't be said of the rest of the city because of its street action. The old sections of Maracaibo are by the docks, south on the lake from the Hotel del Lago, which has an abundance of Dutch influenced structures, and by the Paseo Las Ciencias, which was the original heart of the city, with colonial government buildings, and 17th century churches. The airport, which is small and functional, is about half an hour outside the city, and on the trip in you'll get a glimpse of Maracaibo's periphery.

NOTE

The area around the Hotel del Lago, on the Lake and back a little, is the wealthiest in Maracaibo, with large, gate and alarm protected, North-American style houses, all containing several cars in the garage.

WEATHER AND DRESS

Since it is at sea level near the Caribbean, Maracaibo is quite hot with afternoon temperatures in the 90's much of the year and evenings in the upper 70's. The hottest months are from July - September. Fortunately humidity is moderate and at mid-afternoon virtually daily comes a welcome breeze off the lake. Thus late afternoons and evenings are comfortable and of course air conditioning is ubiquitous. You will be swimming and boating here so dress accordingly. Bring lightweight sport-type clothes.

TIP

Men rarely wear jackets and tie. Unless otherwise indicated, you can forget them when heading out for the evening.

GETTING AROUND TOWN

Cabs are plentiful and cheap. It will cost you about

TIP

The Milagro por puesto will carry you to and from the Hotel del Lago along Avenida 2.

$1.25 to reach most of the city. Since there are no meters, be sure to fix the fare in advance.

Por puestos (jitney-like sedans) travel the main streets continually picking up and discharging passengers. Fares range up to 25 cents.

HOTELS

Like any big city there are many hotels in Maracaibo. The range is from the 5-star Hotel del Lago to 2 x 2 wooden rooms with no bathrooms, if that is your preference – although we don't list them. The majority of the hotels are in Maracaibo's center, and are all pleasant, clean and comfortable; the 4-star hotels an inch away from 5-star. Tourism is light except for Christmas and Easter weeks.

In general rates are about 25% less expensive than Caracas. The star system for hotels is in effect in Maracaibo and we will so indicate the rating.

■■■■■ *HOTEL DEL LAGO 5 ***
Av 2 (El Milagro)
364 rooms
Pool
Phone: 912022, 912000
Telex: 62309
Fax: 914551
Expensive

NOTE

What is most special here is that the lake is its backyard, and makes the hotel sumptuous.

Overlooking Lake Maracaibo, this Intercontinental hostelry is more a resort than a hotel. First class inside and out, the hotel enjoys a fine reputation among North American executives who stop here when traveling with their families. With a fronting long horizontal building, the central tower leaps up above. The inside lobby is windy and long, with rows of stores and five restaurants lining its path. There is a coffee shop, snack bar, at the large glistening pool, a live music bar and Windows restaurant serving nouvelle cuisine. On the grounds are a pool, gym, sauna, steam bath, jogging track, racquetball courts and convention facilities. Boats can be rented from the hotel. The service here is supposed to be unparalleled.

HOTEL KRISTOFF 4 *
Av 8 (Santa Rita) near Calle 68
318 Rooms
Pool
Phone: 72911
Telex: 61396
Expensive

Despite its center city location, the Kristoff manages to retain a countryside quality. Chirping birds help too. Prices are extremely modest considering the comfortable air conditioned rooms and the beautifully maintained grounds.

Its pool is large, and the general atmosphere is very quiet. There are two restaurants by the pool, one informal and the other formal, and past them is a disco. The rooms are not overwhelmingly large, but are very comfortable. There is a gift shop and barber shop in the lobby. The staff speaks fluent English.

HOTEL EL PASEO 4 *
Av 1b at Calle 74 Sector Cotorrera
54 Rooms
Phone: 919744, 919621
Telex: 62581 Paseo Ve
Expensive

With 14 floors and only 54 rooms, this 4-star hotel has quite spacious rooms. A single room borders on a small suite in other hotels, and the actual suites are extensive. With a lavish lobby, featuring a large painting over the reception desk and a large quilt on the wall, the hotel has very good business facilities, with projectors, movie screens, betamaxes, podiums and microphones. There are

NOTE

The hotel can also boast Venezuela's only rotating restaurant, on the top floor.

three other restaurants complimenting the rotating one. There is a pool. The hotel offers spectacular views, being on the lake, of the sunrise and the activity on the lake.

GRAN HOTEL DELICIAS 3 *
Av 15 Las Delicias Square
Calle 70
108 Rooms
Phone: 76111
Telex: 61221
Moderate

Not in the class of luxury as the three previous hotels, the 3-star Gran Hotel Delicias is, nonetheless, modern, stylistic and clean. A tall building with a prominent stone awning, the hotel has a pool, large restaurant, gift shop and parking lot. Very little English is spoken here, but that should not be a deterrent.

HOTEL SAN JOSE 3 *
Av 34 (San Martin)
Calle 82, No. 82-29
30 Rooms
Phone: 914647, 914714
Inexpensive

In a completely different style than the hotels mentioned, the San Jose is a throw back. The hotel has no modern accoutrements, is more like a large private house than a prefabricated hotel, and has a much different kind of comfort – familiar, sweaty (this does not imply that there is no air conditioning, there is) and lazy. It fits the image of Latin America more than any other hotel because of its balminess and rusticity. There is a porch to sit and watch the action, and just think. The restaurant is more like a cafeteria, communal and familial, and there is a snack bar. If you have the time to escape business, this should be the choice.

NOTE

The hotel has been in this one spot for 50 years, and you can smell the sand and water in the twisty hallways.

HOTEL ROMA 2*
Calle 86 No. 3F-76
170 Rooms
Phone: 220868
Inexpensive

Similar to the San Jose, with a tropical laid-back feel, Roma is dominated by its restaurant. The restaurant is very ornamental and Catholic, with pictures of Jesus, Mary and some Saints on the walls, crosses and candles. It is background, there is no genuflecting before dinner. It adds a real Latin touch. When we came in, six men were at one small table drinking beer. Their eyes moved to take in the strangers, but their heads didn't – it was too hot and they were too comfortable to care that much. Air conditioned, the rooms are just as comfortable as a more modern hotel.

HOTEL PALACE 2*
Calle 99, Av 10
Phone: 227806
Inexpensive

A little away from the center of town, Hotel Palace is more modern than the San Jose or Roma, and has 30 rooms. It is quiet and clean.

HOTEL ASTOR 2*
Calle 78, No. 3H-37
Plaza Republica
Phone: 914530
Inexpensive

Clean and spacious, Hotel Astor is centrally located in walking distance from many stores, travel agencies and restaurants.

THE BEST RESTAURANTS

As befits any good sized cosmopolitan city, Maracaibo houses a number of first rate restaurants

NOTE

For convenience we have grouped our selections by type of food served.

including one truly great emporium, Mi Vaquita. By the way, unlike in Caracas, informal dress is standard at most restaurants largely because of the warm climate which means that comfort comes first. A recommended local beer, Zulia, is widely served and yes, you can drink the water in the restaurants below.

It should have been no surprise, but it was, actually, that Maracaibo has so many good and classy restaurants. The diversity is also outstanding. Maracaibo is a city noticeably under construction, and in tandem with that is a growth of restaurants. With its internationalism, Maracaibo's restaurants are predominantly sleek and high-tech – yet the prices are what it would cost for a burger and a coke in America.

NOTE

Most Maracuchos start dinner between 8 and 9 pm.

Remember 10% will be added to your bill for service, add another 5% if the waiter has been particularly attentive. See introduction for description of Venezuelan foods. Prices noted include a four-course dinner, service, cover and tax, but exclude liquor and wine.

Argentine Steak Houses

Argentina's great tradition of superb beef has carried North to Venezuela and particularly to Maracaibo which now boasts two restaurants that would thrive in Buenos Aires and in New York for that matter.

MI VAQUITA
Av 3H No. 76-222
(Off Av 5 de Julio)
Phone: 911990
Open 11 am - 11 pm (Closed Sunday)
Moderate

Mi Vaquita is Maracaibo's most famous and unique restaurant. It is a mythical Old West haunt, and, in many ways embodies the opposites of Maracaibo. The whole theme of the restaurant is an homage and glorification of the American Old West, which, of course, is not whole without the Latin enemy and drawl. American Indian weapons dangle from the ceiling. There is a poster advertising the capture of Geronimo. There are dolls of John Wayne, Jesse James and other folk heros. And, of course, swinging doors for the main entrance. It is fantasy, revering the days when you shot a man for looking at your wife, and respect was only gained behind a gun. This dream is as appropriate to Venezuela as it is to America.

The bar, though, is a homage to modernity. Several hanging televisions broadcast the Mets and Yankees, while a giant video screen shows and plays either rock and roll, country western, or pop.

The house specialties – you need journey no further on the bi-lingual menu – include three dishes any one of which will linger in nostalgic memory long after you've returned home. These are a parrillada mixta Argentina, cooked at your table on a small grill stove; a marvelously tender T-Bone Baby Beef steak whose size may intimidate you; and finally a succulent churrasco (strip sirloin) steak. Instead of plates, you dine on thick wooden platters which heighten the ranch-like ambience. Too, we're partial to the guacamole salad (avocado blended with tomato and onion) and the mixed salad. Need we say more? Yes, make sure each member of your party orders a different main dish and share in the riches jointly. The mashed potatoes are genuinely the best I've ever had anywhere. And remember the sauces are only for cowboys. It is great dining. (Ice cream is also available.) This is the local watering hole for many North Americans employed in Maracaibo. Its a good place to meet them.

TIP

Founded in 1957 by two Americans, the food is exceptional. The parrillada mixta Argentina (mixed meats), cooked at your table, is fantastic.

TIP

Warning: the hot sauces are just that.

■■■■■ **EL GAUCHO**
Av San Martin No. 77-22
(near Plaza Republica monument)
Phone: 82110
Open 5 pm - 2 am (daily)
Moderate

NOTE

*All main dishes come
with potato, yuka,
arepas, garlic bread
and tomato and
lettuce salad.*

If outdoor dining is your cup of carne, El Gaucho should be for you. Of the two dining rooms – one indoors and air conditioned – we prefer the exterior room which has only a tree branch cover between you and the evening sky. Aside from that, the beef is the rage here and you should indulge yourself with the filet mignon, the churrasco, or the inevitable Argentine parrillada. The owner insists that his grilled chicken (pollo bebé a la parrilla) is the best in Venezuela. He may be right.

Criolla Food

■■■■■ **EL TINAJERO**
Av 3C no. 71-80
Phone: 915362, 919020
Open 11 am - midnight (daily)
Moderate

NOTE

*The ceilings are low
and beamed, the
chairs short and hard
leather and the tables
non-fangled wooden
squares – a blatant
Spanish motif, with
columns dividing
each table.*

Easily the best "native" restaurant in Maracaibo, the Tinajero is housed in what was once obviously an elegant private house reconstructed to resemble an underground cave with a colonial Spanish motif. The atmosphere is informal and the food is unique and excellent.

But the atmosphere, no matter how effective, can only carry a restaurant so for. Fortunately, the Tinajero has not neglected gustatory fundamentals and when you try the **camarones** (shrimp) or the **punta trasera** (a steak served with rice and yuka with beans and platano) or the **pabellon criollo** (shredded beef, rice, black beans and platano you will understand why the locals flock here. And the appetizer special, **aguacate Margariteña** (avocado) is especially recommended. Arepas (corn bread) comes with most platters. Watch the sauces, they can bite.

■■■■■■ *SONATA*
Calle 75, Av 4
(Bella Vista District)
Open 12 am - 12 pm
Moderate

Not nearly as well-known or recommended as El Tinajero, Sonata is none the less a good restaurant for Venezuelan food. The staff is nice, and the atmosphere is personal. Their special dish is **Canon de Mariscos** (shellfish).

■■■■■■ *RESTAURANT EL CALAMAR*
Calle 76, Bella Vista y Santa Rita
Dinner only
Phone: 71660, 79384
Moderate

A typical Venezuelan restaurant in the center of the city, El Calamar has an extended menu that specializes in native meat dishes. Try the Cazuela de Mariscos.

International Restaurants

■■■■■■ *RESTAURANTS GIRASOL*
Hotel el Paseo
Dinner only
Phone: 919621
Expensive

Maracaibo's most physically unique restaurant because of its rotation, Girasol also has fantastic food. The restaurant is spacious and very modern, and like any rotating restaurant you get a slow merry-go-round feel; add that to a few beers and its a wonderfully tipsy evening. The meats are searing

NOTE

*Venezuela's only
rotating restaurant.*

good, and the chicken dishes are also recommended.

CASABLANCA
Calle 67, Cecilo Agosta
Open 12 am - 11 pm
Phone: 919571, 919411
Moderate

Although you would expect Casablanca to be expensive because of its look, it is actually quite moderate, even inexpensive. The food, and the interior design, is not, however. Very chic and modern, and obviously new, the restaurant is dominated by mirrors, has the elegant feel of a European formal haunt, has a central fountain, has modernist and cubist paintings on the wall, a piano bar and plush soft colors. Their pork dish is great, as well as the beef and pastas too.

WINDOWS
Hotel del Lago
Dinner only
Phone: 912022
Expensive

Well reputed in Maracaibo, Windows caters to an international crowd, and has a nouvelle cuisine menu. The fish is outstanding, and the service superb. The view, fitting for a restaurant called Windows, is also superb.

MANSION COLONIAL
Calle 67, 3G
Open 12 am - 12 pm
Phone: 912930
Moderate

An established and interesting restaurant, Mansion Colonial is fittingly in colonial decor and has an international menu that is quite good.

HOTEL KRISTOFF
Dinner only
Phone: 72911
Moderate

Tucked away in the back hall of the lobby, the restaurant is relatively small, yet plush and comfortable. The menu is not overwhelming, but the meats are good.

MUTINI
Av 71, Calle 9b
Dinner only
Moderate

A former private house that has been modernized, the restaurant shares its space with a bar and disco. Reservations are recommended.

Italian Food

LA TRATTORIA DEL CESAR
Costa Verde Shopping Center
Lunch and Dinner, closed Mondays
Expensive

TIP

Italian food is popular and Italian restaurants are usually crowded. Reservations are advised.

La Tratttoria del Cesar has excellent food, and many people know it. An informal typical set-up, the design is irrelevant because of the high quality food. The **insalata cesar** is great, and the **funghe panna** (mushrooms) also great. Maybe Maracaibo's paramount Italian restaurant.

EL TAVOLIERE
Av 8, Santa Rita
Lunch and Dinner
Moderate

El Tavoliere is next to Hotel Kristoff, and has a set-up similar to any Italian restaurant in America – pictures of Italy adorn the walls, the tables have checkered and tomato slobbed tablecloths, it is crowded and unprivate and unhushed. Run by an

Italian family, the pastas are, as predicted, always pertinent, but the fish, particularly the trout, is bravissimo.

PIZZERIA NAPOLITANA
Avenue 5 de Julio
(corner Bella Vista)
Open 5:30 pm - 5 am (daily)
Moderate

This 30-year-old restaurant, practically an institution here, is typical of the great old Italian restaurants you find in the Little Italies of New York, San Francisco, and even Buenos Aires. The house specialities are of course the inevitable pizzas as well as enormous pasta dishes. Every dish we sampled can hold its own anywhere, but oddly a simple spaghetti and sauce dish seemed to mesmerize us. We became conspicuous consumers. Dine in the rear garden or in either of the two indoor dining areas. Ideal too for a late night take-back-to-your-hotel pizza. Look for the chefs in front feeding the huge pizza ovens.

Chinese Food

LA ESTRELLA
Av 4, Calle 77
Lunch and Dinner
Phone: 76476
Moderate

Typically Chinese, harking back to the styles of Hong Kong; noisy, ornamental and Oriental. La Estrella has very good pork dishes, and noodle dishes.

LOTO DORADO
Calle 76, No. 3-H-91
Lunch and Dinner
Phone: 78952
Moderate

The Spanish-English-Chinese menu is well organized and clear, and will be the path to good Chinese food. The **wor sui opp** (boned duck in mushroom sauce) and the **chow fun see** (shrimp, pork and ham with noodles) are reeling.

LAGO DEL OUESTE CHINA
Calle 76, No. 3H-02
Lunch and Dinner
Phone: 912120
Moderate

Across from Mi Vaquita, Lago del Oueste China is as formidable for Chinese food as Mi Vaquita is for meats. Its large Oriental facade glitters at night.

CHINESE HUE CHIE
Av 8, Calle 69
Lunch and Dinner
Phone: 73458
Moderate

A solid, typical and reliable Chinese restaurant.

Japanese

SAMURI
Av 20, Calle 69
Dinner
Phone: 518806
Expensive

Well known and frequented by Maracuchos, Samuri is alone in Maracaibo for Japanese food. The entrance is a bridge over a large aquarium (for a restaurant) and fountain, and the set-up is typically Japanese, with low tables, pillows, grills at each table, and a sushi bar. The staff speaks English. **Camarones Sakura** is their best dish. There are many soup dishes on the menu that set the proper mood. The friendly staff will explain all daily specials.

French Restaurants

███████ **CHEZ NICOLAS**
Calle 78, Av 18 and 19
Dinner
Phone: 511801
Expensive

Excellent French food, Chez Nicolas is formal, personal and proper. The food is the rival of any restaurant in the States, and the **beef bourgonuine** is tremendous. A classy restaurant.

███████ **RESTAURANT AISKO'S**
Av 13, No. 77-40
Lunch and Dinner
Phone: 78559
Moderate

Restaurant Aisko's is a fine restaurant with an intimate elegant setting. Try the duck dishes for a real treat.

Sea Food

███████ **CASA PACO**
Av Bella Vista No. 70-49 (Av 4)
Open 11 am - 1 am
Phone: 77040
Expensive

NOTE

The adjoining discotheque has dancing to records late in the evening on a dance floor that's designed to resemble a bull ring.

The motif is Spanish bull ring (circa 1940) but the food fresh from the sea is of a high order. In particular, you should investigate the **shellfish casserole** and the **pargo** (red snapper) which is a find. The locals clamor for the mero (bass), a delectable dish in a tangy sauce. The bi-lingual menu also features steak and chicken platters.

███████ **TABERNA VASCA**
Av 3
Lunch and Dinner
Moderate

Very modern and spacious, Taberna Vasca has good snapper, trout and bass. The setting is old Spain. Good second choice.

Spanish Food

RESTAURANT TOLEDO
Av 76 no. 3H-74
Phone: 74665
Open 11 am - 11 pm
(closed Sundays)
Moderate

A long canopy provides an attractive approach to the inviting and comfortable Toledo where the paella and arroz marinera are highly recommended. Another favored dish is the red snapper habanera. Steak lovers should try **lomito al jerez**, steak cooked in sherry. Though small, there are two dining rooms which seem packed whenever we stop here.

Swiss Food

CHALET SUIZO
Calle 78 Av 3G-65
(near Plaza de la Republica)
Phone 914370
Open 6:30 pm - 11 pm (daily)
Moderate

This tiny restaurant which manges to create a Swiss atmosphere via decor as well as paintings and posters features a **fondue** that is outstanding. Regulars are partial too to the **bistek chihuahua**, a ham and cheese blend on steak that comes with a tangy sauce, as well as the **chuletas with sauerkraut**. Different and pleasant.

FAST FOODS

Maracaibo is packed with quick eateries. Anywhere you walk there will be a snack bar, coffee shop or pizza joint. Here is a list of several.

PIZZA JOINT, BURGER KING
Costa Verde Shopping Center

No description necessary.

TICO'S SNACKS
Av 3, Calle 74

Hams, papitas, empandas

HELADERIA (Ice Cream) AND PIZZERIA
Calle 77, Bella Vista

HABANA LUNCH
Calle 76, Bella Vista

DE CANDIDO
Calle 70, Santa Rita

Pizza and fast food.

LOS FAROLES PIZZA
Calle, 67, Bella Vista

Pizza, of course.

FUENTE DE SODA POPIA
Av Bella Vista, Calle 67

Coffee Shop, sandwiches, ice cream

MARACAIBO SUNUP TO SUNDOWN

The way to get to know any city is on foot and accordingly we recommend a walking tour of Maracaibo beginning with the Old Colonial Section in the downtown dock area.

Hop a cab to Avenida El Milagro (also known as Avenida 2) and Calle 100 where the city projects

TIP

A perfect time to stroll the narrow streets – if the day is cool – is during the siesta hours (12:30 - 3 pm) when stores are closed and the streets are quiet. If temperatures tend to discourage mid-day walking then wait until late afternoon when breezes make things comfortable. Here's our walking tour.

TIP

Bargaining is very much in style but in Spanish only (English is truly a foreign tongue here). Key words to remember: demasiado caro (it costs too much).

NOTE

The huge statue you see at the park entrance is of General Rafael Urdaneta, a revolutionary hero born nearby who fought with Bolivar.

into Lake Maracaibo. This is the heart of the bustling dock area and from dawn to dusk shoppers throng the open stalls overflowing with fruits, vegetables, meat and clothing. The stallkeepers vie with hawking salesmen for the attention of bargain hunting customers. Food odors dominate the senses, particularly oranges and grilled frankfurters. When you've had enough of the dock section, stroll away from the lake along Avenida El Milagro for four blocks until you reach the Indian Markets on Calle 95. As you amble along the narrow streets, note the brilliantly-painted colonial-style buildings that appear to be windowless. Wisely, the builders put the windows on the inside facing peaceful inner patios.

Once at the Indian market, note the handmade **mantas** (long dresses) worn by most of the women. These are particularly good buys here. More common in the stalls are **ruanas**, pom pom slippers, beaded bags, and miscellaneous low-cost souvenirs.

It's time to turn left on Calle 96 and three blocks beyond at Avenida 5 is the city's colonial center – **Plaza Bolivar**. Typically, the plaza is dominated by an equestrian statue of Simon Bolivar and there are benches, greenery, shrubbery and foot paths. Perfect for a rest. So relax for a time. Look around at the government buildings and **The Maracaibo Cathedral** which faces the plaza. The two white colonial-style structures are the **Municipal Building** and the **Government Palace**.

When ready, walk along Avenida 5 to Calle 93, turn left, and two blocks down is the beautiful **Urdaneta Park**, which is adjoined by the lovely **Plaza Urdaneta.** Oddly, the park resembles in some ways a Japanese setting what with shooting fountains illuminated at night with colored lights, foot bridges over the fountains and pagoda lanterns. Try to come at dusk when the fountain lights are turned on.

A block up from Urdaneta Park at Calle 91 are the tall gray Grecian-style columns marking the entrance to the block-long **El Museo Urdaneta**, erected on the site of General Urdaneta's birthplace. Here you will see colonial weaponry and other war memorabilia. The hours are: 9 am - noon and 3 - 6 pm (Monday - Friday); 9 am - 3 pm (Sunday); closed Saturday.

Modern Maracaibo

Avenida 5 de Julio – from the Plaza de la Republica (Avenida 3Y) to Calle 15 – is considered the commercial center of new Maracaibo. You can walk the stretch in 30 minutes and on the way you will stroll by the city's major shops, restaurants and night clubs. Another interesting street to walk along is Bellavista (Av 4). It runs through the entire city and has many modern office buildings, banks and shops.

Paseo De Las Ciencias (Science Walk)

The Science Walk (actually a sculpture walk) stretches from the Cathedral and Plaza Bolivar at one end to the **Basilica of Chiquinquira** at the other end. The area is bustling and active, with the street west of the Walk lined with shops. Paseo de las Ciencias was named after a previously important Maracaibo street, and is about seven blocks long. On the Walk are predominantly sculptures, modern designs done by Venezuelans. The idea, it seems, is a public art gallery, and its interspersed small parks and benches enhances the idea of a lazy lunch-break art space; an opportunity for artists and non-museum going citizens to connect. There are also nice gardens, fountains and a sundial. The street paralleling the Walk to the east is a colonial relic (it is this part of town which was the original heart of Maracaibo); the buildings are ornamental, have wrought-iron balconies and fronting columns. In the middle of the walk is the **Church of Santa Barbara**, with a blue stuccoed fairyland facade and stone withered base. The church dates from 1865 and was refixed in 1940.

Plaza Bolivar

Forming one boundary of the Science Walk, Plaza Bolivar is, of course, highlighted by the horse-ridden statue of Bolivar.

La Catedral

Next to the Plaza Bolivar, La Catedral is associated with a strange tale. One of the relics in the Cathedral is an old and famous cross with Christ, called Cristo de Gibraltar (Black Christ). Originally in the church in Gibraltar, the town and church were leveled by the Quiriquire Indians in 1600. The image of Christ was so beatific, it is said, that even though the cross it was on was burned, the image was only charred. The Christ image was given to the church in Maracaibo for safeguarding until Gibraltar's church was redone. But the image acquired such notoriety that the clergy in Maracaibo broke the contract and kept it. The ensuing dispute went to the top reaches of the Church authorities, and their decision was to put the image in a canoe and see which way it floated, towards Maracaibo or Gibraltar. Well, the winner is obvious now.

The cathedral is open 8 - 12, 4 - 8.

Basilica de La Chiquinquira

Finding a plain white board on the beach never interrupted her thoughts for more than a moment. The woman who found the board experienced nothing more than utilitarianism, and thus took it home with her to use as a cover for jars. Unexpectedly noticing a religious painting on the board, she nonetheless did not change her spirit but merely changed the location of the board from jar to wall, for decoration. Then, one day, the board began banging, and when the woman turned her attention to it it was resplendent and glowing with the image of Nuestra Señora de la Chiquinquira. She screamed "miracle," and her neighbors witnessed it also (her street was named El Milagro, now Av 2). The clergy wanted to put it in the local church, but upon carrying it there its weight grew exponentially until it was too heavy to move. Scratching their heads, it was randomly suggested that the Virgin might want to be taken to the Church of San Juan de Dios; this was the correct assessment because the board went back to its original weight.

NOTE

The Crown of the Virgin is a jewel of gold and stones that is, aside from revered, very valuable. All the gold and jewels in it were gifts from parishioners.

The Basilica of Chiquinquira, at the other end of the Science Walk, was originally begun in 1686 on the site of the Church of San Juan de Dios. But when Pope Benedict XV, in 1917, decreed the coronation of the Virgin of Chiquinquira, the church was reconstructed where it is now. The Basilica is large and yellow and has two domed towers shouldering a middle gothic structure. There are leaf paintings on the facade. Inside the Basilica are complex minute blue and white carvings, and white pulpit.

The plaza in front of the Basilica was redesigned as part of the Science Walk construction. It is wide and a magnet for the sun. There are two fountains.

Concejo Municipal

Constructed on the site of the house in which the last Spanish governor of Maracaibo lived, the Concejo Municipal (Municipal Council) replaced the house in which Maracaibo's independence was signed. South of the Plaza Bolivar, the Concejo has the **Municipal Museum of Graphic Arts** on the ground floor, which is open all day except from 12 - 2:30 in the afternoon.

Plaza Baralt

Formerly the apex of Maracaibo's business, politics and shopping, Plaza Baralt lost that status as a result of oil money and time and demographics. Plaza Baralt is one block south of the Science Walk on Av 6, and is now a mall that is closed to traffic. The previous waterfront market, famous in its time, is now closed. The **Mercado de las Pulgas** was built in 1927; it is supposed to reopen as a market for local crafts.

Parque Urdaneta

North of the Science Walk at Calle 93 between Av 7 and 9, Parque Urdaneta brings you closer to the water, and temporally away from the colonial look and history of the Paseo de las Ciencias. It is a new park, bragging modernity with a band-shell, many pools crossed by bridges, and fountains that are illuminated at night.

Museo de General Rafael Urdaneta

General Rafael Urdaneta was Maracaibo's most famous Independence War hero. The museum is on the site of his birthplace, and is devoted to heirlooms of the Urdaneta family and the history of the city. Included are paintings of the family, colonial weaponry and other memorabilia. The hours are 9 -6 Monday - Friday; 9-1 Sunday.

Lake District

Hugged by Avenida El Milagro (Avenida 2), the lake district is where Maracaibo's docks are located and is a shopping center. From dawn to dusk, shoppers

TIP

Almost no English is spoken at the Indian market so be prepared with either a phrase book or translator, or to stutter.

throng the open stalls that sell fruits, vegetables, meats and clothing. Also in the area is the Indian Market, which specializes in mantas (long dresses) that are worn by the Indian women of the region. Also for sale are slippers, beaded bags and other crafts.

Plaza de La Republica

The Plaza is in the modern section of Maracaibo, between Calle 78 and 77 (Avenida 5 de Julio) and is a good jumping-off point for a walk around this part of the city. In the center of the Plaza is a tall obelisk, which is supposed to honor all Venezuelan states. The area around the Plaza is Maracaibo's economic center, and the infrastructure is near perfect, the buildings new and the area infested with shops and banks and travel agencies and airlines from around the world. With all this internationalism Maracaibo's spirit has stayed traditionally slow and friendly, and this neighborhood is no different.

Plaza del Buen Maestro

Translated as the Plaza of the Good Teacher, this rocket-shooting water jet (supposedly able to make the water reach the height of 165 ft.) is another testament to "black gold" riches. At the intersection of Avenida 4 (Bella Vista) and Avenida 2 (El Milagro), the jet is a bit of a let down; although if fully operational, at night there are rotating lights.

El Monumento de La Marina - El Mirador

NOTE

The stages of the battle are depicted on the sides of the Monument.

This monument, the Marine Monument, is in commemoration of the naval victory that overcame the last obstacle to Venezuela's independence. There is also the bust of Commander-Admiral Jose Prudencio Padilla.

The 164 ft. observation tower, El Mirador, offers fantastic views of the lake and city, and is highly recommended so as to take in Maracaibo's sprawl, the lake's massiveness and the derricks in the distance. The elevator is open everyday from 3 pm - 10 pm.

Centro de Bellas Artes

The Fine Arts Center is dedicated to the showcasing of all of Maracaibo's artistic strands. With this purpose, the Fine Arts Center has a litany of events and regular shows. Also on Sundays, at 11 am, a film or play for children is presented. And on Thursdays at 8:30 pm the 100-piece Maracaibo Symphony Orchestra gives a concert.

The Fine Arts Center has a little theater where concerts, plays and other shows are given. (The local papers have the schedules.) The Maracaibo Players, who perform in English, use this space.

The Centro Bellas Artes is located at Avenida 3F and Calle 68A.

EXCURSIONS

Rafael Urdaneta Bridge and Oil Town

This short excursion will highlight the country's monetary mainstay. The bridge is six miles long, and at sunset wonderful to drive over. It is seemingly infinite, and gives an indication of the lake's size; it is also the route to oil town. Unexpectedly, the oil rigs do not dominate the skyline, are in fact invisible from the center of town. Seeing them, from the bridge, from El Mirador, from the top of the Hotel El Paseo, or from the shore of Maracaibo or Cabimas, they have the capacity to be majestic, technologically regal. They are like, if your mind is set free, immobile Godzilla's in the sunset. For a peaceful, slightly surreal, excursion, see the oil rigs and bridge at night.

Sinamaica Lagoon and Los Filudos

Sinamaica Lagoon is about an hour's ride north of the city. The easiest way, but not necessarily the cheapest, is to rent a taxi. The boat trip of the lagoon is as long as you want it to be, and if you get as intoxicated by it as we did you might make it last for hours.

The central part of the lake has rows of traditional **bohios**, houses, that are made from a papyrus-like reed that grows in the shallows. Gardens are grown in hallowed-out logs, ditched canoes, and dot the lake. On the trip you can stop at El Barrio where there is a general store and school. Also, in the center of the lake is a bar and restaurant for tourists that is built in the same way as the bohios are built.

Physically, the Lagoon is a slice of dense vegetation; hot, tropical and jungle-like. The lagoon is cut-up like a maze, with minute water avenues slinking under the overhanging trees. The birds are abundant and audible, and with the water lapping up at the sides of the boat, you can dream yourself into the heart of the jungle.

Continuing north from Sinamaica Lagoon, en route to Los Filudos, you will begin to see the houses of the Guajira Indians, some similar to the bohios, and the Guajira women in their long mantas. The multiplicity of cows is because cattle is their currency.

It is estimated that there are 50,000 Guajira Indians, and they live, when not moving, on the Guajira peninsula which span both Venezuela and Colombia. These modern borders are irrelevant to them, as they persist in their traditional ways – nomadic, matrilinial and violent. Actually, most of the Guajiras are on the Venezuelan side.

NOTE

Their constant movement is spurred by the seasonal watersupply, and when travelling take their houses with them.

The women, who always are robed in their mantas, are the power bloc of the society. They do most of the work and are the spiritual mediators of the tribes: Each tribe has its symbolic animal, which is branded on the cattle and tattooed on the women.

The only route to the market is by dirt road which makes a jeep or truck the only means of transportation.

Still sectioned by intertribes, disputes erupt easily and often, and can be bloody. This way of life has been very lightly touched by the modern world, although some Guajira men hire themselves out to work in construction or on other people's ranches.

The men, dressed in loin cloths and cowboy hats, are the herders and hunters.

The Guajiro Market, Los Filudos, an hour or so further from Sinamaica Lagoon, is not a market to buy Guajiro crafts, but a market from which the Guajiros buy goods themselves. In essence, it is a chance to see the Guajiro society in action. The market opens at 5 in the morning on Mondays and is ostensibly open all day; the grind is actually between 5 am and 10 am.

The market is made-up of trucks selling plantains, corrals with cows, meat shops and shops for hides. The women cook for the shoppers.

SPECTATOR SPORTS

Horseracing

Track fans will be interested in the (8:30) Friday and Saturday night races at the **Hipodromo La Limpia** in the **Francisco Miranda** section. Admission is 75 cents, and the minimum bet is $1. Check the Panorama newspaper or your hotel clerk for entries. A cab will cost you $2.

Baseball

From October-January fans flock to the **Estadio Luis Aparicio** at the **Polideportivo**. Games are played nightly and on Sunday afternoon. General admission is $2. By the way, Hall of Famer, Luis Aparicio, the great (all star) White Sox shortstop of yesteryear, was Venezuelan.

MARACAIBO AFTER DARK

The diversity of night life in Maracaibo is great. All the good hotels, in particular Hotel del Lago and El Paseo, have piano bars and discos. And there are many independent discos and piano bars around town. Current U.S. and European films are shown around the city, primarily in the theater in the **Costa Verde shopping center**. Concerts at the Bellas Artes are an option. There is bowling at Pin Zulia. And finally, you can watch the Yankees or Mets at Mi Vaquita.

Concerts and Opera

Longhairs (1950 variety) should haunt the **Centro de Bellas Artes,** Avenida 3F and Calle 67, the city's main cultural hall where visiting artists and troupes regularly appear. Your hotel clerk will keep you informed.

Bowling

Enthusiasts need go no further than Pin Zulia, in the Centro Comercial Internacional, Avenida 5 de Julio.

Discotheques

There are several in town, each charges $2-$3 per drink.

> ■■■■■ *MUTINI CLUB*
> *Av 71 Calle 9B*
> *Open 10 pm - 3 am*
> *Singles admitted*

NOTE

One bar is connected with the disco and the other bar for piano listening and chatting.

Mutini actually has two bars and a disco. The club is very modern and slick, with a more middle-aged clientele. The club is set-up like a glass box, shiny and waxen. The architecture favors the bar, with the dance floor off to the side. There is a bouncer that carries a gun.

■■■■■ CLUB LENVILL
Costa Verde Shopping Center
Open 10 pm - 4 am
Singles admitted

NOTE

American music is interspersed with Venezuelan, Brazilian and Latin music.

Much more loud and active than Mutini, Lenvill caters to a more youthful crowd. The club is not large but centered around the dance floor. A bar hangs above the dance floor, and the voyeurs sit there and watch. There are booths for couples and for groups. And there are seats adjacent to the dance floor. Strobe lights adorn the walls, and everything feels strangely claustrophobic; but that is the way Marachuchos like it, according to the bouncer/maitre de.

■■■■■ JET SET
Costa Verde
Open 9 pm - 4 am
Singles admitted

All black, Jet Set, vies with Lenvill for the most popular youthful joint, and is raucous and energetic. They are on opposite side of the shopping center.

■■■■■ HOTEL KRISTOFF
Open 9 pm - 3 am
Singles admitted

The Kristoff has both a piano bar and disco. The disco is the largest one we saw in Maracaibo, and contains many booths. The place is great for dancing. The piano bar is pretty and quiet, good for relaxing and talking.

■■■■■ SONATA
Calle 75 Av 4 Bella Vista
Open 9 pm - 2 am
No singles admitted

The disco is very intimate, and that is why coming as a couple is mandatory here.

▰▰▰ LA CONGA DISCO
Av 13 Calle 77
Open 9 pm - 4 am
Singles admitted

Loud hyperactive and a little bit off the main stream, La Conga seems geared to a less international crowd.

▰▰▰ MAGIC DISCO
Av 8 Calle 77
Open 9 pm - 4 am
Singles admitted

A little run-down but good for Latin dancing.

FOR MEN ONLY

Any cab driver will direct you to some of Maracaibo's clubs catering to men on the prowl.

▰▰▰ CHEZ MIMI
Av 8 Calle 76

Flesh is the name of the game here, lots of it too.

▰▰▰ LA MATHQUENA
Calle 87 Av 9

Similar to Chez Mimi.

SHOPS AND SHOPPING

Maracaibo has two major highlights in shopping – shoes and Indian crafts and clothes. Maracaibo has many shopping areas (one across from Hotel Kristoff, another in the radius of Bella Vista and Calle 77 and another by Mi Vaquita) that have a spate of international goods that are slightly cheaper than in America. Shop hours are 9 am - 12:30 pm and 3 pm - 7 pm. Most shops are open on Saturdays.

TIP

Leather shoes locally made are best buys in Maracaibo

Costa Verde, Av 5 de Julio and Calle 65-67, is the primary and largest shopping complex in Maracaibo. It is jammed with stores, but the clothes are somewhat expensive. On the other hand, shoes, Italian shoes, are very cheap – a pair that is $150-200 in America is $50-60 here.

Guajira handicrafts and clothes represent the most unique shopping available in the city. Mantas, the long colorful psychedelic robes worn by Guajira women, carved out gourds, pouches, duffle bags, Christmas ornaments and the popular Guajiran hammocks are all available in Maracaibo for cheaper than anywhere else. The price range can be vast.

The **Mali Mai** shop, attached to the Centro de Bellas Artes, features all these items. Guajira rugs are complex, intricate and beautiful, and can be sampled or bought from this shop. The rugs are designed by Luis Montiel, and are made in his small factory further north than Los Filudos market. All the items at Mali Mai are special, and will give you an idea of the work that is done, the quality that can be expected, and the price range.

ARTESANIA NACIONAL
Av 5 de Julio at Santa Rita (Av 8)

Heavy in Indian crafts, this small store carries handbags, belts, maracas, and Indian-style long dresses called mantas that are much like our granny dresses. Prices for the better items are $10 and up.

ARTESANIA DEL HOGAR
Av 9 and Av 5 de Julio

Operated for charity, the thrifty Artesania del Hogar sell items such as stuffed rag dolls, stuffed animals, and woven wall hangings, all handmade by indigent women working at home. Prices are quite low, $3 and up. Good values.

▬▬▬ *INDIAN MARKET*
Av 1C at Calle 96

Indian families gather here daily to sell homemade goods in wooden stalls set up in this old section of the city. Best buys are colorful ruanas, shoulder bags, belts, beaded slippers and pom pom slippers. We purchased a warm lovely ruana for $10. Prices in general start as low as $1. Reportedly this area is slated for leveling as part of an urban renewal project so check with your local hotel clerk before you journey here.

ETCETERA ETCETERA

AUTO RENTALS

Hertz, Avis, and Volkswagon all have agencies here. Rentals can be arranged through your hotel. You must be 21 and licensed.

Avis

Calle 67 Av 3F
Phone: 913540
Aeropuerto, Phone: 344524

Budget

Calle 76, Av 13 No. 13-08
Phone: 70107

National

Aeropuerto, Phone: 344486

ACO

Edificio Aco Occidente No. 86-A-50 Av 4
Phone: Aerpuerto, Phone: 349846. Renting a car without a credit card can be a problem.

AIRLINES

Avensa and **Aeropostal** are the two domestic air lines traveling solely within Venezuela.

AVENSA

Edificio Boulton, Calle Aurora
Phone: 225357, 7348, 7366
Aeropuerto, Phone: 344582, 4625, 4333

LAV-AEROPOSTAL

CC Primavera, Calle 75, Av 13A
Phone: 82395
Aeropuerto, Phone: 349363, 9346

Also in Maracaibo is: **Pan Am**, **Air France**, **Alitalia**, **British Airways**, **Iberian**, **KLM**, **Lufthansa** and **Varig**.

AMERICAN CONSULATE

Edificio Matema
Av 15, Calle 78-79
Phone 522605

BANKS

First National City Bank of New York has a branch here on Avenida 5 de Julio. The Banco Royal Venezolano, the largest domestic bank, has its main office on Avenida 5 de Julio at Avenida 9B. Banking hours are 8:30 am - 11:30 am and 2:30 pm - 4:30 pm (Monday-Friday).

BOOKS

English-language books, magazines, and periodicals are available at the Hotel del Lago gift shop and at the Libreria Universal, Avenida 5 de Julio and Avenida Bella Vista as well as in other bookstores throughout the city and at the airport. The Daily

Journal, an outstanding English-language daily published in Caracas, is sold at the Hotel del Lago for 20 cents daily and 25 cents on Sundays, same price as in Caracas.

HORSERACING

There is a popular racetrack packed on weekends. Check with your concierge.

DR. SCHOLL'S

The footweary should head to the good doctor at Avenida 5 de Julio between Avenidas 4 and 8 (Also called Bella Vista and Santa Rita.)

PAN AM

The local office is at Avenida 5 de Julio corner of Santa Rita, Phone: 704111.

PANORAMA

This Maracaibo daily newspaper lists all sport events, films, and cultural programs in town. Price is 8 cents daily, 12 cents Sunday.

PHARMACIES

These are plentiful all over and most carry a full line of North American over-the-counter medicines.

VIASA

Venezuela's international airline has an office here at Avenida 3 and Calle 98, Phone: 25855.

Venezuela

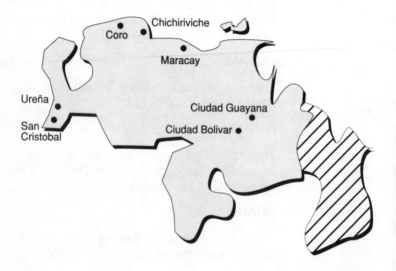

AROUND VENEZUELA

CIUDAD GUAYANA and CIUDAD BOLIVAR

(Bolivar State)

Many Venezuelan financiers point to the gold, diamond and other mineral wealth of Bolivar as representing the economic future of Venezuela. And that may well be, for this state is huge – larger than all of New England plus West Virginia. It embraces a quarter of Venezuela's land mass, much of its plains, jungle and mountains. The Orinoco and four other major rivers cut through the region. Understandably, visitors throng here to view Angel Falls, the world's highest, Devil Mountain, and the jungle camps at Canaima.

The new city of **Ciudad Guayana**, carved out of the jungle much like Brasilia in Brazil, was formed in 1961 by joining the towns of Puerto Ordaz and San Felix at the junction of the Orinoco and Caroní Rivers. Key to the City's rugged beauty are the Cachamay Falls, which cascade near the city center. Travelers are charmed by Caroni Park and by the order of the well-planned streets and highways. Serious hunters and fishermen embark on their trips into the mountains from here. For luxurious accommodations stay overnight at the 205-room **Hotel Intercontinental Guayana** (air conditioned) which offers a stunning view of the La Llovizna Falls. Make reservations at the Hotel Tamanaco in Caracas or the Hotel Del Lago in Maracaibo.

Sixty-five miles west is the old colonial city of Ciudad Bolivar.

Founded late in Venezuelan history, Ciudad Bolivar was, nonetheless, the most important city during the Independence War.

Founded in 1764 by Governor Joaquin Sabas Moreno de Mendez, the city was originally known as Angostura.

It early history was mainly formed by its location on the Orinoco River, Venezuela's largest. With that geography, it became a segue point for trade into the interior. Easily reached from the Atlantic, it was, and is now, an important city for trade and import.

During its early growth its elegant colonial infrastructure was layed out: cobblestoned streets, austere cathedrals, and fine homes – these have been preserved, in great part, today.

Yet Angostura reached its fame during the Independence War. It was the base of operations for Bolivar and the independence forces. It was finely suited for this role because of its interior location. It was easily defended, and really, it was never threatened. Bolivar, and his troops and advisor, were able to work and plan in peace; Angostura served as an unchallenged home for the forces, enabling much work to get done.

From Angostura, on February 15, 1819, the Second Congress of the Republic of Venezuela was held. The Constitution was hammered out here, and in fact, most of Bolivar's and future Venezuela's structure was in embryo form in Angostura.

It might be called the most important city during the Independence War.

On May 3, 1846, Angostura became Ciudad Bolivar, for obvious reasons. It is the capital of the state of Bolivar, the largest State in Venezuela. It is a prosperous city because of trade and location, and has wonderful and pretty new suburbs. The University of the East, Schools of Mines and Medicine are located here, giving the city a cosmopolitan and cultural feel also.

Today, the city retains a colonial flavor through its architecture despite extensive rebuilding and development. Flights to Canaima stop here for refueling. Some sights here would be the **Talavera** (colonial **Museum**, the ruins of the **Fortress of the Vulture**, and Orinoco Avenue, a two mile promenade along the river's bank.

CORO

(Falcon State)

Architecture buffs should hardly delay a moment before journeying to Coro, some 280 miles west of Caracas on the Caribbean. As Venezuela's first colonial capital, and the departure points for numerous Spanish expeditions in to the interior, Coro developed an authentic colonial architecture in its homes, churches and government buildings after its founding in 1527.

HISTORY

One of Venezuela's oldest cities, Coro was reputedly founded on July 26, 1527 by Juan de Ampies. Ampies had good relations with the local Caquetio Indians, but Coro's history changed drastically the same year.

The Province of Venezuela at the time consisted of the region of present day State of Falcon and Zulia, and the eastern coastal region. Charles V leased the province to a family of German bankers called the Welsers. The first German governor arrived on Coro on February 24, 1529. He immediately set the tone. Using Coro simply as a base for expeditions into the interior, the Welsers were unconcerned with establishing a community, or having good relations with the local Indians. Their interest was profit, and they pillaged and explored the interior for natural resources, holding their fingers tight with expectation. It was Charles V's idea, in leasing the area out to the Welsers, for them to begin some profit making industry. But their attempts failed, eventually, and in 1546 their lease was revoked.

Coro, after the Welsers, languished and became decrepit. But in the 18th century Coro was revived by a growing trade with Curacao and the Dutch islands. It eventually became the fulcrum for European goods into Venezuela.

Its economic basis for trade has stayed with it until the present. With a population of 60,000 and the capital of Falcon, Coro has fantastic colonial architecture, with bold Spanish style and Dutch style. It is so endowed with great buildings that it was declared a National Monument, and hence has its history preserved.

SEEING THE CITY TODAY

If time is limited, concentrate on these structures:

The Cathedral

Constructed like a fortress as a result of frequent pirate attacks in the 16th and 17th centuries, it is Venezuela's oldest cathedral. It was declared a national monument in 1957, and was restored to its original design.

The San Clemente Cross and Temple

Symbolizing the martyrdom of Saint Clement, the cross marks the area where the first mass in Venezuela was celebrated.

House of the Iron Windows

Said to be Venezuela's best example of Spanish colonial architecture, this house dates from the 18th century.

Treasure House

The wealthy stored their gold and diamonds here during attacks by pirates.

The Arcaya Family House

Another example of an 18th century home, this one features two floors, massive doors and a balcony that encircles the structure.

The Jewish Cemetery

South America's oldest Jewish cemetery, still in use, was started by Curacao Jews who emigrated to Coro in the 19th century.

Diocese Museum

An 800-year-old statue of St. Peter can be seen here as well as a 450-year-old monstrance.

A word about local food. You should sample the goat meat, either in a curry called **talkary** or in a coconut shell dish.

A recommended hotel is the 66-room air conditioned **Hotel Miranda**, with pool and private baths. Located opposite the airport, the phone number is (068) 510807.

THE DESERT

Just north of Coro is **Los Medanos**, a sweeping desert region that draws many geology students to study the area. Be sure to check it – it's almost eerie in its hypnotic effect.

SAN CRISTOBAL, UREÑA and SAN ANTONIO (Táchira State)

South of Merida, and only 34 miles for the Colombian boarder in the heart of a resort zone is San Cristobal, a city of 100,000 with a near perfect year-round climate that draws tourists from both Venezuela and Colombia. A fairgrounds is the site of the San Sebastian international fair every January and a bull ring draws first rate matadors. Shoppers should seek out ceramic and woven straw gifts. A lovely town with attractive plazas and parks.

A few minutes from the Colombian border is Venezuela's most famous spa, **Aguas Calientes** (hot waters) near Ureña where temperatures of the iron and sulphur-rich springs range up to 123 degrees F. Regulars here attest to the restorative powers of the springs. The hotel stop here is definitely the 28-room **Aguas Calientes**, which offers a private thermal pool with air conditioned room.

Your flight here lands in the boarder town of **San Antonio**, which connects with Colombia via an historic international bridge. On the Colombian side is the old city of Cúcuta where you should do some native crafts shopping since prices are favorable indeed.

Stay at the 113-room **El Tama Hotel** on Avenida 19 de Abril (Phone: 554477) a hostelry with all amenities, including a pool.

MARACAY and CATA BEACH

Situated 60 miles west of Caracas, via excellent highways, Maracay was the home of Venezuelan ruler (1908 - 1935) General Juan Vicente Gómez, who rose from an illiterate cowboy to become dictator. His enormous palace on the grounds of the Hotel Jardin is a must for visitors, particularly the fountains and immaculate gardens. A bullfight aficionado, General Gomez built a brilliant replica here of Seville's world-famous bullring which still today draws Spain's best matadors. Striving for a cultural identity, the general also commissioned an opera house. Open to visitors too is his country home, **Las Delicias**, which is of special interest to children because of the large zoo on the grounds. Understandably, the tomb of General Gomez – who made Maracay the nation's capital for a time – is another tourist draw. Founded in 1607, the city was named for an Indian chieftain.

Today, as the capital of Aragua state, Maracay boasts a growing population of over 200,000 and a steady stream of visitors to the nearby military air base at **Palo Negro** and to the outlying beaches.

The city's 1500-foot elevation provides welcome breezes despite a semi-tropical climate with average temperatures of 77.

CATA BEACH AND RANCHO GRANDE

North of Maracay, 25 miles or so, is the **Ocumare de la Costa** beach area on the Caribbean. Driving there on the El Limón highway you pass the **Henri Pittier National Park (Rancho Grande Park)** noted for its thick tropical vegetation, unusual plant life and restful cascades. Wildlife is abundant and birdlovers will have a feast! There is a small museum on your way up the well preserved mountain road. The Cata Bay area is probably Venezuela's most memorable beach, striking in its beauty what with huge coconut trees and endless sands. To the east along the seacoast is Choroni, another recommended beach and fishing area.

Maracay's best hotels are the 178-room **Hotel Maracay**, a hostelry, with huge pool, golf course and stables with fine horses, and the **El Pipo Internacional** (phone: 41-20-22) on Avendia Principal El Castaño.

PARQUE NACIONAL MORROCOY CHICHIRIVICHE (Estado Falcon)

Want to enjoy a perfect place for snorkeling, sailing, motorboating, diving and camping? Go to Morrocoy – 3 and a half hours from Caracas (West) or one hour from Valencia. Morrocoy is comprised of numerous islets of coral reef, connected by some 35 miles of channels and waterways. At the time of this writing, Morrocoy is being incorporated into the tourist boom, so you will find a few hotels and lots of new activities to make your trip worthwhile. Try to get a reservation in Caracas for **Conjunto Residencial Morrocoy** a place offering 5-star service and excursions to the islets. If you want to do this trip, arrange for an overnight stay.

Half an hour further west from Morrocoy Park (the fishing village next to it is **Tucacas**) you can drive to the village of **Chichiriviche**, surrounded by lovely beaches, lagoons with flamingo birds and the spectacular deep red **coro-coro** birds. You will find moderately priced hotels in Chichiriviche, popular restaurants, even a disco, watersports and island tours. While there, ask to be shown the caves inside 90 feet high coral mountains, where you can admire old petroglyphes.

ADVENTURE TOURS

There are many special tours being developed in Venezuela, for the adventurer. Included are parachuting into the jungle, fishing trips in rivers or in the Caribbean, mountain climbing, trips on the Orinoco River (and others). Also available are hunting trips or visiting one of the far away camps, offering a four or five star service and surrounded by the most exotic fauna and flora and hours away from the next city. These "adventure tours" are being offered through travel agencies, in the major hotels and each month there are additional ones.

You may contact Candes or Intravel International in Caracas. Phone: 751-9124 or 911919 for complete information and service.

INDIAN TRIBES

The Venezuelan government for many years has protected its tribes by trying to preserve their secluded lives. At the same time, efforts are being made to incorporate them into modern society. For the visitor, it is not easy to visit the tribes and governors of the states of Bolivar and Amazonas are restricting the necessary permits to vist the tribes. The town of **Puerto Ayacucho** would be a place from where to start expeditions to the indians of the area. Some private pilots in the Caracas airports offer excursions too. If you are able to make arrangements to visit the indian tribes, it will be an unforgettable journey.

ÃBĆ

HABLE ESPANOL!

s languages go, Spanish is relatively easy to learn. While it is not essential to speak Spanish, your ability to understand and pronounce a few simple words will enhance your enjoyment.

TIPS ON PRONUNCIATION

Vowels – These are always pronounced in exactly the same way, that is a (ah); e (eh); i (ee as in deep); o (oh); and u (oo as in spoon).

Consonants – These are pronounced exactly as in English, with these major exceptions:

double l as in llama is like "y" (yama)

ñ an in niño equals "ny" (neenyo)

j as in jabon (soap) equals "h" (habon)

c before e or i equals "s" as in "central" (sentral)

g before e or i equals "h" as in "general" (heneral)

h as in "hablar" (to speak) is silent (ablar)

English	Spanish
Hello	Buenos dias
How are you?	Como esta usted?
I am fine	Estoy bien
Please	Por Favor
Thank you	Gracias
Excuse me	Permiso
Where is?	Donde esta?
What time is it?	Que hora es?
What's your name?	Como se llama?
I like it	Me gusta
I don't Like it	No me gusta
When	Cuando
Goodbye	Adios (Hasta luego)
Very good	Chevere

Numbers

0	cero
1	uno
2	dos
3	tres
4	cuatro
5	cinco
6	seis
7	siete
8	ocho
9	nueve
10	diez
11	once

English	Spanish
12	doce
13	trece
14	catorce
15	quince
16	diez y seis
17	diez y siete
18	diez y ocho
19	diez y nueve
20	veinte
30	treinta
40	cuarenta
50	cincuenta
60	sesenta
70	setenta
80	ochenta
90	noventa
100	cien

Days of the week

Sunday	Domingo
Monday	Lunes
Tuesday	Martes
Wednesday	Miercoles
Thursday	Jueves
Friday	Viernes
Saturday	Sabado

Months of the year

January	Enero

English	Spanish
February	Febrero
March	Marzo
April	Abril
May	Mayo
June	Junio
July	Julio
August	Agosto
September	Septiembre
October	Octubre
November	Noviembre
December	Diciembre
Relatives	
Aunt	La Tia
Daughter	La Hija
Father	El Padre
Husband	El Esposo
Mother	La Madre
Son	El Hijo
Uncle	El Tio
Wife	La Esposa
Snacks	
Hamburger	Hamburguesa
Hot Dog	Perro Caliente
Salad	Ensalada
Soup	Sopa
Meats	**Carnes**
Bacon	Tocino

English	Spanish
Ham	Jamon
Kidneys	Riñones
Lamb	Cordero
Liver	Higado
Pork Chops	Chuletas de Cochino
Sausage	Salchichas
Sirloin	Churrasco
Tenderloin	Lomito
Tongue	Lengua
Poultry	**Aves**
Chicken	Pollo
Duck	Pato
Hen	Gallina
Turkey	Pavo
Fish	**Pescado**
Bass	Mero
Crab	Cangrejo
Lobster	Langosta
Mussels	Mejillones
Oysters	Ostras
Salmon	Salmon
Snapper	Pargo
Sole	Lenguado
Shrimp	Camarones
Squid	Calamare
Trout	Trucha
Turtle	Tortuga

English	Spanish
Vegetables	**Legumbres**
Beans	Frijoles
Carrots	Zanahorias
Lettuce	Lechuga
Onion	Cebolla
Potato	Papa
Rice	Arroz
Tomato	Tomate
Fruit	**Fruta**
Apple	Manzana
Cherry	Cereza
Lemon	Limon
Peach	Melocoton (Durazno)
Pear	Pera
Pineapple	Piña
Raspberry	Frambuesa
Drinks	**Bebidas**
Beer	Cerveza
Coffee	Cafe
Milk	Leche
Tea	Te
Water	Agua
Wine	Vino
Desserts	**Postre**
Cake	Torta
Cheese	Queso
Ice Cream	Helado

English	**Spanish**
Pudding	Flan

OTHER ALIVE PUBLICATIONS

RIO ALIVE	10.95
VIRGIN ISLANDS ALIVE	10.95
BUENOS AIRES ALIVE	10.95
GUATEMALA ALIVE	10.95

Venezuela
7 DAYS FOR $110*
AIRPASS is your ticket to an affordable, unique vacation: unlimited air travel in Venezuela. Seven days for $110, 14 days for $125, or 21 days for $139 (Children 50%). Choose from 28 destinations plus Aruba. Mountains, beaches, sophisticated cities, jungle mystery, all in surprising Venezuela. Only one airline can take you all the way. Call your travel agent or AVENSA for a free brochure. Today. In NY 956-8500, U.S. 800-872-3533.
AVENSA AIRPASS
*Non-refundable if partially used. Some restrictions apply.

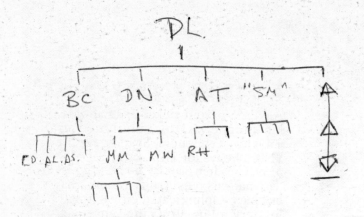

1. Run Agents
2. Sell Foreign
3. Travel Extensively.
4.